Finding God in the Singing River

"Mark Wallace's latest book, *Finding God in the Singing River*, represents a breakthrough in contemporary Christian theological reflection on nature. . . . Elegantly written, this accessible work will be appropriate for Christian study groups as well as seminary students and undergraduates in upper-level religion and environmental studies courses. It especially deserves a wide readership among Christian theologians and laypeople, but it is also a must read for all who are tracking the evolution of Christian environmental ethics."

BRON TAYLOR
University of Florida, Gainesville

"Wallace enchants the reader not only by his passionate commitment to earth justice, but by his skill in navigating through entrenched positions. . . . Ethicists will appreciate Wallace's efforts to place responsibility for all ecosystems at the heart of morality, and his grace in steering a middle way between the essentialist/constructionist debate."

MARY C. GREY
University of Wales

Finding God in the Singing River

Christianity, Spirit, Nature

Mark I. Wallace

Fortress Press
Minneapolis

FINDING GOD IN THE SINGING RIVER
Christianity, Spirit, Nature

For illustration acknowledgments, see page viii.

Cover photo: Vermont River © 2001 John Newcomb (20th c. American)/Superstock
Book design: Becky Lowe

Library of Congress Cataloging-in-Publication Data
Wallace, Mark I., 1956–
 Finding God in the singing river : Christianity, Spirit, nature / Mark I. Wallace.
   p. cm.
 Includes bibliographical references.
 ISBN 0-8006-3726-7 (alk. paper)
 1. Human ecology—Religious aspects—Christianity. 2. Nature—Religious aspects—Christianity. I. Title.
 BT695.5.W345 2005
 261.8'8—dc22
                              2004025449

The paper used in this publication meets the minimum requirements of American National Standard for Information Sciences—Permanence of Paper for Printed Library Materials, ANSI Z329.48-1984.

Manufactured in Canada
09   08   07   06   05   1   2   3   4   5   6   7   8   9   10

Contents

To Ellen, Katy, and Christopher

"But the fruit of the Spirit is love"

—Galatians 5:22

Illustrations

Preface

MOST MORNINGS I GET OUT OF BED and walk into my front yard where I turn and face the four cardinal directions. I weave a circle of gratitude and praise as I turn and look in each direction, and I thank God for the day that is about to begin. As I celebrate the bounty of the good earth God has made I pray that I may be a person of compassion who lives in balance and harmony with his surroundings—even as the animals and plants around me perform their own important and complementary roles in sustaining the web of life. When I first started this ritual, I didn't know east from west or north from south. I didn't know in which direction the sun rose; or where the migrating birds flying above me were headed in their journeys to their overwintering homes in Central America; or where the day ended in the long twilight of languid summer evenings; or in which direction the first cold Canadian blasts of winter originated. One morning as I spun my circle under a black walnut tree close to the edge of the yard, a squirrel dropped a large woody nut down on top of my head. Was this a random mistake, a sign of greeting, or a gesture of irritation? I wasn't sure, but the feeling that I was connected to other life-forms deepened my sense of relationship with the wider earth community during my morning ritual. I am a college professor, so I have a lot of facts in my head. But prior to beginning this ritual, there was not much music in my heart, or juice in my body; now this simple inaugural routine, sometimes accompanied by walnut fragments in my mop of early morning hair, has restored my sense of vigor and belonging to the life-giving flow patterns that make human existence vibrant and meaningful.

This daily activity—an alchemy of Christian prayer of thanksgiving and Native American sacred hoop ritual—goes to the heart of the vision that animates this book. I believe that earth and sky, human beings and other beings, everything that lives and grows in its own time and according to its own nature, is pulsing with a green life force that is sacred, that is eternal, that is God. I also believe that the central biblical teaching that the Holy Spirit is God's abiding and animating presence in the world—

the ongoing incarnation of divine energy that gives breath and life to all things—is an extraordinarily fecund expression of the power of this life force in the visionary language of Christian faith. Reactualizing the power of this ancient life force in my morning prayer wheel ritual is a daily reminder to me that the earth is sacred and should therefore be protected as the place that God indwells and maintains for the well-being of all of us, humankind and otherkind together.

We all need some way to experience a deep sense of belonging to the earth, whether or not we are denominationally religious. Indeed, unless we have that sense of belonging, I fear that the prospects for our continual habitation on this planet are not good. Without a spiritual basis for ecology—without a deeply felt sense of kinship with other life-forms—I think that it will be difficult for us to feel motivated to exercise concern for the welfare of the planet and its inhabitants. Reawakening our spiritual relationship to animals, land, and water forges that primal sense of connection to the lifeweb that is necessary for long-term commitments to sustainable living.

My own contribution to enlivening this primitive feeling of connection to the biosphere is to recover the rich biblical collection of images and stories about God as an earthen being who sustains the natural world with compassion and thereby models for humankind environmentally healthy ways of being. The particular earth-centered theological notion I develop in this book is the idea of the Holy Spirit as the fleshly, carnal bird God of the Bible who lives in all things and who enables in us a heartfelt desire to work toward the preservation of earth community in our time. In the Bible and historic Christian thought, the Holy Spirit is a wholly enfleshed, avian life-form made up of the four primitive elements—wind, water, fire, and earth—that are the key components of embodied life as we know it. As the dove who alights on Jesus at his baptism in the Gospels, God as Spirit is not a distant, invisible abstraction in heaven far removed from earthly concerns. On the contrary, God as Spirit is a sacred animal—a living, breathing life-form like all other life-forms on the planet—who shows Godself to us concretely by living in and through the earth. The message of Christian faith, therefore, is that as God loves and cares for the earth, we are to do the same. Thus God and the earth, Spirit and nature, Christianity and environmentalism are one.

Many colleagues, friends, and family members have generously contributed to the writing of this book. Jürgen Moltmann offered early support for the direction of my thinking at a conference on the Spirit at

Marquette University in 1998 organized by Lyle Dabney and Brad Hinze. In that same year, Dieter Hessel, Mary Evelyn Tucker, and John Grim gave me the opportunity to present my work on the wounded Spirit and Chester, Pennsylvania, at a Harvard University conference on Christianity and the environment. I am grateful to Darby Ray for the invitation to be the Summers lecturer at Millsaps College in 2003, a further occasion for developing my spiritual ecology concerns. Bron Taylor provided a thoughtful reading of the early manuscript and made many helpful suggestions regarding my interpretation of radical environmental movements today. Stephen Dunning similarly read parts of the manuscript and helped me to sharpen my thinking on the relevance of my project to traditional norms in Christian thought. Roger Latham supplied an engaging evaluation of the book's final chapter regarding the Crum Creek in Pennsylvania. Roger Gottlieb, Nathaniel Deutsch, Steven Hopkins, and Mark Cladis have been faithful dialogue-partners in my intellectual journey and I owe them much gratitude for their insights into the topics explored herein. Zulene Mayfield in Chester, and Wilford Guindon in Monteverde, Costa Rica, represent to me the strength and pathos of a prophetic challenge to the world domination system in our time. I am grateful to them for their leadership and friendship.

Paul Ricoeur says that to be moral is to aim at the good life with and for others in just institutions. Two institutions that seek to embody the good life for their members have provided me with consistent support in this book project. The Constructive Theology Workgroup at Vanderbilt University, organized by Peter Hodgson, Paul Lakeland, and Serene Jones, has created a dialogical forum for the kind of progressive theological thinking advanced here. Within the larger workgroup, the members of the Spirit subgroup in which I have participated—Jim Perkinson, Sharon Welch, Ada María Isasi-Díaz, Catherine Keller, Walt Lowe, Barbara Holmes, and Serene—have energized my green spirituality hopes with their provocations and insight. As well, Swarthmore College granted me sabbatical funding by supporting my application for an Andrew W. Mellon New Directions for Scholars-Teachers Fellowship that enabled me to finish this book. And my Swarthmore Provost Connie Hungerford went the extra mile by making available a subvention to the publisher to print the book's color illustrations. At Fortress Press, Michael West, Becky Lowe, Bob Todd, and Beth Wright have energetically shepherded the book to the final publication stage. I have appreciated the Fortress staff's attention to my needs and their hands-on approach to publishing quality books in religion that have a contemporary edge and are resonant with classical Christian themes.

This book would not have been possible without the support of my family. My parents, Homer and Shirley, and my sister, Darice, have always been the incubator for giving life to my creative work. My children, Katy and Christopher, are an abiding source of joy in my life, irrepressibly and exuberantly full of life; my hope is that I can continue to live toward a better future for our sacred, wounded earth both for their sake and with the hope and enthusiasm they embody. My wife, Ellen Ross, is a daily source of love and energy in my life. Sharing our job at Swarthmore College, summertime walks along the beach, fall afternoons at our children's soccer games—life with Ellen is a gift and a wonder. Ellen's overall sense of my theological direction and her careful eye for grammar and detail have made this book a much better piece of writing than it would have been otherwise. I am grateful to her for her patience and affection.

René Magritte's painting included here, *La grande famille* ("The Great Family"), speaks directly to the vision of God as Spirit I put forward in this book (see plate 2). As I interpret the painting, the winged Spirit broods over the waters of the earth in the same manner that the Spirit broods over the great egg of creation in the opening verses of Genesis: "In the beginning God created the heavens and the earth . . . and the Spirit of God hovered over the face of the deep" (1:1-2). In Magritte's portrayal the Spirit is radically immanent to the natural world—the Spirit is an earthen life-form, a bird, whose very being indwells creation as shown by the transparent sky and cloud patterns that constitute the Spirit's aerial shape. Magritte's image of *la grande famille*—the great family of creation—is dynamically woven together by the four primitive elements. In the *wind* that swirls in and around the Spirit, the movement of the Spirit's wings enlivens the cloudy atmosphere; in the ocean *water* below, the deep is teeming with an abundance of life that sustains the health and well-being of the biosphere; in the *fire* of the sun that appears to emanate from the luminous great bird itself, the ocean surf is charged with warmth and sparkles with light in its never-ending movement toward the shore; and at the horizon line of the watery *earth* itself, just visible underneath the wing feathers of the cosmic bird, we see the eternal oneness of God and nature in an eternal dance of unity and love. Rediscovering God's presence in the everyday rhythms of natural life is the promise of this painting—and the hope and dream of this book as well.

Introduction

The River God

THE PALPABLE EXPERIENCE OF GOD in the earth is one of my earliest childhood memories. As a boy, my family often traveled from Los Angeles, where I grew up, to coastal Mississippi, the site of my mother's homestead. Along the shores of the Singing River near Biloxi, Mississippi, my mother told me the story of the Pascagoula Indians who inhabited the banks of the river many generations ago, and the story of my great-grandmother, Frances Hawkins, a Seminole woman who migrated to the Mississippi Gulf Coast probably sometime in the 1890s. Little is known about her, but my grandmother, Winona, used to carry with her a dog-eared photograph of her mother in tribal garb. Throughout my childhood, the story of my great-grandmother's travels to Mississippi was intermixed with the other Native American story told to me by my mother and aunt about the early conflict between the Biloxi and Pascagoula Indians. Through this story, I experienced the power and mystery of Earth God present within the ebb and flow of the Singing River.

According to ancient legend, the two Indian communities had peacefully coexisted along the banks of the Singing River generation after generation. The Biloxi Indians, however, were a warrior clan while the Pascagoula peoples were more peace-loving. A mutual détente had held between both groups since earliest memory. This nonaggression pact entailed the proviso that the Biloxi would never attack the Pascagoula as long as no intermarriage between the two peoples took place. But the pact became threatened by the fledgling relationship between a young man of the Pascagoula families and a young woman of the Biloxi clan. Star-crossed lovers, the boy and girl's growing affection toward each other threatened to disturb the peace and stability that existed between the two communities. Fearful of an attack by the Biloxi on their population, and not willing to take up arms against their neighbors, the Pascagoula opted for a united course of action to prevent a massacre. They decided to put themselves to death. And they did so, according to the legend, walking single file into the dark waters of the Singing River—and singing a mournful, tribal song in the process.[1]

As a child I was fascinated and troubled by this account. But what I found particularly compelling about this story was my mother's claim that the song sung long ago by the Pascagoula could still be heard in the cadences of the river's waters. If you swim under the waters of the river and listen hard, you can hear the ancient dirge of the drowning people. My mother explained that while the Singing River is technically the Pascagoula River, most local people refer to it as the Singing River in recognition of the ongoing power of the legend. As a child I believed my mother's account: I swam in the river and heard the plaintive song of this lost community. In the undulating swish-swish of the water flow, I could hear the distant echo of the Pascagoula's river music mysteriously preserved in this underwater environment (see plate 1).

As a child swimming in the river, all of my senses were keenly attuned to the possibility of hearing the song of the Pascagoula. In some rough sense, I felt I was encountering God in the river. The river was a site of numinous powers, greater than myself, that both transcended and interpenetrated the everyday world of boyhood activity I normally inhabited. God, I sensed, was in the river, but God was also beyond the river. As an adult reflecting on the theological import of my childhood river experience, I now believe that the ancient tribal music I heard in the river deeps was made possible by God's presence within the muddy waters. Down in the dark water of the river, God actualized the ancient song and made it a reality to my listening ears. In this sense, as I now realize, my experience went beyond a hearing of the river song, as strange and miraculous as this might be; rather, it entailed an encounter with the divine life who made possible the transmission of the native dirge to my comprehension. I cannot exactly explain this double sensibility I felt at that time—how the hearing of the Indians' song was felt by me to be an instance of God's presence. Yet I knew, somehow, that the God I had learned about in my home and church and Sunday school as a child, this same God, now present to me in the river, was mediating to my understanding the death march music of the Pascagoula.

In claiming that the power to hear the river music was generated by the same God witnessed to in the Bible, it may appear that I am co-opting Native American spirituality by subsuming the story of the Pascagoula under the Christian notion of an all-encompassing God. What I am suggesting, however, is that God—or the Sacred or the Real—is a living and dynamic presence within the natural order who is greater than the theological models of God within any one particular religion, be it Christian or Native American. The spiritualities of biblical communities and America's Gulf Coast Indians have their own meaning and integrity and should not be collapsed into one another. Nevertheless, in the light of my own Christian upbringing and my hearing of the ancient dirge in the river, it made sense to me then, and it does again now, to understand the significance of these two dimensions of my life as having a common origin, a divine origin. Alternately, God is the same reality *witnessed to* by the biblical stories and the *source of* my encounter with the plaintive song still reverberating within the Pascagoula River. This double awareness has led me as an adult to embrace a multicultural vision of Christianity as a distinctive—but not absolute—worldview that draws its strength both from its time-honored scriptures and from its ongoing relationships with other religions and cultures. All that is good and wonderful springs from a common source—a divine source—toward which the world's religions and cultures strive to understand, and sometimes worship, in their own partial and fragmented ways.

Submerging myself within the waters of the river allowed me, then, to hear the river song and understand that its message sprang from the God of biblical faith. This twofold sensibility should not come as a surprise. Throughout my young life at the time, I had been taught Bible stories in my home and church in which the divine life was regularly figured as a nature deity. I had learned that God fashioned Adam and Eve from the dust of the ground, spoke through Balaam's donkey, arrested Job's attention in a whirlwind, used a great whale to send Jonah a message, and appeared as a dove throughout the New Testament. If these stories were true, then, similarly, is it impossible to imagine that God could speak again to an eight-year-old boy through a Mississippi river song?

The pedagogical import of the self-sacrifice of the Gulf Coast Indians was, to my early understanding, very clearly ethical in nature. This is why I thought God was in the river. In my young mind, the divine message embodied in the river music was clear: the preservation of this tribal melody was an undying memorial to the spiritual power and moral integrity of the Pascagoula. In order to prevent bloodshed, the community opted to perish collectively in the dark waters of the river. Tragically, horribly, the Pascagoula laid down their lives in order to prevent an internecine conflict from destroying their nation and the Biloxi. The model of giving the gift of one's own life so that another might live became the sacred teaching I took away from the river.[2] Bathed in the music and message of the river, I felt the divine presence in a direct, tangible fashion that I will never forget. I met God in that river and heard God's *moral* voice speak to me through the ancient song.

But while my boyhood encounter with the religiously charged river bore profound spiritual meaning for me at the time, as I grew older, and later learned to practice Christianity more reflectively, I drifted away from any sustained realizations of God in the natural world. Now I believe I know what I had encountered in the Pascagoula River—the God of Christian faith revealing Godself to me as a river God—but as a teenager and young adult I had become mistrustful of my earlier experiences as exercises in wishful thinking, even delusion. Sadly, as I now realize, this drift was aided and abetted by the historic indifference of Christian practice to, and even its hostility toward, the discovery of God within the environing earth.

In the main, historic Christianity understands the divine life as a *Sky God*. In nursery rhymes, sermons, hymnody, iconography, and theological teachings, God is pictured as a bodiless, immaterial being who inhabits a timeless, heavenly realm far beyond the vicissitudes of life on earth. Of course, in the person of Jesus, God did become an enfleshed life-form in ancient history. But the incarnation is generally understood as a long-ago, punctiliar event limited to a particular human being, namely, Jesus of Nazareth. Tragically, for many Christians, the incarnation of God in Jesus does not carry the promise that God, in any palpable sense, is continually enfleshed within the natural world as we know it. Rather, for the better part of church history, the divine life and the natural world have been viewed as two separate and distinct orders of being. Occasionally, God may intervene in the natural realm in order to achieve some other-worldly objective—as in the case of sending Jesus to earth in order to redeem humankind from its sins. But occasional divine visitations do not entail the continual presence of God in the earth. Indeed, the majority theological judgment is that any suggestion that God is somehow embedded in the earth smacks of heathenism, Paganism, and idolatry. Whatever else God is, God is not a nature deity captive to the limitations and vagaries of mortal life-forms. God is not bound to the impermanent flux of an ever-changing earth. God cannot be regarded as existing on a continuum with creaturely life-forms. It is for these reasons, according to mainstream opinion, that biblical religion forbids the fashioning of graven images as representations of the divine life: God is not a bull or a snake or a lion. On the contrary, so the majority argument goes, God abides in an eternally unchanging heavenly realm where bodily suffering and death are no more and every tear is wiped dry for the privileged believer who dwells there.

My experience of the sacred river instilled within me an abiding uneasiness with the majority argument against God in nature. It was here—in the swift current of the river—that I had my first experience of God as a numinous power within a natural landscape. But as I grew older, as I have said, I found it easy enough to discount this experience. What had begun for me as an encounter with God in the underwater cathedral of the river evolved, over time, into a distant memory of a youthful enthusiasm. As a young adult, I questioned whether I really did experience God in the river as a boy. I speculated that I was an impressionable victim of autosuggestion. Based on my mother's tale, I entered the river primed to hear the music of the Pascagoula and, accordingly, thought I heard the ancient song when, in reality, it was simply the roar of the river's underwater power that I was hearing. In following through this line of questioning, however, I began to realize that I was making war against my deepest sensibilities. I was doing damage to my soul. If a person cannot trust his or her innermost stirrings, then we are all captive to the voices of others with no ability to plumb our own internal depths and discover therein what we know to be true. As an adult, I resolved to trust my inward certainties and suspend the majority theological conviction that God could not possibly appear and speak profound messages in natural landforms such as the Singing River.

If God long ago spoke through Jesus as the Word of God, is it impossible to imagine that God today could speak again through the muddy waters of a Mississippi coastal river? Alongside Christianity's time-honored source of revelation—the biblical texts—could God speak again through an alternative medium to a child primed to hear the song of the river? For me, in those early boyhood swims, the God of the biblical testimonies was a river deity who said to me—through the requiem of the Pascagoula—that one should always live one's life in the service of others—even as the Pascagoula did in their mass migration into the river. I found this ethical message to be in perfect harmony with the biblical teachings. It neither contradicted nor undermined these teachings. It only deepened them. Or perhaps, I now realize, it is the other way around—namely, that the biblical teachings have their peculiar depth and power in my life because these teachings are fundamentally rooted in earth-centered, spiritually charged events in my formative years, such as swimming in the sacrificial stream of the Singing River.

Landscapes of the Sacred

In this book I want to explore the promise of Christianity as an earth-centered, body-loving religion.[3] I want to explore the promise of Christian faith to heal human beings' exploitative environmental habits through its nature-based teachings concerning the enfleshed presence of God in all things. Sadly, we are living at a time when plant and animal species are being wiped out at an unusually rapid rate. Unlike previous mass death events in our planet's evolutionary past, this contemporary "Sixth Great Extinction," as Niles Eldredge puts it, is being caused by our own rapacious habits.[4] We need a fundamental attitude adjustment in order to address the contemporary crisis, and Christianity has the potential resources for changing hearts and minds for enabling greener lifestyles. Christianity is a treasure trove of rich images and stories about God's loving the earth and living in the earth that can set free robust, environmentally sustainable ways of being.[5]

For this book, in particular, I want to retrieve a central but neglected Christian theme—the idea of God as carnal Spirit who imbues all things— as the linchpin for forging a green spirituality responsive to the environmental needs of our time. Theologically speaking, I believe that hope for a renewed earth is best founded on belief in God as Earth Spirit, the compassionate, all-encompassing divine force within the biosphere who inhabits earth community and continually works to maintain the integrity of all forms of life. Like the river deity I encountered in the Singing River as a boy, in green spirituality God is the *Earth God* who indwells the land and invigorates and flows with natural processes—not the invisible *Sky God* who exists in a heavenly realm far removed from earthly concerns.[6]

In antiquity, early Christians identified the Spirit as coequal with God the Father and God the Son, a constituent member of the divine Trinity, and the supreme and all-encompassing presence of God in the world. But this ancient understanding of the Spirit seems to have little purchase on contemporary religious thought and life. One exception to this general trend is the practice of charismatic and Pentecostal believers who encounter the work of the Spirit in their everyday lives. Through the gifts of the Spirit—speaking in tongues, miracles of healing, and words of prophecy—members of the Pentecostal movement are baptized in the Holy Spirit and experience directly the tangible energy of the Spirit through different signs and wonders. But many other persons (and I count myself among this number) are not always comfortable with such spectacular exhibits of divine power, and such persons look for God's presence in equally palpable but less demonstrative displays.

Unfortunately, however, this search for God's presence outside Pentecostalism's signs and wonders is often not successful because it cannot locate the more subtle traces of the Spirit's presence in the world around us. The upshot of this fruitless search is that the ancient Christian experience and understanding of the Spirit as God's radical presence in the here and now is lost to many of us. Thus the reality of the Spirit has dropped out of the experience of many Christians. Indeed, many contemporary Christians, if they think about the Holy Spirit at all, now visualize the Spirit as the passive and retiring member of the Godhead, the mysterious and unknown member of the Trinity who, unlike the Father and the Son, lacks personality and definition.

This way of thinking restricts Christianity to being a religion of the Father and the Son and deadens our awareness of the Spirit's critically important work in the world today. To offset this tendency, I propose a nature-based model of the Spirit as the "green face" of God. The Spirit is the divine power who sustains the integrity of the natural world and brings together all of creation into one common biotic family. This earthen doctrine of the Spirit offers hope at a time when the future prospects of the planet are increasingly dim. A new vision of the Holy Spirit as the Spirit of the earth has the potential both to bring meaningful renewal to many persons and to invigorate public policy discussions about how best to ensure the well-being of all members of our planet home.

For this change to take place, however, the dominant model for understanding the Spirit has to be significantly overhauled. Unfortunately, the vernacular definition of the Spirit as the "Holy Ghost" in common parlance and the historic liturgy of Christianity renders this task especially difficult. Translated from the ancient Hebrew and Greek texts, early English versions of the Bible mistakenly translated the phrase "Holy Spirit" as "Holy Ghost." The clear sense of the original biblical texts is that the Spirit is to be understood as God's visible and benevolent power in the cosmos, not a spook or ghost. The Spirit is not a heavenly phantom—immaterial and unreal (and perhaps a bit scary as well!)—but God's all-pervasive presence and energy within the universe. Nevertheless, the Holy Spirit,

God's power for goodness and healing in the world, has been handed down to us as a shadowy, unearthly apparition, the Holy Ghost. It is not surprising, therefore, that many contemporary persons have little sense of identity with this specter of sorts.[7]

Understanding the Spirit in ghostly terms makes the Spirit unreal and immaterial. From this perspective, the Spirit is not a bodily, physical reality like the rest of things in creation; it is not of the same nature as other animate and inanimate life-forms on the earth. Thus this ghostly model of the Spirit fuels the standard polarities in Western thought (including Western theology) with which many of us are now familiar: mind versus body, the supernatural versus the natural, God versus nature, and Spirit versus material reality. These oppositions undergird a wide chasm that separates the world of the Spirit and the world of matter, rendering the Spirit an invisible, incorporeal, and, finally, unreal theological fiction.[8]

The biblical descriptions of the Spirit do not square with this ghostly model. The biblical message seeks to bring together God and the earth, the spiritual and the natural, mind and matter, but this message is often missed. The apostle Paul's rhetoric of spirit versus flesh, for example, is often mistakenly read as an endorsement of a state of war between God and human passions, but this is not Paul's point, as I will attempt to demonstrate later on. The vast majority of the biblical texts undercut the oppositional set of terms that legitimizes the split between the spiritual and the material.

In particular, on the topic of the Spirit, not only do the scriptural texts not divorce the spiritual from the earthly, but, moreover, they figure the Spirit as a creaturely life-form interpenetrated by the material world. Indeed, images of the Spirit drawn directly from nature are the defining motif in biblical notions of Spirit. Consider the following metaphors and descriptions of the Spirit within the Bible: the *animating breath* that brings life and vigor to all things (Genesis 1:2; Psalms 104:29-30); the *healing wind* that conveys power and a new sense of community to those it indwells (Judges 6:34; John 3:6; Acts 2:1-4); the *living water* that vivifies and refreshes all who drink from its eternal springs (John 4:14, 7:37-38); the *cleansing fire* that alternately judges wrongdoers and ignites the prophetic mission of the early church (Acts 2:1-4; Matthew 3:11-12); and the *divine dove*, a fully embodied earth creature, who births creation into existence, and, with an olive branch in its mouth, brings peace and renewal to a broken and divided world; this same bird God hovers over Jesus at his baptism to inaugurate his public ministry (Genesis 1:1-3, 8:11; Matthew 3:16; John

1:32). The Spirit is an earthen reality who is biblically figured according to the four primitive, cardinal elements—earth, wind, water, fire—that are the key components of embodied life as we know it.[9] In these scriptural texts, the Spirit is pictured as a wholly enfleshed life-form who engenders healing and renewal throughout the abiotic and biotic orders.

As I perform a retrieval of the Spirit's *earthen* identity in this book, I also hope to recover the Spirit's *female* identity.

As God's indwelling, corporeal presence within the created order, the Spirit is variously identified with feminine and maternal characteristics in the biblical witness. In the Bible the Spirit is envisioned as God's helping, nurturing, inspiring, and birthing presence in creation.[10] The mother Spirit Bird in the opening creation song of Genesis, like a giant hen sitting on her cosmic nest egg, broods over the earth and brings all things into life and fruition. In turn, this same hovering Spirit Bird, as a dove that alights on Jesus as he comes up through the waters of his baptism, appears in all four of the Gospels to signal God's approval of Jesus' public work. The maternal, avian Spirit of Genesis and the Gospels is the nursing mother of creation *and* Jesus' ministry who protects and sustains the well-being of all things in the cosmic web of life. Early Christian communities in the Middle East consistently spoke of the Spirit as the motherly, regenerative breath and power of God within creation. These early Christians believed that the Hebrew feminine grammatical name of the Spirit – *rûach* – was a linguistic clue to certain woman-specific characteristics of God as Spirit. As these early Christians rightly understood that God transcends sex and gender, their point was not that God was a female deity, but that it is appropriate alternately to refer to God's mystery, love, and power in "male" *and* "female" terms.[11] In this book I will take the liberty of referring to the Spirit as "she" in order to recapture something of the biblical understanding of God as feminine Spirit within the created order.

Far from being ghostly and bodiless, then, the Spirit reveals herself in the biblical literatures as a physical, earthly presence—a life-form both like and unlike all other life-forms—who labors to create and sustain humankind and otherkind in solidarity with one another. As the bird God in Genesis and the Gospels, the life-giving breath of the Psalms, or the tongues of fire in Acts, the Spirit is an earthen being who infuses all things with the power for growth, change, and renewal. Nature itself in all its many manifestations is to be understood as the primary mode of being for the Spirit's work in the biosphere. In this green model of the Spirit, the earth's waters, winds, fires, and various life-forms are to be celebrated as living and tangible expressions of the divine life itself. So if we wonder where God is in the world today we need only go outside our bedroom window. There we will hear a robin sing to its mate, we will observe an ant carry its daily sustenance on its back, we will watch a hosta plant strain toward the sun in the miracle of photosynthesis, and there we will find God in the viscous, fecund, and rich soil of the earth around us.

The Earthen Bible

The sensibility of this book is rooted in the deep well of the Bible. I go to that well often in my personal devotions and theological reflection for nurture and renewal. I find the Bible to be a fertile source of sensuous earth imagery that depicts the common kinship between humans and the natural world, one of the driving concerns of this book.

In this book I read the Bible with green eyes. My goal is to recover the startling originality of the scriptures from a self-consciously environmental perspective. I celebrate this biocentric framework for biblical understanding and suggest such a framework opens up new vistas of meaning that have gone unnoticed by previous interpretive approaches. Everyone reads the Bible from one orientation or another; no one comes to the biblical texts innocent of her (or her community's) own "working canon" or "canon within the canon." This does not mean that biblical meaning is hostage to unexamined interpretive biases. But insofar as meaning is not "in" the text but rather happens "between" text and reader, my suggestion is that the biblical reader always operates within her own interpretive horizon as the enabling context for understanding new possibilities of meaning.

What does it mean to understand biblical meaning as an event that happens between text and reader? The Bible, as a great classic, is best read in the spirit of a living dialogue between the interpreter and the text itself. Like all of the classics, biblical meaning emerges in the dynamic space between reader and text; it is generated in the to-and-fro movement between the reader's expectations and the text's provocations. From this perspective, the Bible should not be viewed as containing an obvious, univocal message that imposes itself on the obedient reader, nor should its meaning be understood as controlled by the privileged reader whose presuppositions determine what the text can and cannot say. Making sense of the Bible should avoid the Charybdis of authoritarian biblicism and the Scylla of vulgar deconstruction. Biblical meaning is neither a timeless *property* of the text that subordinates the subservient reader to its predetermined message nor the *product* of the entitled interpreter whose learning and sophistication disallow the possibility that the biblical texts could articulate their own reader-independent voice. Biblical meaning is not in the text, nor is it foisted onto the text by the reader; rather, genuine meaning happens between text and reader in moments of sustained encounter and discernment. Neither a bank of preset ideas nor a blank page that gets filled in by the reader's imagination, the Bible is a contested site where a living body of stories and symbols comes face-to-face with a reader who is willing to suspend her everyday assumptions and experience life-changing transformations through this encounter.

Textual understanding always operates, therefore, within an animating "hermeneutical circle"; there is no neutral starting point by which a reader begins the interpretive process. This hermeneutical circle need not be a vicious circle, if the reader is intentional about owning her particular set of assumptions and does not purport to follow a purely "objective" (read: presuppositionless) model of textual interpretation. The hermeneutical circle is productive whenever the reader construes the meaning of a particular scriptural passage in the light of her own founding assumptions and then checks the validity of these assumptions against the possible lines of meaning within the text itself. Assumptions are read against the text and in turn the text is understood in reference to the founding assumptions. Thus biblical meaning takes flight within ever-widening circles of interpretation: it is produced by the give-and-take dialogue in which both reader and text are mutually engaged. In the contrapuntal movement between my own organizing framework and the provocations of the text I have found earth-centered reading to be a liberating source of new meaning and understanding.[12]

I am self-conscious about my earth-centered hermeneutic and believe that such a hermeneutic allows the Bible to speak again from the center of its love and passion for the good creation God has made. God is not distant from our planet, unmoved by earthly concerns, dispassionate and unaffected by the environmental degradation that despoils the bounty and beauty of the created order. Rather, from a green spirituality perspective, we learn that God loves the earth, manifests Godself as an earthen being in the human Jesus and corporeal Spirit, and suffers deeply from the environmental abuse that causes pain and loss to all beings. Of course, there are many other, and equally legitimate, hermeneutical templates, other than a green template, that readers can use to hear the biblical texts' claims to our attention. For example, a reader, or a larger interpretive community, might want to understand the biblical texts from a feminist perspective and discern the significant roles women play in biblical stories; or she might use an evangelical hermeneutic to privilege the place individual salvation plays in Paul's letters; or she might use archaeological evidence or other historical-critical methods in order to illuminate biblical teachings in the light of the ancient cultural milieu that produced them. All of these hermeneutical approaches are, in principle, productive means by which to sustain vital encounters between reader and text.[13]

Consider one example of a green hermeneutic at work on a particular biblical passage, namely, Jesus' teaching about the lilies of the field. In this book I focus on the Spirit in biblical literatures, the earthen bird God who renews and sustains all members of the lifeweb in fellowship with one another. But this same hermeneutic could be applied to a deeper understanding of Jesus' earth-centered mission and message as well. Jesus' teaching about the lilies of the field in the Sermon on the Mount is a good case in point. In Matthew we read, "Consider the lilies of the field, how they grow; they neither toil nor spin; yet I tell you, even Solomon in all of his glory was not arrayed like one of these" (6:28-29). The simplicity and elegance of this passage is difficult to fathom. Here Jesus says that everyday field lilies, in just being what they are, are more glorious and wonderful than was King Solomon in all his regal splendor and power. Solomon, whose royal court was legendary for its grandeur and magnificence, is deemed less resplendent than the wildflowers that grace the meadows enjoyed by Jesus in his journeys throughout the Israel of his day. In this passage, Jesus, the environmental trickster, reverses the priority we assign to grandiose built structures and favors instead the quiet beauty inherent in the natural order of things. The most spectacular architectural treasures of the ancient world are inferior to the rich colors and textures that shine forth from the highways and byways of Jesus' earthly ministry.

One of my favorite summer delights is the discovery of Turk's-cap lilies during nature hikes my family takes in coastal Rhode Island. Beautiful, tall, flowering lilies grow through the crevices of the stone walls we encounter along the wooded path we follow to the ocean from our summer rental cottage. Turk's-cap lilies are large, native wildflowers with showy, curved-back petals that resemble a style of cap supposedly worn by early Turks; they are spectacular orange flowers with elongated, dangling stamens that bounce in the summer breeze. Across the surface of the rounded petals are reddish-brown spots that nicely contrast with the pure orange color of the petals and the deep green of the stem. The rolling fields alongside whose edges we encounter these lilies come alive in a riot of color and movement when these floral gifts arrive in Rhode Island every summer.

Could King Solomon's grand palaces pale in insignificance to these graceful flowers randomly scattered throughout the meadows and woods of coastal New England? Jesus' teaching about wild lilies is a challenge to our aesthetic conventions and ingrained habits of seeing. How many of us would subordinate the beauty of Michelangelo's David or the grandeur of the Eiffel Tower to everyday flora in an uncultivated field? How many of us would regard the majesty of the Empire State Building or the charm of the Taj Mahal as inferior to the beauty and wonder of simple flowers along a common roadside? In my experience, however, Jesus is right: catching a glimpse of Turk's-cap lilies in an open meadow on a summer walk is truly awe-inspiring. If we could learn again, like Jesus, to see the world with green eyes, then we could catch Jesus' vision of an earth charged with a natural grace and beauty more profound than anything we can imagine. A green world alive with color and fragrance—the restrained elegance of lilies in an open field—is the supernatural food Earth God offers to us to feed our hungry bodies and souls.

Christian Paganism

Another source of vision for this book is contemporary Pagan spirituality. Today many Pagans celebrate the immanence of the sacred in everyday, earthly life through seasonal festivals (Samhain/Halloween and Summer Solstice), rites of passage ceremonies (birthing, croning, and death), magic and witchcraft (vision quests and healing practices), and other rituals of earth celebration and earth healing ("shamanic" drumming and political action on behalf of endangered species and habitats). Neopaganism is a modern earth-centered spirituality that draws much of its vitality and symbolism from pre-Christian ceremonies and belief systems. Like ancient Greek and Roman Pagans, contemporary Neopagans believe that all life is sacred; nature, our life-giving mother, is the place where our common lives are nurtured and where sacred power is revealed to us. The "at home" attitude toward the earth in early Celtic, Teutonic, and Nordic religions, now reactualized by modern-day Pagans, offers a healing alternative to the toxic anti-earth attitudes sacralized by certain emphases in Western monotheistic religions.[14]

Pagans celebrate nature as hallowed ground, as a sacred community of interconnected beings rather than an exploitable resource designed to serve human beings' self-aggrandizing interests. They celebrate nature as all beings' common home instead of regarding the earth as a passing phenomenon inimical to people's spiritual growth and in need of future redemption. They regard nature as the bio-spiritual web of life that connects the human and more-than-human worlds rather than an impediment that must be overcome in human beings' march toward salvation in a disembodied heavenly realm. Neopagans' celebration of seasonal festivals and earth-based ritual practices are markers of their deep kinship with the natural world and its cyclical processes. For Pagans, the earth is all we have—there is no distant or better world beyond this world—and it is incumbent upon all of us to protect this rich and fragile ecosystem. Nature is the sacred, interconnected matrix that generates all life-forms and allows them to survive and flourish. Nature is not an object under the dominion of its human caretakers, to be used (and sometimes abused) to serve human ends.

Paganism is sometimes confused with Satanism and worship of the devil: evil, sinister beliefs and practices that destroy life rather than nurture life. But Neopagans consider Satanism to be an egoistic, power-hungry religion that exploits Christianity's polemic against the devil in order to foment dark magic and the harmful manipulation of natural forces. Many Neopagans self-identify as witches in the sense that they are practitioners of a time-honored craft of healing and renewal (so the definition of Neopaganism as the "Craft" or *Wicca*). But contemporary Pagans are good, not evil, witches, because they practice the ancient arts of healing human beings' diseased relationships with other persons and other life-forms. Of course, magic and witchcraft can be pressed into the service of evil ends (as is the case with any religious or ritual tradition). However, modern Pagans do not worship Satan and thereby seek to increase their own personal power at the expense of other persons and other life-forms. On the contrary, Neopaganism is an intensely communal religion that celebrates nature's strengthening, life-giving forces in order to harness these forces to restore the lost balance that at one time defined the natural harmony between humankind and otherkind.

The emphasis in Neopaganism on community-centered, earth-based religious life is a vital resource for developing a green Christian imagination. But there are important differences between the two religions that should not be overlooked. For those Pagans who are theistic, their vision of divinity is pluralistic and immanentist, while orthodox Christianity understands God to be one and fundamentally transcendent. It appears, therefore, that a rigid line of division separates the two traditions: Paganism is polytheistic and this-worldly, while Christianity is monotheistic and otherworldly. But upon closer inspection of the historic and symbolic affinities between Christianity and Paganism, it becomes clear that the two forms of spirituality are not polar opposites.

From its origins two thousand years ago, Christianity matured and flourished in the fertile soil of Judaism, on the one hand, and the indigenous Pagan religions of Greece and Rome, on the other. From the Jews, Christians learned respect for law, belief in the Bible, and an understanding of God as a unitary, heavenly Father who rewards the just and punishes the wicked. From the "mystery religions" of Hellenized and Roman cultures, Christians learned about the immortality of the soul, the magic of physical healing, and the redeemer myth of a god who rises from the dead. But Christianity is not merely an extension of Judaism and Paganism: Christianity, while indebted to its forbearers, charted its own original course and developed beliefs and practices independent from its ancient cultural origins.

While Christianity evolved away from its formative predecessors, it still bears some fundamental affinities with both of its originary religious heritages. And while it may appear radically distinct from its root sources, it continues to carry within itself a deep strain of Pagan this-worldliness and a vision of God that borders on *animism*—even while maintaining its fidelity to Jewish monotheism. Animism is the belief that the sacred permeates all living things; in Christianity, the belief that God's Spirit imbues all creation roots biblical faith in the Pagan animist soil of its primitive origins. In particular, the animist tendency in Christianity is apparent in the Christian doctrine of the Trinity, the idea that God is one *and* three, both transcendent to the world and immanent in the world, all at the same time. The idea of God as Trinity stresses both the unity and the plurality of the Godhead and also, paradoxically, the notion that God is both "other" and, at the same time, pervasively "present" in all things through the Spirit of God. In the Trinity, the Godhead is a unitary relationship of three persons in one being—Father, Son, and Holy Spirit—in which God is both external to the world and fundamentally internal in the world at the same time. Paradoxically, God is one and not one; God is transcendent and immanent; God is alternately and at the same time, without confusion or division, both beyond the world and everywhere in the world. God in Christianity is both the far-removed "One" and the ever-present "Many."

In dialogue with Neopaganism, this dialectic of the One and the Many in historic Christianity opens up a renewed understanding of Christianity's ecological potential for our own time. If, according to orthodox belief, God is always already both "up there" and yet still "everywhere" at the same time, then Christianity is not opposed to Paganism (even as it is not opposed to Judaism) but a rearticulation of the radically earthen sensibility of Paganism in a new biblical idiom. Christianity is not an anti-body and anti-worldly religion, but rather a holistic spirituality that pictures all planetary life, indeed the whole universe, as infused with God's presence through the power of the Spirit. The promise of the Trinity, then, is not a new mystical arithmetic by which to cogitate God's one-in-threeness. The promise of the Trinity, rather, is a deep green, cosmically pluralistic model of God's immanent indwelling of all earthen life-forms *along with* the insistence that God, in some sense, also transcends this divine enfleshment in all things. The promise of the Trinity is that God is beyond and in everything and thereby wonderfully present everywhere, infusing all things with the vigor and power of the Spirit. As in Neopaganism, nothing is dead and matter is not inert because all things are charged with the sacred power of the Spirit. All things God has made—Cooper's hawks, manure worms, ripe asparagus, feral cats, ancient redwoods, everyday pigweed, and Turk's-cap lilies—are beings or life-forms bodying forth the love and presence of God's Spirit.

As Christianity needs to heal its relationship with Judaism and overcome centuries of Christian anti-Semitism, so also does it need to repair its relationship with Paganism and overcome its historic antipathy to the body and nature. In this healing, Christianity rediscovers its Pagan roots and becomes what it has always been—a thoroughly biblical and biocentric source of personal and communal well-being. With particular reference to Paganism, this healed relationship allows Christianity to reawaken itself to its belief in God as both "beyond" and "everywhere"—what we might call its "transcendental animist" history and identity. Christianity's transcendental animist identity consists of a twofold belief that all of nature is infused with God's presence, on the one hand, and that God is not collapsed into nature without remainder, on the other.

In spite of Christianity's orienting affinity with Neopaganism, the dialogue between the two traditions has not been constructive to date. Oftentimes, both groups treat each other with suspicion, even hostility. On the Christian side, Carl E. Braaten sharply contrasts "the gospel" and "neopaganism" by defining "the word 'gospel' in the broad sense of the whole message of Jesus Christ" whereas "'neopaganism' is a word used [as] a catchall for everything opposed to Christianity." Braaten continues that in particular he "will use the term ['neopaganism'] to refer to modern variations of the ancient belief of pre-Christian mystery religions that a divine spark or seed is innate in the individual human soul."[15] The Christian gospel for Braaten stands for the message that every person by nature is broken and in need of redemption, whereas the teaching of Neopaganism, he writes, is that there is something of God in all of us. I do not think the traditional Christian idea that we all need the good news of the Gospel and the Neopagan conviction that the seeds of God's presence are implanted within all of us are opposing beliefs. But for Braaten there seems to be no middle ground that brings together these two belief systems.

Braaten's comments are representative of much of conservative and mainstream Christian thinking about the inherent differences between the two traditions. On the Neopagan side, by contrast, Christianity is often identified with witch burning and the general oppression of Pagans. Loretta Orion summarizes this judgment in narrating the "Christian" arson of the earth-loving, nature sanctuary home of Micha de Liuda, a Wiccan practitioner, in Vermont in 1993:

> The night of the fire there had been a Christian conclave in a town about twenty minutes from de Liuda's land; the flier for the event had urged followers to "illuminate the night with Christ's righteousness."[16]

In general, then, as many Neopagans are distrustful of Christians as stridently opposed to earth-centered religion, many Christians do not recognize the origins and ongoing vitality of their religion in biblical and Pagan teachings that the earth is holy and that all things are filled with the Spirit—that all things carry an "innate divine seed," as Carl E. Braaten (disparagingly) puts it. Neopagans are often wary of Christianity as a destructive ideological force intent on emptying the natural world of any signs of sacred presence even as Christians question any earth-passionate belief system that blurs the particularity of their understanding of the Gospel message. That all things, wonderfully and powerfully, are filled with the presence of the divine life is the common feature of both religions, but a feature generally lost in the current acrimonious climate.

It may seem, therefore, that in the light of Paganism's emphasis on this-worldly theism and Christianity's belief in a transcendent deity that Neopagans and contemporary Christians have little to say to one another. I have sought to show, however, that the two communities have much in common in spite of their mutual recriminations and important differences. In particular, with reference to my attempt to reestablish Christianity on the firm ground of its ancient earth-centered teachings, Paganism is crucial for reawakening Christian faith to its deep-seated passion for the integrity and goodness of the earth and the body. The Pagan conviction that the whole earth is sacred rekindles the ancient Christian trinitarian doctrine that God as Spirit imbues all things. In short, therefore, Paganism helps to return Christianity to its earthen beginnings and the best of its ecological insights and potential. Surprisingly and paradoxically, Christianity, which historically waged war against "heathen" fertility and Goddess cultures, can now recognize itself as the bearer of the very earth-centeredness that it initially inveighed against. That Christianity *is* animism and animism *is* Christianity is an insight that is now possible as a result of a new, healed relationship between biblical religion, on the one hand, and earth religion, on the other. The Spirit and the earth are one, the Sacred and the planet are one, God and nature are one—so begins a new adventure in the return of Christianity to its green future as a continuation of ancient Pagan earth wisdom.

Deep Ecology

Along with the Bible and Neopaganism, this book has another important source as well—namely, the contemporary environmental philosophy of "deep ecology." Deep ecology further informs the root metaphors and basic orientation that animate this project. The core insight of deep ecology is that all living things are equal in value and worth and possess the inherent right to grow and flourish. As opposed to "shallow ecology," which views the natural world as a manageable resource subordinate to human needs and control, in deep ecology the natural world has intrinsic and not merely instrumental value: all life is worthwhile in and of itself independent from its usefulness to the human community. All life is inherently valuable and important whatever its utility might be for furthering human interests.[17]

Deep ecology flattens out the value hierarchy, intuitive to most of us, that ascribes supreme significance to human beings over and against all other life-forms. It knocks humankind off the top of the "ontological pyramid" that privileges human beings as bearers of more worth and value than other life-forms. In deep ecology, since all things subsist in common kinship with one another, it follows that no one particular species, including the human species, is more important than any other. Deep ecology, then, is vigorously opposed to anthropocentrism, the worldview that locates human beings at the apex of a Great Chain of Being that begins with God, moves to humankind, and then locates all other life-forms as lower and less significant in the Great Chain. Opposed to anthropocentrism, deep ecology stresses that humankind and otherkind are of equal worth and that humans, therefore, need to learn to share the planet with other living things. Thus, endangered North American shorebird populations should be accorded the same right that humans' enjoy to birth and feed their young within the coastal ecosystems that human beings like to use for recreational purposes. Since all things depend upon one another for their health and well-being, all beings should be allowed to realize their own natural ends without becoming the objects of callous misuse.

The ethical corollary to this "live and let live" insight centers on equal regard for all species populations. Insofar as all life-forms are codependent members of the biosphere, the traditional value distinctions that prioritize the interests of humankind over otherkind are consistently effaced. Conventionally speaking, it has been said that because human beings are smarter or more sentient or more complex than other life-forms it follows that humans are more worthwhile than other beings and should therefore be given more resources to live and flourish. On the contrary, deep ecology stresses the supreme value of preserving the integrity of whole ecosystems—that is, integral communities of living beings in their native habitats such as temperate grasslands or tropical forests. This emphasis on protecting the health of natural systems effectively subordinates the particular interests of any one species—including the human species—to the larger welfare of the whole ecosystem. Deep ecologists label as "speciesist" the assignation of superior worth to one species over another, and they refer to "biotic egalitarianism" as the reverential attitude of equal regard human beings should have toward nonhuman species.

Deep ecology stresses an attitude of equal regard for all life-forms as the highest good humans can seek to live by in their interactions with the natural world. Since all organisms, from single-celled bacteria to highly developed mammals, are coequal centers of biological activity, the maintenance of healthy environments in which the realization of a biocommunity's life cycle can be sustained is the primary good deep ecology valorizes. The moral stance that results from this commitment to green integrity is variously formulated as the "duty of noninterference," the "principle of minimum impact," or "the rule of letting nature be." This stance entails a hands-off, live-and-let live behavioral norm that encourages our copartnership with nature in order to assist particular ecosystems in helping them realize their own natural ends. "Green teleology" is the watchword of deep ecology: loving and working with living systems toward the end that their growth and fruition are enabled in a manner consistent with their deepest biological impulses.

Deep ecology informs current practices of earth healing by different human groups, some of which are religious and some of which are not. It provides the baseline philosophy that guides thoughtful human efforts to live lightly on the earth and thereby shrink our "environmental footprint," so to speak, so that other communities of beings can enjoy a rich and fruitful existence. Thus, in conflict situations where humans and nonhuman others have competing claims to resources and habitats, the ethical goal should be to develop policies that register no or as little negative human impact as possible on the natural world. Practically, this would entail that in circumstances where *nonessential* human interests are furthered by the destruction of plants and animals (for example, in the case of doing irreparable harm to a native grassland in order to make room for a housing development), the decision should be to make little or no provision for such environmental impact. On the other hand, however, in situations where the *essential* integrity and well-being of a species population is at stake, human or nonhuman, more latitude should be given to measures that will benefit the needy population in spite of the negative effects on the other populations not benefiting from the measures in question (for example, in cases where a sustainable drawdown of river water for human consumption might temporarily depress the flourishing of native biota). Nevertheless, the same rule applies in both situations, namely, the rule of "minimal impact as much as possible" regarding other species.

In religious terms, deep ecology emphasizes the sacredness and holiness of all things living in harmony and balance within the natural order of creation. Spiritually oriented deep ecologists refer to healthy and diverse ecosystems as "sacred places" or "holy ground," terms that may sound oddly misplaced for religious persons used to reserving the language of "the sacred" or "the holy" for God alone. Referring to the created order in religious terms challenges the common understanding of traditional orthodoxy that only God can be said to be holy and that sacredness inheres in God alone, not natural systems. In conventional theological terms, it is wrong to say that the creation God has made is sacred because such honorific language is uniquely applicable to God and appears to detract from the glory of the Creator. Such language appears idolatrous, exchanging worship of God for reverence of the earth.

I recently enjoyed a nature retreat led by Lorraine Fox-Davis, an American Indian healer, in the mountains of southern Colorado. Along with other retreat participants, our group hiked and camped in the foothills of the Sangre de Christo mountain range (named, according to legend, by Spanish missionaries for the mountains' deep, red, eucharistic colors at sunset). On the retreat we bathed in a cold mountain stream, had morning devotions in the still quiet of a cottonwood grove, and watched deer and elk graze in the meadows beneath our campsite. This bucolic existence was interrupted late one evening by two black bears, who entered our camp and proceeded to root around in search of food. In the morning our campsite was a mess, but we escaped otherwise relatively unscathed. Some of our fellow campers' personal vehicles, however, were not so fortunate. Some of the campers had left their cars and trucks, filled with open containers of food, too close to the wilderness area where we were staying. Though these automobiles were locked tight and their windows generally rolled up, the hungry bears smelled the food and proceeded to break into and tear apart the interiors.

Many of my retreat fellows were angry and upset at what they called the "destruction" wrought by the bears' search for food. Some members of our cohort whose vehicles were broken into were crying; they all were apoplectic with frustration about the damage done to their prized Jeep Cherokees and Nissan Pathfinders. But Lorraine Fox-Davis explained to us that the reason their vehicles were attacked was because a few of us had brought large foreign objects loaded with food into a wilderness area. The fault does not lie with the bears, she gently chided the campers, but with us. The Sangre de Christo mountains are part of a harmonious and fragile ecosystem that has survived intact for thousands of years in spite of many human incursions. These mountains are sacred, she said, because the Spirit of God lives in the mountains and the mountain ecosystem is richly diverse and naturally balanced. We should treat the mountains—including their animal denizens and natural systems—with awe and respect. But when we disrupt nature's balance with our SUVs, processed food, and leftover trash, we sometimes are "judged" by the Spirit of the Mountains and reminded of our natural places in the great scheme of things. Our retreat leader said that the bears were God's special emissaries sent to our campsite to remind us to treat the Sangre de Christo mountains as holy ground.

Lorraine Fox-Davis's theology of the mountains is rooted in a deep ecology sensibility. In green Christianity terms, since God as Spirit lives in the earth, and since all natural systems are inherently valuable in and for themselves, we can refer to God's creation in sacred terms and mourn the loss of the lifeweb that nourishes and supports all of us as an attack on the sacred order of things, as a desecration. My sojourns in the southern Colorado high country, while probably not particularly enriching for the bears and elk and hummingbirds I met along the way, were deeply important to my own recovery of my identity as an earthen being whose essence is rooted in the organic lifeways and cycles of the natural world. Nature is an integrated whole, it is sacred ground, and when I live in harmony with my surroundings I live in harmony with myself and rekindle the spark of God that is within me and all other beings. Deep ecology is a refreshing tonic in contemporary Christianity that invigorates and restores human persons' sense of identity with the larger biotic community to which we all belong.[18]

The Cruciform Spirit

The biblical, Neopagan, deep ecology framework of this book emphasizes the unity of the Spirit and the natural world. Whether manifesting herself as a sacred animal—such as the biblical bird God in Genesis and Jesus' baptism stories in the Gospels—or as a nonsentient life-form—such as the mighty wind in the creation story in Genesis and transforming fire in the Pentecost narrative in Acts—the Spirit labors to lead all creation into a healthy and robust relationship with herself. Spirit and earth, therefore, are bound up with one another, without confusion or division, each living through and with the other in symbiotic unity. By breathing the breath of life into all kinds, God as Spirit becomes a grounded being and undergoes permanent change within Godself. No longer an invisible heavenly deity divorced from earthly things, God in Christian faith is a landed reality who lives in the ground, swims with the oceans, and flows through the atmosphere that surrounds us and gives us life. God is now a body. God is now an earth being. God has become one of us.

Christianity often acts like a "discarnate" religion—that is, a religion that sees no relationship between the spiritual and the physical orders of being and, at times, discriminates against the needs of the flesh as inferior to the concerns of the soul. In the history of the church some early apostles rejected marriage as giving in to sexual pleasure, and greatly revered saints and martyrs starved their bodies and beat themselves with sticks and whips in order to drive away earthly temptations. In many regards, Christianity has a sorry record as a religion that is conflicted about, or at times even at war with, the deep and genuine human need to reconcile the passions and drives of physical pleasure with the aspirations for spiritual transformation.

In fact, however, Christianity is not a discarnate religion. On the contrary, beginning with its earliest history, Christianity offers us a profound vision of God's nature-centered identity through its ancient teaching that God at one time enfleshed Godself in Jesus, or became incarnate. Long ago God poured out Godself into the mortal body of one human individual, Jesus. But that is not all. Christians also believe that since the dawn of creation, throughout world history and into the present, God *in and through the Spirit* has been persistently infusing the natural world with divine presence. The Spirit is the medium, the agent, or, in terms more felicitous for a recovery of the Bible's earth-centeredness, the *life-form* through which God's power and love fill the world and all of its inhabitants. Through green Christian optics, we can now see that the gift of the Spirit to the world since time immemorial—a gift that is alongside and inclusive of Jesus' death and resurrection—signals the beginning and continuation of God's incarnational presence. As once God became earthly at the dawn of creation, and as once God became human in the body of Jesus, so now God continually enfleshes Godself through the Spirit in the embodied reality of life on earth. In this sense, God is carnal, God is earthen, God is flesh. The Spirit has always and continues to indwell the earth as its inmost source of life and breath, and the earth has always arrayed, and continues to array, the Spirit in the garments of the cardinal elements.

It is theologically proper to say, therefore, that the world is the "form" God takes among us, that the earth is the "body" of the Spirit we encounter daily. But with this affirmation comes considerable danger to God. In an earth-centered model of the Spirit, God is a thoroughgoing incarnational reality who decides in freedom, and not by any external necessity, to indwell all things. But in making this decision, God as Spirit places herself at risk by virtue of her coinherence with a biosphere that suffers continued degeneration. If God's body—this small planet that is now under siege by continued global warming, deforestation, the spread of toxins, and the chronic loss of habitat—continues to suffer and bleed, then does not God, in some sense real but still unknowable and mysterious to us, also suffer and bleed? If God's earthen body undergoes deep environmental injury and waste, does not God in Godself also experience pain and deprivation? Since God and the earth, Spirit and nature, share a common reality, is it not possible that the loss and degradation of the earth might mean loss and degradation in and for God as well?

If it is the case that when the earth, God's body, suffers, then God's Spirit suffers as well, then we can say that the Spirit of God is "Christlike" or "cruciform" because the Spirit suffers the same violent fate as did Jesus—but now a suffering not confined to the onetime event of the cross, as in the case of Jesus, but a suffering that the Spirit experiences daily through the continual debasement of the earth and its inhabitants. In agony and sorrow, Jesus bore his cross as he climbed Golgotha and was crucified for human sin. Also in pain and suffering, the Spirit bears the cross of a planet under siege as she lives under the burden of humankind's ecological sin. Indeed, the lash marks of human sin cut into the body of the crucified Son of God are now even more graphically displayed across the expanse of the whole planet as the body of the wounded Spirit bears the incisions of further abuse. The Spirit in the earth, the body of God for us today, is being crucified afresh.

In this earth-centered model, the Spirit in our time is the "cruciform Spirit" who, like Christ, takes into Godself the burden of human sin and the deep ecological damage this sin has wrought in the biosphere. But as Christ's wounds become the eucharistic blood that nourishes the believer, so also does the Spirit's agony over damage to the earth become a source of hope for communities facing seemingly hopeless environmental destitution. As Paul says in Romans 8, the earth, in and through the ministry of the Spirit, groans and moans, like a woman in labor, as the earth awaits its deliverance from human sin—and now we can say, its deliverance from human *ecological* sin. The Spirit's abiding presence in a world wracked by human greed is a constant reminder that God desires the welfare of all members of the lifeweb—indeed, that no population of life-forms is beyond the ken of divine love, no matter how serious, even permanent, the ecological damage might be to particular communities of living things.

Green Christian spirituality envisions God as present in all things and the source of our attempt to develop caring relationships with other life-forms. This perspective signals a fundamental revaluation of characteristic Christian themes. Christians speak of the embodiment of God in Jesus two thousand years ago, but now all life is the incarnation of God's presence through the Spirit on a daily basis. Christians speak of the miracle of the Eucharist, in which bread and wine become Christ's flesh and blood, but now the whole earth is a living sacrament full of the divine life through the agency of the Spirit who animates and unifies all things. Christians speak of the power of the written word of God, in which God's voice can be heard by the discerning reader, but now all of nature is the book of God through which one can see God's face and listen to God's speech in the laughter of a bubbling stream, the rush of an icy wind on a winter's day, the scream of a red-tailed hawk as it seizes its prey, and the silent movement of a monarch butterfly flitting from one milkweed plant to another. The hope of this book is that readers will discover a new sense of intimacy with God and the earth through finding traces of the Spirit in all of creation.

Chapter One

God Is Green

The Earth Crisis Is a Spiritual Crisis

TODAY THE SINGING RIVER is an endangered watershed. Failed septic systems, storm water runoff, lawn fertilizers, timber-cutting waste, and industrial chemicals have degraded the water quality and compromised the health of the diverse plant and animal species who depend on the river for their sustenance and well-being.[1] Today I would be cautious about swimming in the river in order to hear the lost music of the Pascagoula. Like many waterways the world over, the Singing River is at risk because human communities abuse it in order to pursue their technological and commercial interests. But why are the world's riverways—indeed, all landforms affected by human incursion—in such deep trouble? Could it be that current religious beliefs and practices—and, in particular, the distinctive beliefs and practices of Christianity—are responsible for present-day environmental degradation?

The burden of this book is to sound the depths of Christianity's vision of a whole earth community in oneness and harmony with itself. I want to help realize the *promise* of Christianity to ameliorate our exploitative anti-environmental habits through a return to Christian faith's earth-centered teachings about the enfleshed presence of God in all things. But to accomplish this task I also want to explore Christianity's *culpability* as a sacralizing force that legitimizes humankind's exploitative treatment of nature as well. Christianity is a gold mine of empowering images and stories that can enable a vigorous, nature-based lifestyle, but it can also be partially blamed for our current plight.

Thus a twofold concern undergirds my articulation of green spirituality here: How has Christian faith contributed to the current crisis? And is
it possible that a reinterpretation of the Christian tradition might help to
resolve this crisis? With these questions in mind, let me turn to examine
the origins of the ecological crisis in the history of Christian thought and
then move to a retrieval of a central but neglected Christian theme—the
idea of God as carnal Spirit who imbues all things—as the key element for
forging a green spirituality responsive to the needs of our time.

We face today an environmental crisis of staggering proportions. We
now know this. But we seem confused as to how to address the crisis in a
manner that will engender long-term sustainable growth for human communities without sacrificing the vital needs of nonhuman communities
to survive and flourish. All of us—liberal and conservative, religious and
nonreligious, rich and poor, members of underdeveloped and developed
countries—claim to want a balance between satisfying essential human
needs and preserving the biodiversity that makes our planet a rich and
invigorating place in which to live. Yet we apparently lack the heartfelt
commitment to sustainability required for ensuring the integrity of humankind and otherkind in unity with one another.

But why is this the case?

Is the cause of our collective inability to address adequately the earth
crisis a cognitive failure to understand what it will take to build sustainable
communities? Is the problem, in other words, essentially technological,
so that if we only had, for example, better pollution controls to protect
against the greenhouse effects of carbon-based emissions, we might then
be able stem the deleterious impact of global warming on public health?
Or is the real reason behind our failure to practice sustainable living and
earth healing a matter of the heart? That is, do we not know *how* to solve
the problem, or, rather, do we not *care* enough about planetary integrity
to feel motivated to address the predicament at hand?

I believe that the fundamental cause of our collective inability to confront the global environmental crisis is our deep-seated unwillingness to
change our consumption-intensive habits and embrace greener lifestyles.
The problem is a matter of the heart, not the head. The problem is not that we do
not know how to avoid our current plight, but rather that we no longer experience our co-belonging with nature in such a way that we are willing to
alter our lifestyles in order to build a more sustainable future. Of course, in
terms of both technological innovation and public policy, we will all profit
through increased knowledge about how we can better stem the tide of

environmental degradation. But unless at the core of our deepest selves we are fundamentally committed to sustainable living, no amount of eco-efficiency in business and industry will make for long-lasting change.

Moreover, insofar as the environmental crisis is a matter of the heart, the crisis at its core is a spiritual crisis. The environmental crisis is a spiritual crisis because the continued degradation of the earth threatens the fundamental interconnections that bind human beings to one another and to all other forms of life. "The frog does not destroy the pond in which it lives," says an Indian proverb, but we no longer experience the natural world as the great pond that sustains us and to which we owe moral obligations. We need a "conversion to the earth," as Larry Rasmussen argues, a radical turn to re-earthing our identities as bonded with all of creation.[2] But at a very deep level we no longer feel our common kinship with other living things; we do not understand ourselves as needing to rely on the interconnected tissue of natural systems for the support of our existence. We think of ourselves as part *of* nature but not *as* nature itself; we regard ourselves as living *in* nature but we do not regard nature itself as *why* we are alive at all. We have lost our primordial sense of belonging to the unified lifeweb that our kind and otherkind need for daily sustenance.

In saying that the earth crisis is a spiritual crisis, I mean something else as well. I also mean that the problem is explicitly a *religious* problem in the sense that the promulgation of particular biblical and theological teachings has led to the ravaging of earth systems and habitats. In the Christian tradition, for example, one interpretation of the Genesis creation story is that God, a heavenly monarch far removed from the concerns of the planet, created human beings in God's image to be God's vice-regents and to exercise dominion over the earth. I submit that this kingly interpretation of the Genesis creation account has had more to do with religious justifications of environmental degradation in the Western world than any other reading of biblical and classical literature. According to this royal reading of Genesis, human beings are to "subdue and have dominion over" the natural world: to bend earth community to their will, to fill it with their own species and adapt it to their own needs and interests.

> Then God said, "Let us make [human beings] in our image, after our likeness; and let them have dominion over the fish of the sea, and over the birds of the air, and over the cattle, and over all the earth, and over every creeping thing that creeps upon the earth." So God created [human beings] in his own image, in the image of God he created them;

male and female he created them. And God blessed them, and God said to them, "Be fruitful and multiply and fill the earth and subdue it; and have dominion over the fish of the sea and over the birds of the air and over every living thing that moves upon the earth." (Genesis 1:26-28)

In this central biblical passage, God gives to his image-bearing earth wardens the right to govern the animal kingdom along with the right to propagate their own kind. In what Sallie McFague calls the "monarchical" reading of this passage, God is a distant potentate who has handed over to his human subjects the whole created order as a resource under their oversight and for their own use and benefit.[3] God is a faraway king who has ceded control of all the animals and plants to his human servants; God instructs his human assistants to rule over what has been entrusted to them. If God, the heavenly monarch, has given the whole created order over to us, his earthly stewards, then why not do with it what we want? Is this not what the Bible is teaching us in this passage?

Lynn White, in a now famous essay, writes that the legacy of the kingly interpretation of the Genesis creation story has undergirded Christianity's indifference—and at times contempt—toward the welfare of the natural world.[4] He goes on to argue that this antinature orientation paved the way for Christianity's early attacks on Paganism's belief that the sacred imbues all of nature. By criticizing Pagan pantheism, Christianity effectively sacralized the exploitation of nature by putting forward a notion of God as a disembodied deity uninterested in earthly affairs. White writes that Western Christianity's attack on Paganism effectively stripped the natural world of any spiritual meaning and thereby made possible the widespread practice of environmental degradation. Christianity opened the door to abusing earth community by replacing animism, the belief that a sacred life force animates all things, with the doctrine that God is a bodiless divinity whose true residence is in heaven, not on earth. "By destroying pagan animism," White writes, "Christianity made it possible to exploit nature in a mood of indifference to the feelings of natural objects."[5] The belief that the sacred is in rivers and trees and animals was supplanted by the belief that God is a discarnate and dispassionate reality uninterested in affairs of the lowest order of being.

White's analysis is telling in many respects. The impact of Christianity's monarchical reading of the Genesis cosmology, and corresponding anti-Pagan teachings, have tended to empty the biosphere of any sense of God's presence in natural things in many people's minds. Fueled by the

"subdue and have dominion" interpretation of Genesis along with Christianity's historic antipathy to Paganism, God is now pictured as a Sky God
with little if any connection to natural processes. In turn, human beings,
as bearers of God's image, are not viewed as genuine members of earth
community, but regarded instead as "souls" taking up temporary residence
in their earthly bodies and awaiting their deliverance into a disembodied
heavenly eternity. In this schema, we are all transient denizens of a material world from which we will be set free in death in order to return to
the disembodied Source from which we have originated. Along the way,
these teachings imply or state outright that God is against nature, with the
result that they inculcate in human beings an absence of family feeling for
other biotic communities. The ecological crisis is fundamentally a spiritual crisis because certain distorted Christian teachings have blunted our
ability to experience any significant co-belonging with other life-forms,
rendering us unable to alter our self-destructive course and plot a new
path toward sustainable living.

Ecocidal Addiction

My thesis, therefore, is that "ecocide"—a habit of life and thought that makes
war against earth community—is a spiritual disease. Like alcoholism—
another disease, as Carl Jung said, that is essentially spiritual in nature[6]—
ecocide is rooted in addictive behaviors that undermine human persons'
health and well-being. The spiritual origins of ecocide are apparent in our
headlong rush to environmental disaster; as in the case of the alcoholic, we
know we are undermining the quality of our lives but we can no longer
stop ourselves from doing so. In theological parlance, our predisposition
toward environmental abuse is an instance of the "bondage of the will," in
which we find ourselves unable to stop behavior that we know to be self-
destructive.[7] Why else would the human community push itself further and
further toward certain environmental catastrophe—global warming, irre-
versible ozone depletion, massive deforestation, chronic loss of arable land,
daily extinction of numerous species—unless it were addicted to toxic attitudes and habits from which it can no longer escape?

But if the root of the environmental problem is deeply spiritual or
religious at its core, it is also the case, ironically, that an answer to the
problem lies in a rehabilitation of the earth-friendly teachings within the
theological tradition that has at times been most openly hostile to nature,
namely, the Christian tradition. If ecocide is a disease of the soul, then it

requires spiritual medicine—the medicine of healthy, rather than toxic, Christian values and ideas—to heal this disease. This paradox should not be surprising to us. It is often the case that the seeds for positive change lie deep within the very thing that is the source of the seemingly incorrigible impediments to change in the first place.

Recently, I finished treatment for a severe allergy to bee stings that consisted of taking incremental amounts of bee venom in order to build up my immune system in the event that I would be stung again by a bee, wasp, yellow jacket, or hornet. Over time, my system became gradually desensitized to the effects of a bee or wasp sting through venom injection therapy. The regimen I endured was an exercise similar to *homeopathy*—"like treats like"—and it proved successful as a remedy from the near-fatal bee-sting attacks I had suffered since childhood. In my view, Christianity vis-à-vis the earth crisis is like the venom I took to overcome my bee-sting allergy: it is both the origin of the problem and its solution. In relation to potential planetary destruction, Christianity is part of the "cause" of the ecocidal "disease" from which we suffer because it mediates many of the founding stories and images that teach us, in the Great Chain of Being, to exercise lordship and dominion over the created order. At the same time, Christianity is essential to the "cure" of ecocidal "sickness" insofar as it provides nonmonarchical scriptural and ethical resources for a healthy mind-set toward nature that is a prophylactic against nature-hostile attitudes and habits. In my struggle to overcome a fatal allergy to bee stings, I had to inject the very thing that made me sick in order to become well again. Likewise, it behooves all of us to digest thoughtfully Christianity's understandings of nature—for good and for ill—in order better to understand our ecocidal tendencies *and* to heal the world around us through utilizing the green resources within certain constructive Christian teachings.

Part of my justification for the claim that Christianity is both a central cause of and a vital cure for our current planetary crisis is historical influence. As one of the regnant cultural systems in Western society—along with modern science and technology—Christianity has played a privileged role in shaping humankind's place within the natural world. In this third millennium, it is unclear whether Christianity will continue to play its central role in molding modern society's understanding of the environment or whether another primary symbol-system—for example, global capitalism or information technology or Islam—will set the terms for articulating the most fitting relationship between humankind and otherkind. I believe we are moving into an era when a variety of competing thought systems will vie for control over the debate regarding sound environmental policy.[8] Thus the verdict is out as to whether Christian ideas will continue to play an authoritative role in our environmental thinking in the future or whether this role will be ceded to other players in the debate. Nevertheless, the need is urgent for excavating the deep and complicated origins of the crisis in the foundational Christian texts and symbols fundamentally responsible (at least up to this point) for the causes—and the solutions—of the global earth crisis.

If Christianity is both disease and cure in regard to the ecocrisis, then what role can the ancient earth wisdom within Christianity play in making our respective bioregions vital places in which to live and work? The potential of Christian faith to address the current crisis is rooted in the central biblical notion of God as earthen Spirit. The Spirit is the promise of God's material, palpable presence within the good earth God has made for our sustenance and the health of all beings. God continually pours out Godself into the cosmos through Earth Spirit, the driving force within the universe that brings each thing into its natural fruition. In this sense, God is *carnal*: through the Spirit, God *incarnates* Godself within the natural order in order to nurture and bring to fruition every form of life. The Holy Spirit is an enfleshed being, an earthly life-form who animates life on earth as an outflowing of God's compassion for all things. In ecumenical Christianity, the foundational Nicene Creed in 381 CE names the Spirit as "the Lord, the Giver of Life." I make sense of this ancient appellation by reenvisioning the Holy Spirit as God's invigorating corporeal presence within the society of all living beings.

Unfortunately, however, many contemporary Christians experience and understand the Spirit—if they think about the Spirit at all—as the forgotten member of the Trinity, the shy member of the Godhead, the left hand of God. As I said earlier, in the lived practice of God's presence in many noncharismatic Christian communities today, the promise of the Spirit to fill and renew all of God's creation is generally overlooked. This oversight renders present-day Christianity a binary religion, a religion of the Father and the Son, with little if any awareness of the Spirit's critically important work in the world. This neglect of the Spirit saddles Christianity with a backward-looking orientation. It undercuts one of the most important promises of the Gospel, namely, that the departure of Jesus from the world two thousand years ago entails the gift of the Spirit in the future for all who seek the truth. In the Gospel of John Jesus says,

I tell you the truth: it is to your advantage that I go away, for if I do not go away, the Counselor will not come to you; but if I go, I will send him to you. . . . When the Spirit of truth comes, he will guide you into all the truth. (John 16:7, 13)

The hope of Christianity is the promise of God's omnipresent Spirit to fill the earth with power and love so that all of God's creatures, human and nonhuman alike, can be brought into a healing and restorative relationship with the truth.[9] In its best moments Christian spirituality consists, simultaneously, of *remembering* with gratitude God's goodness and love in the mission of Jesus, and *looking forward* with hope and expectation to the continuation of that mission, now under the power of the Spirit, in the new situation of the present and future. The "new situation" that now confronts us is the earth crisis. Jesus has departed this world, but in his absence God offers to us the all-encompassing work of the Spirit—the Spirit's work of renewal and restoration in a world badly wounded by chronic environmental abuse. We live in the age of the Spirit, in a time when the Spirit expands Jesus' work into the full expanse of the whole created order.

Yet many Christians, because of their understandable but almost exclusive identity with the story of Jesus, are today unable to track the new work of the Spirit in a world loved by God but under siege by human arrogance. To counteract this tendency, I offer here a forward-looking, nature-centered model of the Spirit as the Earth God, who sustains the natural order and unifies all of God's creation into one common biotic family. From a religious perspective, this earth-centered doctrine of the Spirit—as reminiscent of Jesus' love for all creatures testified to in the Gospels—is the best grounds for hope and renewal at a point in human history when our unchecked appetites seemed destined to destroy the planet. A new vision of the carnal God as the Spirit of the earth has the potential to invigorate all of us in our struggles to love and protect the gift of creation.

The Historic Agon of Spirit and Flesh

In traditional Western thought, however, the Spirit is not understood as a friend of the earth but as a ghostly, bodiless entity far removed from the concerns of the created order. I have noted how conventional understandings of the Spirit evoke images of a vapid and invisible phantom ("the Holy Ghost") divorced from the tangible reality of life on this planet as we know it. These popular notions are rooted in the canonical definition of the Spirit as an incorporeal, bodiless, nonmaterial being that stands over and against the physical world, which is not of the same nature as the Spirit. As one theological dictionary puts it, the Spirit is "immaterial or nonmaterial substance. . . . The term *spiritus* can therefore be applied to God generally [or] to the Third Person of the Trinity specifically."[10] Much of Western thought—including religious thought—operates according to a series of binary oppositions that separate spirit from body, mind from matter, and God from nature. These dichotomies not only divide the spiritual world from the physical order but also order the two terms in the polarity in a valuational hierarchy by positing the first term (spirit, mind, God) as superior to the second term (body, matter, nature). Western thought has pitted the spiritual world and the physical order against one another; moreover, it has subordinated the one to the other. In this schema, the Spirit is regarded as an eternally invisible and incorporeal force superior to the earthly realm, which is mired in contingency and change.

This bipartite and hierarchical division between spirit and matter has a long and tenacious history in Western philosophical and religious traditions.[11] Plato's philosophical anthropology, for example, is controlled by metaphors of the body as the "prison house" and the "tomb" of the soul. The fulfillment of human existence, according to Plato, is to release one-self—one's soul—from bondage to involuntary, bodily appetites in order to cultivate a life in harmony with one's spiritual, intellectual nature.[12] Origen, the third-century Christian Platonist, literally interpreted Jesus' blessing regarding those who "have made themselves eunuchs for the sake of the kingdom of heaven" (Matthew 19:2) and at age twenty had himself castrated. As a virgin for Christ no longer dominated by his sexual and physical drives, Origen, in his mind, became a perfect vessel for the display of the Spirit.[13]

But in the Christian West, Augustine is arguably most responsible for the hierarchical division between spirit and nature. Augustine maintains that human beings are ruled by carnal desire—*concupiscence*—as a result of Adam's fall from grace in the Garden of Eden. Adam's sin is transferred to his offspring—the human race—through erotic desire that leads to sexual intercourse and the birth of children. In their fleshly bodies, according to Augustine, infants are tainted with "original sin" communicated to them through their biological parents' sexual intercourse. Physical weakness and sexual desire are signs that the bodily, material world is under God's judgment. Thus, without the infusion of supernatural grace, all of creation—as depraved and corrupted—is no longer amenable to the influence of the Spirit.[14] This long tradition of hierarchical and antagonistic division between Spirit and matter continues into our own time—an era, often in the name of religion, marked by deep anxiety about and hostility toward human sexuality, the body, and the natural world.

At first glance, some of the biblical writings appear partial to this binary opposition between body and spirit. Consider Paul's rhetoric of "spirit" versus "flesh" in the books of Romans and Galatians as cases in point. In Romans 8:5-13, Paul emphasizes that "life in the flesh leads to death while life in the Spirit leads to life." This juxtaposition lends credence to the received notion that the material and spiritual orders are fundamental opposites in the New Testament. But while this reading of Paul is understandable given the force of his rhetoric here and elsewhere, it is a mistake because, in fact, Paul assigns positive, saving value to the body. In reality Paul's thought utilizes a threefold anthropology that trades on the terms *sarx* ("flesh"), *soma* ("body"), and *pneuma* ("spirit"). In this schema the Christian subject is an embodied self (*soma*) who experiences the inner warfare between impulses that resist life in Christ (*sarx*) and a power within the self that brings the self into relationship with Christ (*pneuma*). Each of these terms carries a particular value in Paul's "systems" theory of the self: *soma*, as the human person in her essentially positive, bodily state, is the environment within which the battle between the negative tendencies of *sarx* and the beneficial influence of *pneuma* is carried out. Paul values somatic, bodily life as the site of God's power to renew and transform all persons. Far from the body's being a negative concept in Paul's thought, the body is the locus of God's saving, healing activity in the life of the individual. For Paul, the body is a sacred site because it is the privileged point at which God becomes real in human existence: the body is the place where God comes alive in the human person.

This reverence for the body is further expressed in 1 Corinthians 6:19-20, where Paul writes, "Do you not know that your body (*soma*) is a temple of the Holy Spirit (*hagiou pneumatos*) within you, which you have from God? You are not your own; you were bought with a price. So glorify God in your body." To be a person is to be a temple of God, a temple of the Holy Spirit. To be an earthen being—a fully enfleshed being with bodily appetites and physical drives—is to be loved by God as a tabernacle of the Holy Spirit. The embodied, somatic Christian subject is a sacred dwelling place—a temple—inhabited by the Spirit of God. God loves our bodies and reveres our bodies as testimonies to the Spirit's presence in the world. The Spirit and the body, therefore, are positive and complementary ideas in Paul's thought.[15]

Along with Paul, the vast majority of the biblical texts undermine the split between God and nature by structurally interlocking the terms in the polarity within one another. In particular, on the question of the Spirit, the system of polar oppositions is consistently undermined. In terms of the Spirit, rather than prioritizing the spiritual over the earthly, the scriptural texts figure the Spirit as a carnal, creaturely life-form always already interpenetrated by the material world. Granted, the term "Spirit" does conjure the image of a ghostly, shadowy nonentity in both the popular and high thinking of the Christian West. But the biblical texts stand as a stunning countertestimony to the conventional mind-set—including the conventional theological mind-set. Indeed, the Bible is awash with rich imagery of the Spirit borrowed directly from the natural world. The four traditional elements of natural, embodied life—*earth, air, water,* and *fire*— are constitutive of the Spirit's biblical reality as an enfleshed being who ministers to the whole creation God has made for the refreshment and joy of all beings. In the Bible, the Spirit is not a wraithlike being separated from matter, but a creature like all other created things made up of the four cardinal substances that compose the physical universe.

Earth, Air, Water, Fire

Numerous biblical passages attest to the foundational role of the four basic elements regarding the earthen identity of the Spirit.

(1) As *earth* the Spirit is both the *divine dove*, with an olive branch in its mouth, that brings peace and renewal to a broken and divided world (Genesis 8:11; Matthew 3:16; John 1:32), and a *fruit bearer*, such as a tree or vine, that yields the virtues of love, joy, and peace in the life of the disciple (Galatians 5:15-26). Pictured as a bird on the wing or a flowering tree, the Spirit is a living being who shares a common physical reality with all other beings. Far from being the "immaterial substance" defined by the canonical theological lexicon, the Spirit is imagined in the Bible as a material, earthen life-form who mediates God's power to other earth creatures through her physical presence.

(2) As *air* the Spirit is both the *vivifying breath* that animates all living things (Genesis 1:2; Psalms 104:29-30) and the *prophetic wind* that brings

salvation and new life to those it indwells (Judges 6:34; John 3:6-8; Acts 2:1-4). The nouns for Spirit in the biblical texts—*rûach* in Hebrew and *pneuma* in Greek—mean "breath" or "air" or "wind." Literally, the Spirit is pneumatic, a powerful air-driven reality analogous to a pneumatic drill or pump. The Spirit is God's all-encompassing, aerial presence in the life-giving atmosphere that envelopes and sustains the whole earth; as such, the Spirit escapes the horizon of human activity and cannot be contained by human constraints. The Spirit is divine wind—the breath of God—that blows where it wills (John 3:8)—driven by its own elemental power and independent from human attempts to control it—refreshing and renewing all broken members of the created order.

(3) As the *living water* the Spirit quickens and refreshes all who drink from its eternal springs (John 3:1-15, 4:14, 7:37-38). As physical and spiritual sustenance, the Spirit is the liquid God who imbues all life-sustaining bodily fluids—blood, mucus, milk, sweat, urine—with flowing divine presence and power. Moreover, the Water God flows and circulates within the soaking rains, dewy mists, thermal springs, seeping mudholes, ancient headwaters, swampy wetlands, and teeming oceans that constitute the hydrospheric earth we all inhabit. The Spirit as water makes possible the wonderful juiciness and succulence of life as we experience it on a liquid planet sustained by nurturing flow patterns.

(4) Finally, as *fire* the Spirit is the *bright flame* that alternately judges evildoers and ignites the prophetic mission of the early church (Matthew 3:11-12; Acts 2:1-4). Fire is an expression of God's austere power; it is viewed biblically as the element God uses to castigate human error. But it is also the symbol of God's unifying presence in the fledgling Christian community where the divine *pneuma*—the rushing, whooshing wind of God—is said to have filled the early church as its members became filled with the Spirit, symbolized by "tongues of fire [that were] distributed and resting on each one" of the early church members (Acts 2:3). Aberrant, subversive, and creatively destructive, God as fire scorches and roasts who and what it chooses apart from human intervention and design—like the divine wind that blows where it wills.

But like the other natural elements, fire should be understood as functioning in the service of maintaining healthy earth relations. Fire is necessary for the maintenance of planetary life: as furnace heat, fire makes food preparation possible; as wildfire in forested and rural areas, fire revivifies long-dormant seed cultures necessary for biodiverse ecosystems; and when harnessed in the form of solar power, fire from the sun makes possible safe energy production not dependent on fossil-fuel sources. The burning God is the God who has the power to incinerate and make alive the elements of the lifeweb essential for the sustenance of our gifted ecosystem.

God as Spirit is biblically defined according to the tropes of earth, wind, water, and fire. In these scriptural texts the Spirit is figured as a potency in nature who engenders life and healing throughout the biotic order. The earth's bodies of water, communities of plants and animals, and eruptions of fire and wind are not only symbols of the Spirit—as important as this nature symbolism is—but share in the Spirit's very nature as the Spirit is continually enfleshed and embodied through natural landscapes and biological populations. Neither ghostly nor bodiless, the Spirit reveals herself in the biblical literatures as an earthly life-form who labors to create and sustain humankind and otherkind in solidarity with one another.

To refer to the Spirit as "life-form" is to signal the Spirit's identity as a living being, a being whose nature is the same as all other participants in the biotic and abiotic environments that make up our planet home. Running rivers, prairie fires, coral reefs, schools of blue whales, equatorial forests—the Spirit both shares the same nature of other life-forms and is the animating force that enlivens all members of the lifeweb. As the breath of life who moves over the face of the deep in Genesis, as the circling dove in the Gospels who seals Jesus' baptism, or as the Pentecostal tongues of fire in Acts, the Spirit does not exist apart from natural phenomena as a separate, heavenly reality externally related to the created order. Rather, all of nature in its fullness and variety is the warp and woof of the Spirit's work in the world. The Spirit is an earthen reality—God's power in the land and sky that makes all things live and grow toward their natural ends. God is living in the ground, swimming through the oceans, circulating in the atmosphere; God is always afoot and underfoot as the quickening life force who yearns to bring all denizens of the sacred earth into fruition and well-being.

Can a recovery of the ancient, biblical idea of the Spirit as the green face of God provide the necessary grounds for the practice of earth healing in our time? The answer to this question has been the focus of this opening chapter. I have proposed here that one of the most compelling *religious* responses to the threat of ecocide lies in a recovery of the Holy Spirit as God's power of life-giving breath (*rûach*) who indwells and sustains all life-forms. I have suggested that the answer to the increasing environmental degradation in our time is not better technology—a matter of more know-how—but a Spirit-motivated conversion of our whole way of life to sustainable living— a matter of the heart. Such a change of heart can occur through an encounter with Christian earth wisdom. This wisdom for our troubled times can be found in the rich biblical imagery of God as Spirit who sustains and renews all forms of life on the planet; the corresponding belief, since the Spirit vivifies all things, in the interdependence that binds together all members of the biosphere in a global web of life; and the concomitant ethical ideal of working toward the healing of various communities of plants and animals whenever they suffer ecological degradation.

Chapter Two

The Mother Bird God

God on the Wing

THERE ARE MANY INDICATIONS of a nature-centered vision of the Spirit within historic and contemporary Christianity. These earth-based descriptions of God as Spirit are based on the *interrelational* character of the Spirit in friendship with the other members of the Godhead. In Western spirituality, the work of the Holy Spirit is consistently understood in relational terms—the Spirit is the power of reciprocity, communion, mutuality, oneness, unity. Early Christian writers conceive of the Spirit in the bosom of the Trinity as the source of mutual interconnection among the three persons of the Godhead. The Spirit is the "flame of love" within the divine life—the union of mutual love in the Trinity who unites the three persons in reciprocal relationship with one another. Basil of Caesarea writes that, as the love that brings together God in Godself, the Holy Spirit is the agent of mutuality, openness, and unity within the Trinity.[1] Analogously, Augustine analyzes the role of the Spirit in terms of the "bond of love," what he calls the *vinculum caritatis*, which he understands as the divine power of relationship that binds the three members of the Godhead together in dynamic intercommunion.[2] "And if the love whereby the Father loves the Son and the Son loves the Father displays, beyond the power of words, the communion of both," Augustine writes, "it is most fitting that the Spirit who is common to both should have the special name of love."[3] The Spirit is God's love connection; the Spirit ties together the members of the Trinity in an eternal embrace.

This classical model of the Spirit as the bond of love leads to the understanding of God's intratrinitarian life as an exercise in *perichoresis*, a technical Greek theological term that literally means "dancing around" and, in this context, stands for the Spirit's eternal enactment of the sweet and festive fellowship of all members of the Godhead. *The life of God is an eternal dance.* As *perichoresis*, God's inner life is a cotillion of joy and companionship, with the Spirit's performing the role of ensuring the reciprocal love among all three members of this never-ending dance. The Spirit is God's celebratory act of interpersonal unity, the bond of harmony and affection that consummates the friendship and love that define the inner relations of Godself.

Like the early Christian theologians of late antiquity, later medieval artists operate with this same *perichoretic* vision of the Godhead but now do so through color and form. The doctrine of the Spirit as the bond of love in Godself is beautifully set forth in the trinitarian miniature paintings of the medieval *Rothschild Canticles* (see plate 3). The *Rothschild Canticles* comprise an illuminated book from the fourteenth century CE that depicts in words and images the centrality of the Spirit in making possible the eternal spiraling dance of the Godhead. Here the Spirit is figured as an all-encircling, stalwart, dovelike animal whose massive wings wrap up the Father and Son in a protective embrace and whose powerful talons and tail provide the points of intersection and intercommunion for all three figures. The Spirit Bird in the *Canticles* is imagined more like a wild raptor than the stylized pigeonlike birds of church art. She is less like the small, domesticated Spirit birds of traditional "stained glass" art and more like a commanding bird of prey, a force to be reckoned with. This avian power in the *Canticles* reminds me of a falcon or a hawk, birds whose jobs in real life are to protect their young and hunt for meat—pursuits that make them the objects of respect and fear by other birds and animals.

In the *Canticles* the Spirit Bird is a source of awe and power because she is the animating force within the Godhead that spins, twists, and twirls the other two members of the Trinity into newly imagined and wonderfully amorous combinations and permutations. At first, each trinitarian life-form has its own separate personality, but as the *Canticles* progresses each member of the Trinity loses its distinctive identity in a whirling, dizzying blur of erotic passion, movement, and color. Now at breakneck speed, the Trinity—through the compassionate agency of the Spirit—twists and spins itself into new and surprising recombinations. The Father and Son laugh and twirl around the avian Spirit, eternally enacting the union of each figure in the dancing Bird God.[4] In the *Rothschild Canticles* the bird God ensures the interrelationship of each divine person in a ludic celebration of *perichoretic* harmony.[5] God's cotillion is a joyous celebration of the unity of the divine life.

The bird God appears again in contemporary Native American–style artistic depictions of the Trinity. In a series of trinitarian icons that celebrate the cultures of the first peoples of the Americas, Father John Giuliani paints each member of the Godhead in meditative intercommunion with one another.[6] As with the *Rothschild Canticles*, the Spirit in Father Giuliani's images is figured as a sacred animal, specifically, a bird of prey—a falcon in one of the icons, an eagle in the other (see plates 4 and 5). As in the *Canticles*, the raptor God makes possible the rich unity of the trinitarian family; and because Father Giuliani uses a sacred animal to represent the Spirit, the perfect fellowship between the divine, human, and more-than-human orders of being is powerfully witnessed to here. The paintings depict the divine raptor hovering in a state of compassionate equilibrium between a wizened, caring grandfather, on the one hand, and a self-giving young man with arms outstretched to the world, on the other. Both the grandfather (God the Father) and the young man (Jesus) gesture with open hands to the viewer, symbolizing their expansive love for all beings; likewise, the fluttering bird between them (the Holy Spirit) outstretches its wings in a similar gesture of openness and love. The divinity of each figure is marked by a golden halo around their head. And the unity of the human world and the animal world is enacted by locating the hovering Spirit God, the bond of love, at the center of the relationship between God the Father and God the Son.

In these images, Jesus, the young man, wears a finely woven shirt with the image of the medicine wheel, the circle of life, emblazoned on his chest. The cycle of the seasons, the power of the four cardinal elements, and the marriage of God and the earth are all symbolized by this sacred hoop. The sacred wheel is divided into four color-coded quadrants. (1) The red sector symbolizes the sun rising in the east and with it the beginning of new life. (2) The yellow quadrant stands for the warmth from the south that makes all things grow that are good to eat. (3) The black area points to the thunder beings coming from the west who bring life-giving rain along with the danger of storm and flood. And (4) the white section represents the cold wind from the north that cleanses and purifies all of earth's inhabitants. The hoop painted on Jesus' breastplate brings together the primitive elements—red sun, yellow earth, black rain, and white wind—to make the point that the three-person Godhead and the four-color circle of the universe are a unified whole. Again, as we saw in the earlier biblical depictions of the Spirit according to the four elements, God and the earth are one. Father Giuliani's iconography teaches us that the Trinity is an earth-based communion, a fusion of the human and animal orders of being. In this tripartite schema, Jesus is the bearer of the sacred hoop that allows all things to exist in equipoise with one another; the Father is the repository of the ancient earth wisdom that renews and sustains life; and the raptor Spirit is the mediatory force on the earth who brings the two-leggeds and four-leggeds, humans and animals, together in earth-centered harmony.

The Trinity and Paganism

Both the *Canticles* and Father Giuliani's paintings are expressions of a biblically nuanced vision of God with Pagan sensibilities. In Pagan terms, these religious images articulate the presence of God in both human and other-than-human "persons." It may sound odd to refer to the avian being in the *Canticles* and Father Giuliani's paintings as a "person," but these works picture divinity as a personal, living being in a form other than the human form. As Neopaganism defines the notion of "person" to include all of the living creatures that inhabit mother earth—groundhogs, snakes, bluebirds, magnolia trees—in a similar spirit these artworks envision the sacred as bursting the bonds of the human and fusing itself with grand and spectacular birds of prey. Unlike the other "religions of the book," Judaism and Islam, Christianity, in its continuation of Pagan themes, taught that God in Jesus Christ became enfleshed in human form. Pressing this point further, the *Canticles* and Father Giuliani's paintings draw an analogy from God-as-human person to God-as-animal being. This analogy, while not always obvious to some Christians, is wonderfully apt based on the biblical witness. The *Canticles* and Father Giuliani's paintings extrapolate from the biblical imagery of God as hovering mother bird in Genesis and the Gospels to picture God as an "avian person," so to speak, who mediates the relationship between the Father and the Son. I suggested earlier that Christianity is a "transcendental animist" belief system where God as Spirit is both beyond the world and radically immanent to the world as an earthen life-form within all creation. Testifying to God's trinitarian love through the image of the raptor Spirit—imagining God as bodying forth Godself in animal form—highlights Christianity's deep indebtedness to its Pagan origins.

The Spirit Bird is the bond of peace and love universal within the trinitarian imagery of early Christian spirituality and medieval and contemporary iconography. These texts and paintings make the dramatic point that the Spirit is not only the power of relationship within God's "inner" trinitarian life but also the power of relationship between the Godhead and the "outer" world of the whole creation as well. In classic theological terms, the "immanent" or "inner" Trinity and the "outer" or "economic" Trinity are one. The Spirit is the avian divinity who binds together the trinitarian family as well as the many other life-forms that make up our common planet home. Both the humanlike Father and Son and the animal God of the Spirit are figured in the *Rothschild Canticles* and Father Giuliani's paintings as co-members of the same intimate fellowship. Here heaven and earth are one, God and nature come together—here the worlds of divinities, human beings, and animals are bound together in common unity.

In the terminology of church theology, the Spirit is the Creator Spirit, the *Spiritus Creator*, who breathes into all things the breath of life and then brings together all members of earth community through forging a series of interpenetrating relationships of mutuality and support. The Spirit Bird, the *Spiritus Creator*, is the supreme source of life and healing within the created order. *Thus the Trinity and creation are one.* As the Trinity enjoys its common life together in the eternal dance of the Spirit, so also does all creation cavort and frolic together with the Spirit Bird as its "master of ceremony," so to speak. The winged Spirit subsists interdependently—*perichoretically*—within the Godhead to foster communion between the divine persons; in the same manner, the Spirit also performs the role of the bond of love, the *vinculum caritatis*, within creation in order to promote the well-being and fecundity of the whole natural order.

From the perspective of green spirituality, nature is the enfleshment of God's sustaining love. As Trinity, God pours out care and compassion for all life-forms through the integrity and the rhythms of the natural order. The divine Trinity's boundless passion for the welfare of all things is revealed in God's preservation of the lifeweb that is our common biological inheritance. Here God as Trinity is set forth in the Father/Mother God's creation of the biosphere, the Son's reconciliation of all beings to himself, and the Spirit's gift of life to every member of the created order who relies on her beneficence for daily sustenance. God as Trinity is three persons united together: creator (first person), redeemer (second person), and sustainer (third person) subsist in deep friendship with one another and all creation. As *creator*, God is manifested in the ebb and flow of the seasons whose plantings and harvests are a constant reminder of earth's original blessings. As *redeemer*, God is revealed in the complex interactions of organisms and the earth in mutual sustenance—an economy of interdependence best symbolized by Jesus' reconciling work of the cross, where Jesus dies so that others might live. And as *sustainer*, God shows Godself through breathing the breath of life into all members of the lifeweb, a living testimony to the Divine's compassion for all things.

God's presence in the living Christ through the Spirit's maintenance of the ecosphere is the basis for the greening of Christian spirituality. The *then and there* incarnation of God in Jesus is recapitulated in the *here and now* embodiment of the Spirit in the world—an embodiment that harks back to the originary Parent God's birthing of order out of chaos. This trinitarian enfleshment of God in nature represents a threefold movement. The first move to an embodied doctrine of God is signaled by the inaugural hymn of Genesis where the Creator Spirit (*rûach*) breathes the world into existence and thereby enfleshes herself in the creation and maintenance of the natural order. The embodiment of the divine life in Jesus—an earth creature like Adam, who himself was fashioned from the soil—is the second move toward a nature-centered model of the Godhead. And the *perichoretic* union of Jesus in the Spirit—like Jesus, an earth being as well but now figured in the biblical tropes of water, dove, fire, and wind—represents the third move toward an earth-loving, or "biophilic," notion of God. It is the move to *embodiment*—the procession of Godself into the green earth that sustains all life—that expresses the primary basis for oneness within the Godhead. In *perichoresis*, God as Trinity subsists in interpersonal *and* interplanetary unity through incarnating Godself in all things that swim, creep, crawl, run, fly, and grow upon the earth.

The understanding of the Spirit as a creaturely life-form, a sacred bird of prey, emphasizes an earth-friendly model of the Spirit in the history of Western spirituality that is generally not recognized. In theory, the Spirit has always been defined as both the Spirit of God and the Spirit of creation. In her first capacity, we have seen that the Spirit is the power of friendship within the intertrinitarian family; in her second capacity, the Spirit is the vivifying breath of God who indwells and sustains the biosphere. In practice, however, the Spirit, defined primarily as the Spirit of God rather than the Spirit of creation, has been almost exclusively understood in terms of her function as the source of mutuality and love within the Godhead. The result of this neglect of the Spirit's green identity is that the Spirit's role as cosmic nurturer of all creation, including nonhuman as well as human creation, has been consistently downplayed. A green vision of the Spirit, indebted to Christian faith's Pagan and biblical origins, allows for new insight into the gift of Creator Spirit's sustenance of the nurturing earth, the beginning and end of all life. The Spirit brings God and the earth together, enabling us to protect the creatures and sing the song of the seas and the stars in our commitments to earth healing and the renewal of all life.

Is God Female?

The mediation of the Spirit through animal beings (such as birds) and natural elements (such as wind and fire) is deeply resonant to the earth-centered thought of one of the most compelling visionary philosophers in our time, Luce Irigaray. Instead of focusing, as is the case with some contemporary philosophers, on the power of abstract thought as the key to understanding human nature, Irigaray emphasizes the role of everyday, elemental life as the most satisfying model for defining the basic nature of human existence:

> We still pass our daily lives in a universe that is composed and is known to be composed of four elements: air, water, fire, and earth. We are made up of these elements and we live in them. They determine, more or less freely, our attractions, our affects, our passions, our limits, our aspirations.[7]

For Irigaray, to be human is to live in harmony with the elemental dynamics of bodily existence. To be human is to celebrate our unity with the natural order; it is to honor the primordial elements as constitutive of all life on the planet, including our own earthly existence.

Irigaray notes that all ancient philosophy and religion understood the significance of the cardinal elements not only as the building blocks of organic life but also as the proper focus for understanding the meaning and purpose of existence as such. In the cradle of Western civilization, early Pagan philosophers argued that the essence of things is made up of different natural elements. In the sixth century BCE, Thales, for example, understood the nature of reality to be water; Anaximenes said that reality is best comprehended as air; and Heraclitus fixed on fire as the primitive essence of all things. Moreover, the ancient Greeks understood God or the One as the supreme force in the universe who binds together all of the basic elements into an all-encompassing unity.[8] Similarly, we have seen that the Bible also offers a vision of reality grounded in the elemental energies of earth, wind, fire, and water. Analogously, the Bible also envisions God (now God as Spirit) to be the animating and unifying force within the whole created order. Healthy philosophy and religion, according to Irigaray, is elementally based, and functions to celebrate the mystery and wonder of fleshy, viscous, corporeal existence.

Though Christianity carries within itself the seeds to reactualize these vital earthen energies, Irigaray argues that orthodox Christianity substituted an elemental sensibility with an otherworldly symbol-system that posited a disembodied Godhead—Father, Son, and Holy Spirit—as the key to understanding reality in general and religious meaning in particular. Furthermore, this invisible divine reality became understood in strictly masculine terms—*maleness* now becomes one of the essential defining characteristics of the Supreme Being. Respect and awe in the face of natural forces was supplanted by a divine male symbol-system that had little room for women's religious experience, including women's (and men's) experience of the feminine sacred.

For Irigaray, Christian faith is oriented toward a monotheistic God-Man who is alternately one and three at the same time. This trinitarian Godhead—Father, Son, and Holy Spirit—constitutes a male divinity insofar as the first two members of the Godhead are male and the third is of indeterminate gender. To be sure, the mother of Jesus, Mary, is accorded a certain pride of place in Roman Catholic piety, but Mary is a *virgin* mother, which renders her full humanity as an adult, sexual woman problematic at best and denigrated at worst. As well, according to Irigaray, the precise relationship of Mary to God is left unresolved in historic Christian theology (note: if Mary is the mother of Jesus and Jesus is God's Son, then does that make Mary the wife of God, a sort of heavenly queen or divine consort?). The symbol of Mary is a deeply ambiguous symbol and cannot account for women's full-bodied experience. Without an adequate female symbol as an ideal to aspire to for women of faith, argues Irigaray, maleness and divinity remain flip sides of the same coin within Christian thought.

Because of this rough equation between maleness and divinity, Irigaray maintains that Christianity provides a somewhat adequate symbol-system for *male* formation only. The male Christian God has been a haven for men's developmental growth and change, a secure refuge for men's exploration of their nature as physical, gendered, elemental beings. The Bible and the Christian tradition are a rich collection of robust divine male images—images such as warrior, king, caregiver, shepherd, redeemer, prophet, groom, creator, miracle worker, father, and salvation bringer. All of these images guide men in the process of becoming psychologically actualized and spiritually integrated. Though men, in their full humanity, would further benefit from an equally compelling set of divine female imagery, what it means to live a rich and fulfilled life is modeled for men by a male God that shows the way to authentic (if not fully gendered) masculine subjectivity.

But women in Christian cultures do not have a gendered religious paradigm in the same way that men do; there is no complementary divine female symbol-system to aid them in the process of full self-becoming. According to Irigaray, with the death of the Pagan goddesses of antiquity and the rise of the male God of Christian orthodoxy, women do not have a female God that can serve as an enduring and transcendent point of reference in their journey toward selfhood. Aside from the ambiguous Marian imagery, women set sail on the ocean of self-discovery only to find that there is no woman-centered lodestar in the night sky to guide them into the safe harbor of genuine female subjectivity. In Christianity women are offered the "radiant glory of the mother," writes Irigaray, but not the image of "a fulfilled woman." Irigaray continues:

> We have no female trinity. But, as long as woman lacks a divine made in her image she cannot establish her subjectivity or achieve a goal of her own. She lacks an ideal that would be her goal or path in becoming. Woman scatters and becomes an agent of destruction and annihilation because she has no other of her own that she can become. . . . If she is to become woman, if she is to accomplish her female subjectivity, woman needs a god who is a figure for the perfection of *her* subjectivity.[9]

At first glance it may appear that Irigaray's call for a female God as the ideal for women's self-actualization entails the destruction of the male God of established Christian belief. But Irigaray is not an "antimale" iconoclast bent on merely substituting a female God for a male God. Her hope, rather, is to *deconstruct*—that is, to critically analyze but not simply destroy—the normative, trinitarian male imagery of God within Christianity in order to *reconstruct* a female divinity appropriate to women's quest for full and coherent selfhood. It is not enough simply to criticize the received Christian tradition as patriarchal; rather, the crucial and positive task at hand is to make sense of the received tradition in order to construct gender-appropriate models of God that can facilitate the process of full female becoming. As she puts it, "Having a God and becoming one's gender go hand in hand."[10]

With a keen eye on the importance of sexual difference in mature psychological formation, Irigaray successfully makes her case for the need for female language and imagery of God as a means for realizing women's identity in male-dominated Western cultures. But precisely at the point where the reader looks for concrete specificity about what a female God might look like vis-à-vis the male monotheistic belief systems of the West, Irigaray falls silent. "A female God is still to come," writes Irigaray wistfully, but how might this God appear and what would be her role in the current male triumphalist system?[11] Would such a female God be one or many? What would be her relationship to the male divinity of conventional biblical and Christian belief? And would the new female God be similar to or identical with the pre-Christian deities of Greece and Rome—or perhaps the Goddesses or consorts of Hindu South Asia or Buddhist East Asia? That is, would the female God who is still to come be a rehabilitation of an earlier deity (or deities), or a totally new and futuristic projection with little if any connection to the ancient gods and goddesses of earlier civilizations? Irigaray is a visionary philosopher, not a systematic theologian or comparative religionist, and this lacuna in her intellectual project is understandable. But the reader persuaded by her account concerning the deleterious effects of masculine religion on women's (and also men's) psychological well-being still hungers for clear guidelines about what this female God, a God who is still to come, might look like in the future.

Intriguing hints as to the identity of this yet-to-appear female divinity are offered in Irigaray's oblique references to the *feminine Holy Spirit* in Christianity.[12] She notes that the Spirit is traditionally understood as "bird" and "fire" in Christian iconography—animal and animist images that call into question the rigidly male and otherworldly figuration of the Trinity. And she speculates that the Spirit could perform the mediatory role of forging intercommunion between the members of a female Trinity—Mother, Daughter, and Spirit—in the same way that the Spirit's role is now understood in relation to the male Trinity of established orthodoxy—Father, Son, and Spirit. But these Irigarean reflections are inchoate and often phrased in the form of questions. The possibility of the Spirit performing the role of the feminine God as a model for women's becoming and fulfillment is a provocative possibility gestured toward but left underdeveloped in Irigaray's feminist project. But as a theologian interested in recovering the role of the Spirit for a contemporary green spirituality, my interest is piqued by her brief remarks about the feminine Spirit.

Thus I wonder, Could the Holy Spirit be the female God who is to come as prophesied in Irigaray's philosophy?

Biblical Imagery of the Earthen Mother Spirit

Is the Spirit in the Bible and Christian tradition the arrival of the female God proleptically anticipated but not fully described in Irigaray's visionary writing?

A number of intriguing linguistic and biblical references to the feminine identity of the Spirit make a positive answer to this Irigarean-inspired question a strong possibility. Grammatically speaking, the term for Spirit in Hebrew is feminine (*rûach*) and neuter in Greek (*pneuma*), the original languages of the First and Second Testaments of the Bible, respectively. In biblical parlance, the grammatical gender of the nouns for Spirit as feminine and neuter have always been indications of the possibility of a female aspect of the divine life. This possibility was realized in the third and fourth centuries of the common era by Syriac-speaking Christians who wrote about the feminine characteristics of the Spirit in part because of the gendered grammar for the Spirit used in the biblical texts. As Susan Ashbrook Harvey puts it

> The [ancient Syriac] texts present a portrayal of the Spirit with feminine images rising first out of the grammatical gender of the noun for spirit—*ruhâ* is feminine in Syriac, as *rûach* is in Hebrew—and secondly out of the verbs which are used to describe the Spirit's actions.[13]

Syrian Christians identified the Spirit in female terms both because the terms they used (and the terms much of the Bible uses) to refer to the Spirit were grammatically female and because of the woman-centered scriptural descriptions of the Spirit's activity (for example, Spirit as birthing and mothering).

Syrian Christians in antiquity sang to and prayed to the feminine Holy Spirit as the mother God and the bird God who complemented the male father God of Christian piety. It is not that the Syrians were proposing a new Trinity (Mother, Father, and Bird) but, rather, that they wanted to emphasize mothering aspects and attributes of God in order to round out the standard male imagery for God in historic Christian thought. In early hymns and liturgies, the Spirit is referred to as a nesting eagle, a nurturing dove, and a nursing, lactating mother. In one Syriac Ode to the Spirit we read the following:

> As the wings of doves over their nestlings,
> and the mouths of their nestlings towards their mouths,
> So are the wings of the Spirit over my heart.
> My heart continually refreshes itself and leaps for joy,
> like the babe who leaps for joy in his mother's womb.[14]

In this hymn of praise, the Spirit is a birthing mother and mothering bird, hovering over the believer with outstretched wings like a hen who shelters and feeds her young. The Spirit is loved and worshipped as a divine female figure who refreshes and cares for all persons like a mother who enfolds her young in the protection of her womb. Could this early Syriac version of woman Spirit be an anticipation of Irigaray's hope for the arrival of the female sacred in our own time? Generally speaking, historic Christianity has not emphasized this neglected tradition of mother Spirit, but the Christian faith clearly carries within itself the germ of feminine God-language that can and should be productively remembered and reha-bilitated. Irigaray's call for a female God is answered in ancient Christian imagery of the hovering, birthing Spirit who loves and protects the world she has brought into existence.

Using the optics of this early Syriac experience of female divinity, we can see how the Bible's grammatical clues concerning the Spirit's non-masculine *identity* are complemented by the biblical descriptions of the *work* of the Spirit as a loving, mothering, nurturing presence in creation. This recognition of the Spirit's woman-centered work—the identification of the Spirit as female presence—is biblically expressed in the inaugural creation hymn of Genesis. In the Bible's opening verses the Spirit emerges as the Great Mother of Creation. In Genesis, the Spirit is figured as an immense mother bird who "broods" or "hovers" over her earthen nest egg in order to birth into existence all of the hatchlings in her charge. "In the beginning God created the heavens and the earth. The earth was without form and void, and darkness was upon the face of the deep; and the Spirit of God was hovering over the face of the waters" (Genesis 1:1-2).

The Hebrew verb *merahefet* translated as "to hover" in this passage is used in the Bible to describe the activity of mother birds brooding over their nests and caring for their nestlings. The use of *merahefet* in this crucial opening passage signals the identity of the Spirit as the primordial bird God preparing to give birth to her young at the dawn of creation. In a manner reminiscent of the avian Spirit imagery in medieval and Amerindian art we discussed earlier in this chapter, the life-giving Mother Bird of Genesis broods over the watery chaos in anticipation of bringing into existence all of creation's various life-forms and other modalities: light and darkness, heaven and earth, plants and animals, stars and planets, and man and woman. Brooding over the great egg of creation, Mother God enacts the birth of all life.

Catherine Keller lyrically evokes the image of the brooding divine Mother Bird as a powerful statement of God embodying Godself in living systems. In becoming matter, she writes, the Spirit,

> far from effecting a spiritual disembodiment, a flight from the earth, suggests in its very birdiness a dynamism of embodiment: lines of flight *within* the world. Moreover, the etymological connotation of brooding has always emitted the mythical associations of the mother bird laying the world-egg. Despite its precarious biblical legitimacy, the egg has tucked itself into the long history of interpretation—as, for instance, in [the medieval theologian] Hildegard's image of the universe as a cosmic egg.[15]

As Keller puts it, the "very birdiness" of the Spirit's progenerative activity plunges us into the earthy depths of the Spirit's "flight *within* the world"—her this-worldly love and passion for the integrity of the "world-egg" she has produced.

The nurturing, brooding bird God of Genesis emerges in the Gospels as well. The same hovering Spirit Bird appears again in the Gospels at Jesus' baptism to inaugurate his public ministry. Matthew's Gospel says that when Jesus was baptized, "the heavens were opened and he saw the Spirit of God descending like a dove, and alighting on him" (Matthew 3:13-17), and John's Gospel has John the Baptist reporting the same event, "I saw the Spirit descend as a dove from heaven, and it remained on him" (John 1:31-34; also cf. Mark 1:9-11; Luke 3:21-22). These passages recapitulate the Spirit's hovering, nesting work from the Genesis creation story. As before, the Spirit is a ministering presence over a watery surface (in this case, the river Jordan). And in a manner akin to the Spirit's mothering work in Genesis, where the Spirit is on the wing hovering over the expanse of creation, the gospel passages state that the avian Spirit comes down from heaven and then "alights upon" Jesus (in Matthew the verb is *erkomai*, which in this case means "to come upon" or "rest upon") or "stays with" him (in John the verb is *emmeno*, which means "to stay," "persevere in," or "remain with").

The "fluttering" image here is of the winged Spirit coming down from above and gently tarrying with Jesus in this inaugural rite of baptism. Here in the New Testament the Spirit alights on Jesus' head and shoulders, literally touching him with her presence and communicating her abiding love and support to him. The Spirit Bird nestles on Jesus' newly baptized body still dripping wet from his immersion in the river. As the Spirit in Genesis hovers over the chaos bringing new life into existence, so also does the Spirit in the Gospels flutter about Jesus bringing the new work of his public ministry into existence. Like a mother with her child, the Spirit in the Gospels gives birth to Jesus' fledgling ministry even as the Spirit in Genesis gives birth to primitive flora and fauna through her hovering work over all creation.

The story of Jesus' baptism in the four Gospels not only conjures the image of the Spirit as mothering, female presence; it also brings together the cardinal elements into a powerful tableau of ecological spirituality. In Matthew's Gospel, Jesus is water baptized by John the Baptist and perched upon by the avian Spirit as a prelude to Jesus' work of healing and friendship. In this story, as we have seen, we see Jesus emerging from the river Jordan dripping wet and alighted upon by the Spirit Bird. John then announces that Jesus will baptize others with the Spirit and with fire, judging the arrogant and selfish ones with the force of God's displeasure. Consider Matthew's version of events:

> [John said:] "I baptize you with water for repentance, but he who is coming after me is mightier than I, whose sandals I am not worthy to carry; he will baptize you with the Holy Spirit and with fire. His winnowing fork is in his hand, and he will clear his threshing floor and gather his wheat into the granary, but the chaff he will burn with unquenchable fire."
>
> Then Jesus came from Galilee to the Jordan to John, to be baptized by him. John would have prevented him, saying, "I need to be baptized by you, and do you come to me?" But Jesus answered him, "Let it be so now; for thus it is fitting for us to fulfill all righteousness." Then he consented. And when Jesus was baptized, he went up

immediately from the water, and behold, the heavens were opened and he saw the Spirit of God descending like a dove, and alighting on him; and lo, a voice from heaven, saying, "This is my beloved Son, with whom I am well pleased." (Matthew 3: 11-17)

In this passage all of the basic, primitive elements are woven together to create a compelling environmental tapestry of prophecy and judgment. The narrative begins with John's revelation that Jesus will baptize some persons with the purgative *fire* of God's judgment. After this announcement, Jesus then goes down into the renewing *water* of the river and is empowered to do his work of ministry. Coming up through the river, the Spirit Bird, an *earthen* life-form, comes down from heaven on the wings of the *wind*, and alights on Jesus' person, perching protectively on his head and shoulders, as God's voice of parental love and pride is heard by all present, saying, "This is my beloved Son, with whom I am well pleased." In this story of landed spirituality the four primal elements—the fire of judgment, the water of renewal, and the life-giving wind of the earthen Spirit—are fully set forth and integrated with one another. What it means to be pleasing to God and at peace with oneself and one's natural environment is clearly expounded in this account. Here the meaning of earth-centered human existence—to live in harmony with the essential elements of life—is articulated in all its breadth and fullness. Like Jesus, therefore, all persons who undergo baptism by water are now singed by God's fire and invigorated by God's breath to share the gospel to a world in dire need of reaffirming the integrity of the good earth God has made.

Using as my departure point Luce Irigaray's yearning for a female God who is still to come, I have suggested here that we reimagine the Spirit as God's elemental and female presence in the created order. To make this claim, however, is not to say that God is a woman—any more than it is to say that God is a man—but to underscore, rather, that God as Spirit, as figured in the biblical texts, possesses certain female traits that warrant references to the Spirit as "she." Alas, in making this analogy between God and the feminine, one must be careful not to *essentialize* womanhood and claim that compassion and nurture are uniquely female characteristics. Such an essentializing move is bad for some women because it locks them into a narrow range of "female" attributes that some women may need to put into abeyance in order to overcome narrow definitions concerning femininity and become fully actualized individuals. And such a move is bad for many men as well because it deprives them of their nurturing and caring potential. But with these caveats in mind, we have seen how the Bible and Christian tradition understand God as Spirit in maternal, feminine terms, and how this understanding liberates a new model of God as woman and sets aside male-only assumptions about God the Father and God the Son. To say that the Spirit is female is to use rich metaphors for imagining what God is like—God is a mothering bird, God is a nurturing parent—without falling prey to the perennial temptation to put the divine life into a small theological box and limit God to being this or that.

In one sense, therefore, God is a gendered, sexual being: as at one time God enfleshed Godself in the male body of Jesus, so again today God continually enfleshes Godself within creation through the female agency of the Spirit, the Mother Bird of Genesis and the Gospels. In another sense, however, God is beyond sex and gender: God transcends sexuality and cannot be exhaustively contained within any one particular person, gender, or life-form. But to note that God escapes gendered categories should not be a theological license to continue to refer to God, including the Spirit of God, in exclusively male terms. Women and men continue to suffer from exclusive language use for God even while the biblical and Christian image of woman Spirit cries out against such usage. Religious institutions have often given sacred legitimacy to sexist habits of thought and language that are, ironically, undermined by the founding scriptures of these institutions themselves. In this chapter, I have tried to show that since the Spirit linguistically and biblically is often figured as sustaining, earthen Mother Bird, it makes sense to pulse toward a new, which is also very ancient, vocabulary for the Spirit in woman-centered terms. This new as well as ancient vocabulary of Woman Spirit opens up new dimensions of the Spirit's female presence in creation. In the same manner, a retrieval of the aviary characteristics of the divine Mother Bird opens up a new nature-centered understanding of the Spirit's work today.

Water, light, mother, fire, breath, wind, bird—the Spirit reveals herself as a healing life-form in the scriptures and important trajectories within church tradition. These land-based descriptions of the Spirit are the source of my attempt to direct our attention away from the model of God as Spirit whose identity is exhausted by her mediatory, unifying role in the Godhead—as important as this role is—toward a vision of the enfleshed, winged Earth God of the Christian heritage who promises life and renewal for all members of our planet home. This proposed shift in focus is not intended to impugn the historic understanding of the Spirit's role as the power of relationship between the Father and Son. Rather, my focus on the Spirit's carnal, fleshly identity as the earthen Mother God who interanimates all life-forms readdresses our attention to the Spirit's work in *all* of creation—not just the Spirit's work within God's inner life, as crucial as that work is.

Chapter Three

Green Spirituality, Brownfields, and Wilderness Recovery

The Current Environmental Debate

ON A RECENT VISIT to the west end of Chester, Pennsylvania, a postindustrial city outside of Philadelphia where I live, the first thing I noticed was the smell. Waves of noxious fumes enveloped me like the stench of rotting meat. Next I felt the bone-jarring rumble of giant eighteen-wheel trash trucks, dozens of trucks from all over the mid-Atlantic and Eastern seaboard, bearing down on the residential streets I was walking with tons of trash—trash that I knew contained everything from toxic chemicals and contaminated soil to sewage sludge and body parts. Then I looked to the horizon and saw the destination of the truck convoys: a line of giant trash processing plants belching putrid smoke interspersed among the daily comings and goings of Chester residents. Children and families who live and work in Chester are awash in the fumes, noise, and pollution generated by a constant armada of trash trucks and a collection of waste treatment facilities situated on the immediate boundary of their neighborhood homes, schools, and churches. My visit underscored a sad truth: Chester, like other poor American towns and cities, has become a corporate sacrifice zone in order to serve the capitalized interests of the waste management industry.

In this chapter I ask the question, What role can the Spirit play in confronting environmental problems in residential areas such as Chester, on the one hand, or in other localities underinhabited by humans, such as wilderness areas, on the other? What is the role of green spirituality in combating the degradation of the earth in settled human communities or in open spaces relatively unaffected by human development? In response, I have suggested that the promise of Christian faith for our time is grounded in the central biblical image of *God as Earth Spirit*, the compassionate divine force within the biosphere that indwells earth community and continually labors to maintain the integrity of all forms of life. In green spirituality God is the Earth God who lives underfoot and makes holy the encircling earth that protects and nourishes all things. God is not a Sky Deity who dwells isolated and dispassionate in a heavenly realm far removed from earthly concerns. God as Spirit is the enfleshment of God within everything that burrows, creeps, runs, swims, and flies across the earth.

To see oneself as a blessed recipient of the Spirit's daily bread is to feel motivated to enter the political fray and work toward healthy earth-centered living, whether in developed places or in wilderness areas. To know that the Spirit maintains the natural systems on which all life depends is to be inspired to labor on behalf of the integrity of these natural systems. To believe that all life is God's gift is to feel empowered to work toward environmental healing and environmental justice in all different types of degraded communities, human and nonhuman. The Spirit maintains the integrity of the lifeweb in cities and rural areas, in urban areas and in forests and grasslands alike. Whenever the lifeweb is shredded by harmful behavior and bad public policy, persons invigorated by the Spirit's presence in the world feel the need to rise up and work for change.

To understand oneself as a member of Spirit-earth community, therefore, entails a commitment to social justice for all creation. The cry for environmental justice in many distressed areas is a critical issue in our time. But contemporary environmental thinking and activity is openly divided on the question of how best to answer the cry for earth justice. That is, should energy and resources be put toward rebuilding human communities that have suffered from environmental abuse, or should the emphasis be placed on preserving the integrity of open spaces not yet degraded by human settlement? Should urban areas be the focus of environmental renewal where people are at risk (for example, cities such as Chester or Detroit or Los Angeles), or should the focus fall on wildlands where equal rights for all species are the primary value (for example, Rocky Mountain rivers or South American rain forests)? While the two concerns are not mutually exclusive, there is considerable tension between proponents of both orientations. My hope in this chapter is to consider how green spirituality, as a powerful force for enabling social change, offers resources for bringing the two sides together around a common commitment to preserving the lifeweb that binds all things to one another.

Two sides, therefore, make up the global environmental movement today: so-called antitoxics groups organized against environmental hazards in economically distressed human communities, on the one hand, and conservation activists who work toward the restoration of biodiversity in wilderness areas, on the other. Both camps consist of grassroots organizations that emphasize all persons' collective responsibility for healthy environments. Both camps recognize that the consumerist logic of the market-state—"grow or die"—will continue to result in the degradation of clean water and air, animal well-being, and human flourishing. As such, both movements are a frontal challenge to the American capitalist ideal that the pursuit of enlightened self-interest somehow guarantees that all members of the body politic will achieve a reasonable standard of living in relatively healthy home and work environments.

But these affinities between antitoxics and biodiversity activists are initially difficult to discern in the face of the disagreements between the two groups. The antitoxics movement has its origins in the plight of human communities—urban, suburban, and rural—precariously situated in close proximity to health hazards such as waste dumps, polluted water supplies, contaminated soil sites, and toxic storage plants. Antitoxics argue that large industrial polluters in collusion with local public officials look for economically distressed areas in which to build hazardous facilities that promise immediate economic gains for the area's inhabitants. Ideal sites for these operations are the brownfields that dot urban landscapes: vast tracts of environmentally scarred areas left over from previous commercial and industrial (ab)uses. In urban areas, more often than not, poor people of color are most directly affected by living near biohazards; in many suburban and rural areas, middle-class and low-income whites are often disproportionately affected by the use and abuse of their environment and its resources. "Numerous studies have found that those who live in close proximity to noxious facilities are disproportionately people of color or of low income, and race has been found to be the stronger indicator of the two."[1] The antitoxics movement, therefore, is primarily concerned with environmental justice for disenfranchised persons who have suffered from historic racial and class discrimination and now have been deprived of their right to live and work in safe and healthy environments.

The conservationist movement, on the other hand, focuses primarily on the exigency to preserve ecological richness and vitality in unspoiled bioregions that have not been badly damaged by the influx of human populations. Here the emphasis falls on preserving or rehabilitating wilderness areas for the sake of biodiversity rather than on the promotion of justice per se for disadvantaged human communities that have suffered environmental degradation. Otherwise disparate groups and movements such as Greenpeace, the Sea Shepherd Society, Earth First! the Animal Liberation Front, and the Earth Liberation Front are united by their vigorous bioregional attempts to recover the integrity of nonhuman species by conserving their habitats. One such movement, the Wildlands Project, states that its mission is "to help protect and restore the ecological richness and native biodiversity of North America through the establishment of a connected system of reserves."[2] From this perspective, the best way to address the degraded environments of impoverished human cities and towns is to do so only indirectly through the promotion of wild spaces that ensure the welfare of all life, not just human life.

At first glance, then, the differences between antitoxics and conservationists appear stark and irreconcilable: either the focus falls on enabling disenfranchised human communities to overcome historic economic and environmental degradation, or the focus is protecting the ecosystemic integrity of all beings without assigning any special concern to the needs of human beings. The understandable but unfortunate continuation of this disagreement further fragments an already divided environmental movement.

In light of this division within contemporary green populism, I will ask here, What role can an environmentally rich spirituality play in healing this breach? Can antitoxics activists and champions of wilderness preservation find common ground in a "sustainable spirituality," to use Charlene Spretnak's felicitous phrase, that seeks both to fight social injustice and to protect nature for its own sake?[3] Sustainable spirituality—or what I have called green spirituality—is an earthen spiritual vision concerning the deep interrelationships of all life-forms on the planet and the concomitant ethical ideal of preserving the integrity of these relationships through one's religious and political practice.[4] Sustainable spirituality offers its practitioners a powerfully useful root metaphor—the image of all life as organically interconnected—that can enable a fresh reappraisal of the debate between advocates for environmental justice and biocentric conservationists. To address this debate, I will use the organic metaphor of *interdependence* rooted in the core vision of green spirituality to press beyond the impasse in the current discussion.

Toxic Sacrifice Zones and the Quest for Justice

It should not come as a surprise that many local economies in urban and rural America today are dependent upon the production and management of toxic wastes. In economically distressed communities the promise of a stabilized tax base, improved physical infrastructure, and jobs for under-employed residents is almost impossible to resist. The waste management industry offers an immediate quick fix to chronic poverty and instability in declining cities and neighborhoods that can no longer attract government and private investment. The price for allowing the storage and treatment of biohazardous materials in one's community may be long-term environmental problems. But people in the grip of poverty and jobless-ness have few options when their very survival, materially speaking, is contingent upon the construction of a trash incinerator or chemical dump in their neighborhood.

Corporate investors know a good thing when they see it. Waste management facilities cannot be sited where politically empowered middle- and upper-class residents will fight through the courts the establishment of such facilities. Close proximity to hazardous industries immediately depresses property values in residential areas where virtually no one wants to risk endangering his or her physical and economic well-being by allowing such a liability to be built in his or her own backyard. And in those rare instances where such facilities have been built in high-income areas, the residents have the means and mobility to "'vote with their feet' and move away from a high risk place of residence."[5]

Recent popular movements of resistance to the expansion of the tox-ics industry into various communities—poor and middle-class alike—are surprisingly resilient. The 1970s conflict at Love Canal, New York, is the first and best-known example of a modern successful grassroots response to callous irresponsibility in the powerful waste industry. A citizens' move-ment led by Love Canal homeowner-activist Lois Gibbs protested Hooker Chemical's disposal of toxic chemicals into the ground on which homes and schools were later built. The Love Canal homeowners convincingly documented the deleterious health affects that had resulted from living in the middle of a chemical dump and persuaded officials to buy out and permanently relocate town residents.[6] Other recent local antitoxics campaigns are also notable, if not always as successful: the protest against siting a PCB (polychlorinated biphenyl) landfill in Warren County, North Carolina; the movement against building a waste incinerator by the Mothers of East Los Angeles; and the campaign by Native American activists against building a waste-to-fertilizer plant on Native lands in Vian, Oklahoma.[7]

The problems and prospects of antitoxics campaigns in blighted urban areas are graphically evident in the resistance to a series of waste management plants in Chester, Pennsylvania. Chester is an impoverished, predominantly African American community in a largely white suburb, Delaware County.[8] Its median family income is 45 percent lower than the rest of Delaware County; its poverty rate is 25 percent, more than three times the rate in the rest of Delaware County; and its unemployment rate is 30 percent. Chester has the highest infant mortality rate and the highest percentage of low-weight births in the state.[9] In the light of its alarmingly bad public health, Chester would appear to be the last place to build a constellation of hazardous facilities.

Nevertheless, five waste treatment plants have been built on a concentrated site surrounded by homes and parks in a low-income, largely African American neighborhood in Chester. The facilities include the American Ref-Fuel trash-to-steam incinerator; the Delcora sewage treatment plant; the Clean Metal metal-recycling plant; the Thermal Pure Systems medical-waste autoclave (which is not operating, at least for the time being); and the Kimberly-Clark Tissue Corporation's combined paper mill and waste processing facility, which burns a variety of petrochemicals, and now hopes to incinerate millions of old tires a year in order to generate tire-derived fuel.[10] Other waste treatment plants devoted to treating PCB and other types of contaminated soil have also applied to local officials in recent years for construction permits in Chester. At this time the verdict is out as to whether the Pennsylvania Department of Environmental Protection will grant the necessary permits for making the plants operational.

The clustering of waste industries only a few yards from a large residential area has made worse the high rate of asthma and other respiratory and health problems in Chester. It has brought about an infestation of rodents, the presence of hundreds of trucks a day at all hours in the neighborhood, soot and dust covering even the insides of people's homes, and waves of noxious odors that have made life unbearable at times.[11] In a landmark health study of the environmental degradation of Chester, the Environmental Protection Agency (EPA) found that lead poisoning is a significant health problem for the majority of Chester children; that toxic air emissions have raised the specter of cancer to two-and-a-half times greater than the average risk for area residents; and that the fish in Chester waters are badly contaminated with PCBs from current and previous industrial abuses.[12]

The EPA study has made public what many Chester residents have long known: the unequal dumping of municipal wastes in Chester has undermined the health and well-being of its population. Chester is a stunning example of environmental racism. All municipal solid waste in Delaware County is burned at the American Ref-Fuel incinerator; 90 percent of all sewage is treated at the Delcora plant; and, until recently, close to a hundred tons of hospital waste per day from a half-dozen nearby states were being sterilized at the Thermal Pure plant.[13] As Jerome Balter, a Philadelphia environmental lawyer puts it, "When Delaware County passes an act that says all of the waste has to come to the city of Chester, that *is* environmental racism."[14] Or, as Peter Kostmayer, former congressman and head of the EPA's mid-Atlantic region, says, high levels of pollution in Chester would "not have happened if this were Bryn Mawr, Haverford or Swarthmore [nearby well-to-do white suburbs]. I think we have to face the fact that the reason this happened is because this city is largely—though not all—African American, and a large number of its residents are people of low income."[15] In other words, Chester has become a local "sacrifice zone," where the disproportionate pollution from its waste-industrial complex is tolerated because of the promise of economic revitalization.[16] But the promise of dozens of jobs and major funds for the immediate areas around the existing toxics industries have never materialized. Indeed, of the $20 million the American Ref-Fuel incinerator pays to local governments in taxes, only $2 million goes to Chester while $18 million goes to Delaware County.[17]

Chester is Delaware County's sacrifice zone. The surrounding middle-class, white neighborhoods would never allow for the systematic overexposure of their citizens to such a toxics complex. The health and economic impact of siting even one of the facilities now housed in Chester would likely be regarded as too high of a risk. But to build a whole cluster of such complexes in nearby Chester is another matter. Nevertheless, many in Chester have tried to fight back against this exercise in environmental apartheid. The Chester Residents Concerned for Quality Living, a small storefront community organization, led by antitoxics activist (or, as she prefers, "reactivist") Zulene Mayfield, has used nonviolent resistance tactics—mass protests, staged truck blockades, monitoring of emissions levels, and protracted court actions—to block the expansion of the complex. Mayfield, a local homeowner who is struggling to end the degradation of her neighborhood, is an urban Cassandra crying out against the market-driven assaults on the health of her neighbors, especially the children. It is the children who are most at risk, according to Mayfield, because they are the most vulnerable to the release of airborne toxins generated by powerful waste management entrepreneurs. It is the children who are being poisoned by the air now heavy with lead generated in part by the trash facilities sited only a few dozen yards from their homes and playgrounds.

Echoing Mayfield in her opposition to the granting of a permit for operation for still another waste facility to be built in the area, a contaminated soil remediation plant, former Chester mayor Barbara Bohannan-Sheppard concluded her remarks at a public hearing with the following: "Chester should not and will not serve as a dumping ground. A dumping ground for what no other borough, no other township, or no other city will accept. Yes, Chester needs the taxes, Chester needs the jobs. But, Chester also needs to improve its image and not be a killing field."[18] Many Chester residents such as Bohannan-Sheppard and Mayfield have tried to resist the imposition of environmental apartheid in Chester. Mayfield has told me that she sees herself as waging an impossible, long-term spiritual war, a sort of David-and-Goliath conflict. Sadly, she is not confident that she will be successful.

Mayfield understands the spiritual foundations of her singular struggle as a reworking of her Methodist upbringing. She says that her appropriation of the Christian story grounds her belief that all persons are fundamentally equal and that everyone has the right to family stability and meaningful work in a healthy environment. This religious foundation for her work is the basis for her belief in the inherent right to be free from ecological degradation—a right shared by all God's children living together on this sacred earth. But Mayfield's activism has attracted little institutional support from the organized churches in the area. She has approached the local ministerium to support her efforts but found little interest among religious leaders in combating the waste complex. Chester clergy, she says, are committed to so many other important issues that the embrace of the environmental problem seems too much of a stretch. She is not bitter about this lack of ecclesiastical support but realistic that in an economically ravaged community church leaders are limited in their time and resources. Thus Mayfield is generally alone in her work. She cries and gets angry and is sometimes depressed when she considers the bleak prospects for her neighborhood, especially in regard to the local children. I have told her that she reminds me of a biblical prophet. She shrugs and says that she would prefer that someone else or some other group take up the resistance to the waste plants, but that no one else is doing anything and she feels called to confront the problem. Like a prophet she is regularly persecuted for her efforts: she and her mother receive death threats from anonymous callers, and her office was recently broken into and vandalized and sprayed with the initials "KKK" and other racist epithets.

Hope is not lost in Chester.

There is a growing awareness of the injustice being done to low-income, often racial minority communities that have suffered from the unequal distribution of environmental hazards in their neighborhoods. In 1995 Bill Clinton signed an executive order mandating all federal agencies to ensure the equitable location of polluting industries across race and economic lines.[19] But the signs are not good that the Chester Residents organization can successfully combat the expansion of the waste industry in their area insofar as no major environmental organization has taken up the Chester cry against environmental racism as its own. And time is running out as new waste treatment facilities—such as the Kimberly-Clark Tissue Corporation's tires-to-fuel plant—are preparing to overcome the last legal hurdles to bringing their operations on line.

What role can green spirituality play in the struggle against environmental racism in areas such as Chester, Pennsylvania? In response, it should first be noted that few people see it as in their interests to express solidarity with disadvantaged communities that have suffered the brunt of unequal distribution of environmental risks. Many people have become inured to the gradual environmental degradation of their home and work environments and most likely consider the development of occasional toxic "sacrifice zones" and "killing fields" to be a tragic but necessary result of modern technological life and its attendant creature comforts. If everyone has the right to pursue his or her own material self-interests, and if some persons are better able to do this on the basis of their "natural" advantages based on family, national origin, or socioeconomic class, then it follows that some disadvantaged groups will be marginalized in the social struggle for increased wealth, security, and power.

But green spirituality challenges this whole set of assumptions by affirming instead that all persons are fundamentally equal and that everyone has the right to family stability and meaningful work in a healthy environment regardless of one's racial, cultural, economic, or sexual identity. Moreover, green sustainable spirituality affirms the common interdependence of all persons with each other—indeed, of all species with each other—as we all struggle to protect the integrity of the lifeweb that holds together our planet home. Green spirituality testifies to the bond of unity that unites all of God's children together on a sacred earth. As the participants of the First National People of Color Environmental Leadership Summit put it: "Environmental justice affirms the sacredness of Mother Earth, ecological unity and the interdependence of all species, and the right to be free from ecological destruction."[20] Earth-centered religion values the interconnections among all members of the biosphere in contradistinction to the privileged ideal of maximizing self-interest.

My concern here is to reenvision Christianity as an exercise in green spirituality that can productively address the environmental crisis in places such as Chester. But it should also be noted that green spirituality can be more broadly understood as a distillation of the earth-centered sensibilities within different world religions. This approach does not view green spirituality as a syncretism of all global spiritualities into one totalizing theory, but rather as a selective interpretation of many different religious traditions from an earthen perspective. Depending upon one's religious and cultural background and interests, religious ideas, in addition to the green Spirit Christianity proposed here, that could be candidates for inclusion in such a spiritual vision are the following: the Jewish narrative of a common creation story where all species possess inherent worth as the handiwork of the Creator;[21] the Chinese doctrine of Ch'i—the vital force within nature that dynamically integrates all forms of life into common flow patterns;[22] and the Amerindian imagery of the earth as our Great Mother, which entails the values of care and respect for the "body" of our common parent.[23] Alternately theistic and nontheistic, scriptural and preliterate, Eastern and Western, these earth-friendly religious traditions offer a body of rich stories and images for enabling the quest for environmental justice.[24]

In the struggle against environmental injustice green spirituality can serve an important role: to motivate all persons to live responsibly on the earth. Its hope is to inspire people to imagine the world as a communitarian family of beings that mutually depend upon one another in order to liberate sisterly feelings for the many life-forms that populate the earth. Green spirituality empowers antitoxics to go out and fight injustice by offering them spiritually potent visions of an interconnected world that can set free a primal sense of identification with all forms of life—that can set free, as early American theologian Jonathan Edwards wonderfully put it, the union of heart with Being as such.[25] By bearing witness to the underlying unity of all things, green spirituality can sustain communities of resistance over the long haul. While this model cannot directly fund the material needs of antitoxics campaigns, it can stimulate the imagination to see the world differently and empower the will to stand against oppression as members of embattled communities seek to end the inequitable dumping of hazards and toxins in their neighborhoods. The study and use of fact sheets and health reports alone are not enough to enable the struggle over the long term and in the face of overwhelming odds. By motivating all of the participants to better understand their interdependence on one another—to envision the common bond between rich and poor, suburbanites and city folk, people of color and anglos, humankind and otherkind—green spirituality provides the moral and spiritual resources necessary for enduring commitments to combating environmental racism and injustice.

Deep Ecology and Wilderness Activism

Alongside the antitoxics' concern with safeguarding human communities from industrial polluters, the other wing of the environmental movement works to protect and preserve wild places and endangered species from human incursion. If the antitoxics' rationale for stopping polluting industries is basic human concern for healthy cities and neighborhoods, then what is the basis for the conservationist approach to the environment? In essence, the modern wilderness preservation movement is a practical application of the philosophy of deep ecology, which I alluded to in the Introduction. First formulated by Arne Naess in a 1973 article using that name, deep ecology articulates a spiritual vision of nature as the lifeweb where every ecosystem and its members are bearers of equal and intrinsic worth.[26] The core insight of deep ecology is that all living things are equivalent in value and possess the inherent right to grow and flourish. Opposed to human chauvinism, deep ecology is biocentric rather than anthropocentric: human beings are codependent members of the biotic community rather than centers of supreme value independent from and over and against the natural world. Consider how Vietnamese monk and ecomystic Thich Nhat Hanh articulates our primeval co-belonging with the vital support systems that keep us alive:

> Without trees, we cannot have people, therefore trees and people inter-are. We *are* trees, and air, bushes and clouds. If trees cannot survive, humankind is not going to survive either. We get sick because we have damaged our own environment, and we are in mental anguish because we are so far away from our true mother, Mother Nature.[27]

Or consider how deep ecology activist John Seed makes this point regarding his (and, by implication, other human beings') aboriginal kinship with natural systems as the basis for his own rain-forest advocacy work. Seed writes:

> When humans investigate and see through their layers of anthropocentric self-cherishing, a most profound change in consciousness begins to take place.
> Alienation subsides. The human is no longer an outsider, apart. Your humanness is then recognized as being merely the most recent stage of your existence. . . . You start to get in touch with yourself as mammal, as vertebrate, as a species only recently emerged from the rain forest. . . .
> What is described here should not be seen as merely intellectual. The intellect is one entry point to the process outlined, and the easiest one to communicate. For some people, however, this change of perspective follows from actions on behalf of mother Earth.
> "I am protecting the rain forest" develops to "I am part of the rain forest protecting myself. I am that part of the rain forest recently emerged into thinking."[28]

Thus, I am not an independent life-form who lives merely *alongside* nature. Rather, I am the earth *itself*—I am that part of nature recently emerged into thinking, speaking, and moral activity, as Seed says. In the evolutionary scheme of things, I am that particular earthen being who is currently emerging as a joyously active and ethically reflective member of our true mother, Mother Nature, as Thich Nhat Hanh writes. I have my life and sustenance in a wider family of other brother and sister earth beings on whom I depend; in my family of soil, water, and sky I live and move and experience my very being. In value terms, I am neither better than nor worse than the other members of my earth family—and they me. This deep ecology insight provides the underlying warrant for popular conservationist efforts to renew endangered bioregions in order to promote ecological richness and diversity. If I am the rain forest or the watershed or the grassland recently emerged into thinking and action, then preservation of wildspaces is preservation for all life-forms, myself included. The moral rule that results from this biotic kinship orientation, as I noted in the Introduction, is variously formulated as the "duty of non-interference" or the "principle of minimum impact."[29]

Deep ecology philosophy is the worldview that animates much of grassroots environmentalism today. The direct action organization Earth First! and its offshoots, the Earth Liberation Front and the Wildlands Project, represent the leading edge of this movement. Earth First! emerged out of the disillusionment with the protracted environmental policy debates of the 1970s. At that time Wilderness Society staffer Dave Foreman and some of his colleagues broke with a number of mainstream environmental organizations and founded the self-proclaimed "no compromise" wilderness defense movement Earth First! in the early 1980s.[30] Foreman and other Earth First!ers became well known for highly public, colorful acts of "monkeywrenching" or "ecotage" in their efforts to undermine the industrial exploitation and destruction of unprotected wild habitats. Foreman and other militant greens appropriated the species egalitarianism of deep ecology and turned this philosophy into an ideological wedge to support controversial and sometimes illegal forays into saving wild places.

Taking their cues from the deep ecology activism embodied in the novel *The Monkey Wrench Gang* by Edward Abbey, Earth First! members today continue to style themselves as the final line of defense against a rapacious industrial system hell-bent on destroying the last undeveloped areas in North America, with special emphasis on the vast frontiers of the American West. Many green activists believe that while much of America has been and will be destroyed by the industrial machine, the western frontier will be preserved and restored after the machine collapses under its own weight. Earth First!'s vision of saving a green Wild West in the aftermath of a mass ecocide of biblical proportions—a sort of cowboy apocalypticism—is given voice in the figure of George Hayduke in Abbey's novel:

When the cities are gone, [Hayduke] thought, and all the ruckus has died away, when sunflowers push up through the concrete and asphalt of the forgotten interstate freeways . . . when the glass-aluminum skyscraper tombs of Phoenix Arizona barely show above the sand dunes, why then by God maybe free men and wild women on horses . . . can roam the sagebrush canyonlands in freedom . . . and dance all night to the music of fiddles! banjos! steel guitars! by the light of a reborn moon!—by God, yes![31]

Hayduke is an anti-industrial wildman who prophesies certain eschatological doom; his end-time fantasy provides the master metaphors for Earth First!'s apocalyptic rhetoric. Through vandalizing construction vehicles, spiking and performing sit-ins in trees targeted for logging, and generally wreaking havoc with resource extraction policies in wooded areas, Earth First! has emerged as the largest and most successful activist organization for wilderness preservation in the wake of market-oriented, forest-harvesting development policies.

Recently, Earth First! has given birth to two splinter groups. The radical wing of Earth First! has evolved into the Earth Liberation Front (ELF). The members of this faction call themselves the elves because they generally work at night, undetected and underground, to disrupt and destroy the commercial-industrial system that undergirds environmental degradation worldwide. Unlike more traditional Earth First!ers, who are often open to the wider society and the media about their direct action tactics such as tree-sitting, the elves are organized into anonymous, clandestine cells that disallow any public record of their membership.[32] In general, the ELF uses tactics more law-breaking and violent than the monkeywrenching activities employed by Earth First! Eschewing hope of changing the world domination system by working within the system, the elves often resort to arson and destruction of property as their preferred tactics for grinding the domination system to a halt.

Laboratory offices at Michigan State University and the University of Minnesota; housing developments in Phoenix, Philadelphia, and Bloomington, Indiana; fast-food restaurants on Long Island; ski lodges in Vail, Colorado; car dealerships in Detroit, Erie, Pennsylvania, and Eugene, Oregon—all of these targets have been attacked and often firebombed by ELF members as symbols of the capitalist order that support global environmental squalor.[33] ELF activists used to be focused on saving forests from corporate developers, but recent actions have widened their reach to include a variety of polluting business interests deemed hostile to preserving the integrity of natural systems. Hardcore greens have become increasingly expansive and destructive in their direct actions because they now realize that the whole capitalist system—and not just the large paper contractors and government forestry agencies that are developing America's wooded areas—has become hazardous to the health of the planet. With the eruption of anarchist and radical environmentalist violence at the World Trade Organization meeting in Seattle in 1999, the ELF has shifted its focus away from forest preservation to outright and ever increasing attacks against the entire global economic order.

> Beginning in December 1999, the ELF began directing its firebombs against an array of new and sometimes puzzling targets. . . . What happened? In a word, Seattle. When the antiglobalization movement exploded at the November 1999 World Trade Organization meeting, ELF advocates realized two things. First, violence gets attention. Second, their targets were too limited. After Seattle, the ELF realized that its beef wasn't merely with the Forest Service; the problem was global capitalism itself. Any symbol of that system—a new subdivision, a botany lab, a political clubhouse, a car dealership—became a target.[34]

Green violence is an option of last resort for activists who feel the tree-spiking and tree-sitting efforts of Earth First!ers are not enough to stop the escalating threats to the ecological integrity of the planet. But the risks are high for eco-anarchists who get caught destroying symbols of the world economic order. In June 2000 Craig "Critter" Marshall and Jeffrey "Free" Luers were caught by local police after firebombing the Joe Romania Chevrolet dealership in Eugene near the University of Oregon campus. They were convicted of multiple felony conspiracy charges and were incarcerated in the Oregon state prison system for five years and six months and twenty-two years and eight months, respectively. Stunningly, they continue to speak out from prison in favor of green criminal activities, defending the risks to themselves and other persons' property and well-being as necessary in the fight for earth liberation. As Critter puts it:

> It takes all the tools in the toolbox to dismantle the master's machine. . . . More passive people do tree-sits. More active people are comfortable risking their well-being.[35]

Likewise, Free voices his support of the ecodefense movement using inflammatory rhetoric to motivate other would-be ecosaboteurs in the struggle:

> If we are truly committed to getting rid of fascist governments like ours and getting rid of evil corporations, it is going to take a lot more than signs and protests. . . .
>
> Please, people, let's stop being victims. It is time to fight back, pick up a rock, pick up a lighter or pick up a gun.
>
> I'm gonna get in trouble for saying that, but the truth needs to be spoken.[36]

Critter's and Free's anticapitalist militancy advocates extreme and dangerous measures. In my mind, radical ecodefense has taken an ugly turn in recent years at a high price for both the perpetrators of ecoviolence and their targets. Free's exhortation to "pick up a lighter or pick up a gun" strikes me as a call to step over the line that divides green civil disobedience from anarchy and chaos for its own sake. I do not think that hearts and minds will be won for ecodefense by verbal incitements to violence, but I also believe that I understand the pain that animates this kind of rhetoric. For ecoradicals, the continued degradation of the ecology of the planet fuels anger and hopelessness that cannot be assuaged by incremental measures. For activists such as Critter and Free, dramatic ecoviolence that shocks everyday people, along with local and even world governments, now seems more effective than nonviolent actions such as tree-sits and the disabling of construction vehicles. They aver that not just in off-road, distant forests, but right here and now in everyone's backyard—at the local fast-food restaurant, SUV dealership, or university research lab—commercial activities that directly or indirectly fuel global warming and species extinction must be stopped. The sense of outrage and desperation that is palpable among hardcore greens is heartfelt and authentic. They are right that the health of the planet weighs in the balance of decisions consumers and politicians alike are making about future directions of the world economy. While I do not agree with the ecotage tactics that some hardcore greens engage in, I honor the genuine rage and despair that wells up from the depths of the wounded souls of militants such as Critter and Free as they survey the destruction wrought by our destruction of forests, pollution of earth's atmosphere, and abuse and extinction of many species.

The other break-off faction of Earth First!—led by Dave Foreman, who, as mentioned above, was one of the original cofounders of Earth First!—is more conservative and mediational than Earth First! itself, its erstwhile "no compromise" parent organization. Dave Foreman has organized his Earth First! faction into a politically left but mainstream biodiversity research and advocacy organization that publishes the journal *Wild Earth*. *Wild Earth* champions the Wildlands Project, an ambitious network of activists and scientists working to establish an interconnected system of wilderness parks and preserves across much of the wild and underdeveloped spaces of the Americas. This splinter group represents a significant change in philosophy and tactics from the larger Earth First! movement: wilderness *recovery* is now the watchword of this minority group instead of wilderness *defense*. The angry monkeywrenching tactics of civil disobedience (Earth First!) and criminal arson (ELF) have been replaced by the moderate discourse of earth science and public policy studies. Instead of Hayduke-like apocalypticism and extreme ELF ecotage, the Wildlands Project is seeking long-term political solutions to declining biodiversity in wilderness areas. Instead of countercultural hostility toward mainstream bureaucratic environmentalism, the Wildlands Project is eager to make common cause with any pro-wilderness groups—from biocentric grassroots movements to the more conservative Group of Ten environmental organizations such as the Sierra Club and the World Wildlife Fund.

The central focus of the Wildlands Project is the establishment of a system of nature preserves for the sake of furthering biological growth and diversity. This system would consist of interconnected core reserves that would allow genetically diverse populations to cross-fertilize, evolve, migrate, and flourish.

> The mission of The Wildlands Project is to help protect and restore the ecological richness and native biodiversity of North America through the establishment of a connected system of reserves. . . . The environment of North America is at risk and an audacious plan is needed for its survival and recovery. Healing the land means reconnecting its parts so that vital flows can be renewed. . . . Our vision is continental: from Panama and the Caribbean to Alaska and Greenland, from the high peaks to the continental shelves, we seek to . . . restore evolutionary processes and biodiversity.[37]

This mission statement may appear to hark back to the thinking of turn-of-the-last century wilderness promoters such as Theodore Roosevelt. But the goals of contemporary preservationism are much more ambitious than the ideals of the National Park Service and related movements that seek to set aside scenic wild places for the sake of human recreation and edification. Today the concern is with the preservation of whole ecosystems in order to sustain the health of the planet in general, rather than with the establishment of picturesque sites as "outdoor zoos," so to speak, whose purpose is to refresh and uplift the human spirit in particular. What distinguishes this type of contemporary preservationism from its conservationist precursors is its plea for the establishment of large nature preserves as nurseries for comprehensive biodiversity without which, its proponents argue, diverse life on the planet as we know it will be seriously eroded—if not extinguished altogether.

What is the relevance of green spirituality to contemporary conservation efforts? Initially it seems that religion and conservationism have little in common. Indeed, one of the sources of disagreement that led to the split among Earth First!ers in the first place—the split that paved the way for both the ELF and the Wildlands Project—was the contention by Dave Foreman and his allies that the radical environmental movement had been co-opted by spiritually oriented, social justice types who were blunting the hard edge of the movement's originally uncompromising anti-industrial message.[38] But Foreman's protestations to the contrary notwithstanding, my case is that both militant and mainstream forms of wilderness advocacy are deeply spiritual movements at their core.

I have argued here that grassroots nature activism represents the tactical edge of deep ecology philosophy. As such, contemporary direct action biodiversity efforts—from violent ecotage to transcontinental wilderness recovery strategies—are efforts that are animated by a deeply felt spiritual awareness that all of life, human and nonhuman, is profoundly interdependent, has intrinsic and not merely instrumental value, and should not, therefore, be subordinated to the growth needs of greedy capitalist societies. I label this intuitional perspective "spiritual" in this context because its exponents—implicitly or explicitly, and whether they self-identify as religious or spiritual or not—are committed to preserving the integrity of life as such as an ultimate value. Whatever may or may not be said about its scientific merits, though I do not doubt its conservation biology credentials, deep ecology, at its core, is a spiritual vision of the highest order concerning the organic wholeness and biotic equality of all life-forms on the planet. It is for this reason that I suggest that insofar as contemporary conservationism is politically applied deep ecology, it is a bearer of green spirituality to a culture that hungers for authentic religion in an age of corporate development and the degradation of our fragile earth community.

In the same way, then, that green spirituality can empower long-term antitoxics commitments in the face of powerful countervailing market forces, it can also sustain wildland advocates with an ethically comprehensive, emotionally resonant, and spiritually satisfying worldview concerning the sacred, inviolable character of every biotic community. Here the reason for saving wilderness places is not for the sake of human flourishing—though human flourishing would be a direct consequence of such recovery work—but because all members of the lifeweb deserve to achieve their full biological potential as much as possible. In short, green spirituality helps to answer the "Why" question for conservationism, namely, Why care about wild places at all in the first place? The answer is because such places make up the fragile life-support systems that render the earth a vibrant and teeming biosphere of interconnected living things. Wild places are the nurseries that make biodiversity possible; they are the habitats for ensuring ecological health and well-being. Such a holistic, integrative perspective is inherently religious in its thrust. Or, to put it another way, such a perspective is scientific and spiritual at the same time: scientific because it recognizes that wilderness is crucial to maintaining diversity at all levels, and spiritual because this recognition ascribes supreme value to wilderness places as essential to maintaining life as such.

Mediating the Debate, Green Spirituality, and Market Values

To this point I have considered antitoxics activity and conservationism as two movements at some odds with each other—albeit movements that share a comprehensive spiritual vision of restored nature. Yet it is the oppositional character of each movement in relation to the perceived concerns of the other group that is so striking and, at the same time, in dire need of mediation. On the one hand, antitoxics leaders such as Lois Gibbs sometimes appear to see little relationship between combating pollutants in the home and workplace and the environmental movement's typical interest in protecting plant and animal habitats: "Calling our movement an environmental movement would inhibit our organizing and undercut our claim that we are about protecting people, not birds and bees."[39] On the other hand, Dave Foreman sometimes has struck a misanthropic note in order to underscore the dissimilarities between wilderness protection and fighting against the social causes that force some human communities into becoming toxic wastelands: "We aren't an environmental group. Environmental groups worry about health hazards to human beings, they worry about clean air and water for the benefit of people and ask us why we're so wrapped up in something as irrelevant and tangential and elitist as wilderness. . . . [But] wilderness is the essence of everything. It's the real world."[40] To put the differences between the two movements in the most extreme terms, the antitoxics, in their overriding concern for the health of human communities, are sometimes derided as anthropocentric and not truly biocentric, while the preservationists, in their singular interest in preserving wildspaces, are criticized as antihuman and ecofascist.

Today the claim is made, as Roger Gottlieb puts it, that "[a] balance *can* be struck between *preserving* the wild and *reorganizing* our transactions in cities, suburbs, and countryside."[41] But how can such a mediation between antitoxics and preservationists be possible if the one appears to prioritize the needs and interests of discrete human populations while the other appears to prioritize the needs and interests of the organic whole? My thesis is that green spirituality has the resources for forging rapprochement between these two movements by articulating the connectional worldview that is logically entailed by both forms of environmental populism. I am arguing not that this worldview is self-consciously understood as such by adherents of both movements, but rather that it is the mind-set implied by the commitment to the integrity and sanctity of life shared by both groups. This shared, connectional worldview is holistic in its vision of all life as codependent and interconnected; it is prophetic in its despair over the earth's declining biological carrying capacity; and it is interventionist in its struggle against global market forces that have degraded human and nonhuman environments alike.

My suggestion is that green spirituality enables a mediation between antitoxics and conservationists by explicating the common connectional philosophy implied by the beliefs and actions characteristic of both movements. It is important, however, to nuance my claim about the joint status of this implied mind-set, so that adherents in both groups can recognize their own orientation in what I am labeling a common worldview. At its core this worldview stresses unity and interdependence, but for each group the significance of this worldview will carry different weight. For antitoxics, the implicit commitment to ecological unity will still emphasize attention to human needs in systemically unjust situations. For conservationists, on the other hand, the inherent equality between humans and nonhumans means that the question of human welfare is best addressed indirectly by the primary task of preserving the integrity of whole bioregions. Both groups emphasize biotic interdependence, but for antitoxics this stress need not include the explicit espousal of biotic equality in the deep ecology sense, and for green activists this emphasis can locate human concerns within the larger orbit of wilderness recovery.

Rapprochement between the two movements, therefore, need not entail agreement on all issues, including the question of biotic equality. As long as members of both movements can recognize their tacitly held (if not always explicitly articulated) commitment to the unity and integrity of living things, then the ground has been laid for mediating the differing stances the two groups sometimes take in relation to the interests of the other group. If, then, this common ground can be secured—that is, a unitary vision of all organisms and entities as interdependent, if not always coequal members of an organic whole—then the response to the question whether environmental justice or wilderness recovery should be one's primary focus is a response that is tactical, strategic, and contextual—not deep-down philosophical. The problem, then, is not one of disagreement over the fundamental orientation needed to combat further ecocide but over the political focus and practical measures necessary for enacting this core vision of sustainable eco-communities, human and nonhuman alike.

For disempowered communities that suffer from the onslaught of toxins in their homes and workplaces, it is understandable why such communities seek first and foremost to liberate themselves from the killing fields of America's waste industries. To force such communities into the false choice of unsafe livelihoods or chronic unemployment is an unconscionable Catch-22 that results from aggressive industry efforts to dump toxins into neighborhoods that can least afford to house such hazards. Under these conditions it makes tactical sense for antitoxics groups first to labor against the unequal distribution of waste products in degraded human ecosystems close to home before turning to the equally important task of combating the despoliation of wildland ecosystems in more remote locales. I am suggesting that this decision should be understood in strategic terms. It is not that antitoxics activists do not appreciate the basic connection between human health and the welfare of the biosphere—indeed, as I have argued here, the implied commitment to green holism on the part of antitoxics necessitates just such an understanding, at least tacitly—but rather that the direct threat of dangerous pollutants in their immediate neighborhoods propels antitoxics to organize against these threats first and foremost.

By the same token, the imminent decline and eventual extinction of numerous species and habitats across North America—from large predators and shorebird populations to native forests and tallgrass prairies—understandably shoulders conservationists with a heavy burden for the long-term health and biodiversity of the continent. This burden should not and need not be regarded in opposition to the similar but distinct environmental burden of antitoxics; rather, it is one among many counterpoints to the expansive medley of approaches one can take to restoring the harmony among all living things. For embattled citizens of contaminated neighborhoods who are fighting the daily struggle for their health and survival, it makes sense for such persons to take up the antitoxics cause as their own; as well, for individuals and communities whose daily survival needs are not as immediately critical, it is equally understandable why such persons privilege the reclamation and rehabilitation of nonhuman nature and only consider the needs of human populations in relation to sustaining the health of the wider biosphere. In spite of these differences, I believe the bedrock commitment to the integrity and inviolability of *life as such* among antitoxic and biodiversity activists is the common spiritual vision that sustains both movements. While this common vision leads to different strategic interventions on behalf of healing the earth, the reverence for life at the foundation of each group needs to be recalled amid the welter of the claims and counterclaims advanced by defenders and detractors of both movements.

The debate between antitoxics and conservationists may appear initially irresolvable. But when one considers the lived context of the environmental crisis as understood by the different disputants in the debate—for example, the daily stream of pollutants into minority urban neighborhoods, on the one hand, or the ongoing attenuation of biodiversity in wild habitats, on the other—then the debate becomes one over which tactics and strategies are effective in which particular circumstances, and not over which moral claimant is right or wrong. One's social location—urban/rural, rich/poor, black/white, and so forth—could be the primary factor in determining one's appropriate response to the ecocrisis. Who one is and where one lives and what immediate or long-term environmental threats one considers significant can reliably shape the type of response one takes on behalf of the natural world. In this holistic framework, then, nature is not the special preserve of wilderness activists alone; nature, rather, is the lived reality common to humankind and otherkind alike, wherever both kinds live and work and love and eat. Nature is the lead-filled air breathed in by schoolchildren in toxic urban killing fields; nature is the pristine landscapes and watersheds that still survive in rural parks and wildlands. Whether antitoxic or preservationist in orientation, how one responds to the myriad challenges directed at the natural world authentically can be shaped by the particular places one inhabits. Thus the environmental orientations of both groups—groups whose core philosophies are similar but whose organizational approaches are often different—are equally legitimate and equally dependent upon the social, economic, political, ethnic, and religious locatedness of the different participants in the common struggle for ecological balance and wholeness.

Finally, it is important to note that green spirituality is not only valuable as a means for forging a common link among green activists who are alternately justice-oriented and biodiversity-centered, respectively. It also shines a bright spotlight on the exploitative growth philosophy of market individualism that has led to the environmental squalor that characterizes our own time. Even as green spirituality hopes to mediate the dispute between both forms of eco-populism by specifying the animating worldview behind each movement, it seeks to further arbitrate this dispute by identifying expansionist market forces as the real culprit in creating both human sacrifice zones and depleted wilderness areas. When everything is a potential commodity for buying and selling—including whole neighborhoods like Chester, Pennsylvania, or America's current and prospective wilderness reserves, as envisioned by the Wildlands Project—human poverty and biological poverty are the inevitable results. When every organism or entity becomes "thingified"—mere objects to be bought and sold to the highest bidder in the marketplace—then life and world lose their sacred character and everything becomes a commodity for human consumption. When all life-forms, human and nonhuman, only have meaning as "products" or "resources" to enable the growth of the market-state, the prospects for environmental sanity are meager indeed.

Economic competition breeds more competition, market growth breeds more growth, and the needs and values of fragile human and wilderness ecosystems have little hope for survival against these withering assaults. Growth-obsessed market liberalism driven by the "mindless 'laws' of supply and demand, grow or die, eat or be eaten" tears apart the social and ecological fabric that supports life in urban neighborhoods and rural bioregions alike.[42] Green spirituality reminds both the advocates of environmental justice and those of wilderness protection that they share a core vision of healthy and diverse communities living together on a green planet. This visionary role is the priestly function of sustainable spirituality: to inculcate in all who struggle for a green future a common worldview and ethic that can sustain the combatants over the long term. But green spirituality performs a prophetic role as well. It decries the rapacious power of the market to undermine our collective ability to grasp the inherent value and worth of all life found in the biotic communities that make up our planet home. Ecocatastrophe need not be our fate, but it will be if change does not occur. A uniting, connectional vision of a green sacred earth has the potential to renew and sustain antitoxics campaigners and preservationist activists alike in the long struggle against the regnancy of market domination—a regnancy that must be overcome if the prospects for life on the planet in our time are to improve.

Chapter Four

Green Spirituality and the Problem of Humanism

Dr. Seuss's The Lorax

AT BEDTIME I SOMETIMES READ to my son the Dr. Seuss classic, *The Lorax*. The story takes place in a bucolic setting of heavily fruited Truffula Trees, Swomee-Swans, and Brown Bar-ba-loots, a place where "from the rippulous pond/*comes* the comforting sounds/of the Humming-Fish humming/while splashing around." This arcadian scene is invaded by the enterprising Once-ler who discovers that the soft tuft of the Truffula Trees can be harvested to make clothes, or "Thneeds." The Once-ler proceeds to chop down all of the Truffula Trees for Thneeds. But because the Truffula Trees provide food and shelter for the animals that live in this place the death of the trees marks the end of all of the Swomee-Swans, Brown Bar-ba-loots, and Humming-Fish that depended on these trees for their survival.

At this point the destruction of the once beautiful countryside is interrupted by the Lorax, a small walrus-like creature with a big yellow mustache, who prophesies correctly that the Once-ler's rapacious abuse of his immediate surroundings will result in total destruction of the environment. True to the Lorax's prophecy, this sylvan landscape becomes saturated in toxins: the air is filled with "smogulous smoke," and local waters degenerate into "Schloppity Schlopp . . . that is glumping the pond where the Humming-Fish hummed!/No more can they hum, for their gills are all gummed." The Once-ler bemoans, "No more trees. No more thneeds. No more work to be done./So, in no time, my uncles and aunts, every one,/all waved me goodbye. They jumped into my cars/and drove away under the smoke-smuggered stars./Now all that was left 'neath the bad-smelling sky/was my big empty factory/the Lorax/and I." In the wake of this ecocide, the Lorax himself departs from this now ugly world and leaves in his absence a pile of rocks with the word "unless" inscribed in the rubble. In the final pages of the story a young child happens onto this rock pile and is greeted by the Once-ler, who is depressed and alone and living in the boarded-up remains of his once proud capitalist empire. The Once-ler says to the child, "But now, now that you're here,/the word of the Lorax seems perfectly clear,/UNLESS someone like you/cares a whole awful lot,/nothing is going to get better./It's not."

This story is charged with a simple but profound message, namely, that all forms of life need and depend upon one another for their health and survival, and that the gradual destruction of one life-form (in this case, the bountiful Truffula Trees) eventually results, in a ripple-like effect, in the degradation of the whole ecosystem that originally supported the life-form now under siege. *The Lorax* is a whimsical but telling children's story about the biological interdependence that binds all members of the lifeweb to one another. Sadly, it is a story that ends on the plaintive note that *unless* someone decides to care for the integrity of the lifeweb, the destruction of the places that we dearly love is a forgone conclusion—whether these places are the "Truffula lands" of Dr. Seuss's fertile imagination, or the other places we call "home" where we live and work and raise our families.

Like the world of the Lorax, why is the biosphere that we daily rely upon for sustenance and refreshment in such deep trouble? To what degree is our current thinking about and interactions with earth community responsible for the environmental crisis in our time? I have suggested that an important corrective to our ecocidal attitudes and habits lies in a recovery of Christian themes that stress God's ongoing enfleshment within the natural order as the ground for deep intercommunion between human beings and other living things. I have proposed the ecological retrieval of the Holy Spirit—the Earth God of the Bible who infuses all things with her sensuous presence—as the linchpin for putting together a sustainable spirituality responsive to our planetary dilemma. In this model, green spirituality is the foundation for affirming the intrinsic value and coequality of all members of the natural world. But what are the fundamental challenges in contemporary intellectual life that call into question appeals to "God" and "nature" as the basis for equal regard of all species in creation?

A human-centered system of value is one of the orienting world-views in our era that casts doubt upon a spiritual frame of reference for regarding diverse life-forms as bearers of inherent worth. Anthropocentric value systems—which I will refer to here as "humanism," following the suggestion of David Ehrenfeld[1]—posit human welfare as the primary good in moral decision making. Humanism is intuitively self-evident to most contemporary theorists; it enjoys the status of an unquestionable assumption for most thinkers in the modern West. Due to the apparent order of things, human beings have traditionally assigned supreme value to that group of beings—namely, themselves—that appears to be the most significantly developed and sentient of all beings. Through our rational powers, language systems, and forms of cultural organization, we appear to stand alone as the most highly evolved members of earth community. While some other nonhuman animals inhabit their own "cultures" that support complicated tool making and elaborate forms of communication, none of these activities are as sophisticated and refined as human beings' complex order making and social structures, according to humanist assumptions.

Humanism contends that because the facts of highly organized reason and social production are the hallmarks of humankind, it follows that we are the privileged centers of value and worth in decisions about life opportunities and resource allocations. The core belief of humanism, Ehrenfeld writes, is

> a supreme faith in human reason—its ability to confront and solve the many problems that humans face, its ability to rearrange both the world of Nature and the affairs of men and women so that human life will prosper. . . . Because human intelligence is the key to human success, the main task of the humanists is to assert its power and protect its prerogatives wherever they are questioned or challenged.[2]

This pro-human perspective that Ehrenfeld analyzes asserts the primacy of human needs in moral thought and action. It fundamentally challenges the basic assumption of green spirituality that all things are bearers of intrinsic worth and enjoy an equal-to-humans right to realize their own natural ends empowered by the Spirit's coinherence with earth community. The contest between our society's emphasis on human flourishing, and the Earth God ideal of encouraging all things to realize their natural ends, is the focus of this chapter.

The Priority of Human Being

To this point my claim has been that Spirit-infused nature is a bearer of intrinsic value and possesses the inherent right to grow and flourish. But this viewpoint makes little sense to humanist thinkers. From their perspective, the self-evident ideal of moral thought and action is the advancement of human flourishing rather than promoting the aims of nature as such. For anthropocentric thinkers who regard human welfare as the primary center of value, the question of the needs of the nonhuman world, while an important question, should be subordinated to the problem of ensuring human prosperity.

The privileged place of human welfare in the hierarchy of values is one of the signal motifs of the Enlightenment project. This eighteenth-century European-American phenomenon, the so-called Age of Reason, argued that humankind, now liberated from the bonds of oppressive religious and political institutions, should be encouraged to articulate its own rational self-interests.[3] The Enlightenment legacy casts a long shadow over contemporary thought. Instead of subordinating human concerns to the larger interests of the church and the state, the Enlightenment accorded supreme value to the individual person's quest for social and political well-being. This assignment of priority to human needs is rooted in the special standing humans enjoy in relation to other things—a standing based on what is consistently cited as the distinguishing characteristic of the human animal, the capacity for rational choice.

The attribute of reason is both the grounds for the assignment of primary value to the human person and the source of humankind's special responsibility for maintaining the integrity of the nonhuman order. From the perspective of Enlightenment humanism, since human beings alone possess the capacity freely and rationally to choose a responsible course of action within a range of conflicting ends, it follows that humans have the burden and responsibility for exercising this capacity in relation to the whole biotic order. Through reason, humans have the power to make good choices for themselves and other life-forms about the future of the planet. Enlightenment-inspired thinkers aver that while animals can only follow instinct in pursuit of their natural ends, humans can freely imagine an infinite number of ends in relation to many different courses

plate 1 Pascagoula River

plate 2 *La Grande Famille*, René Magritte

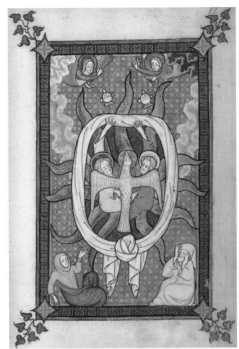

plate 3 *The Rothschild Canticles*, Trinitarian Miniatures

plate 4 *The Trinity*, John Giuliani

plate 5 *The Trinity II*, John Giuliani

plate 6, above *The Holy Spirit*, Bernard Buffet
plate 7, below *The Baptism of Christ*, Bernard Buffet

they are captive to forces outside of their control and not self-legislating moral beings.

John Rawls, contemporary American social philosopher, is a strong exponent of Enlightenment humanist philosophy in the manner of Kant. Rawls's vision of society is of a place where free, rational, moral persons seek to secure their own notion of the good life in a manner that is fair-minded and respectful of the rights of others. A highly functioning society is a place where every person is viewed as roughly equal and allowed to pursue her primary social goods. This self-oriented pursuit is not narrowly egoistic, however. The aim to expand one's share of social goods presupposes the rational capacities of the moral subject to sometimes limit her acquisitions in order to ensure a wider notion of fair play and equal opportunity for all participants in the public order. Thus, in a manner that counsels self-restraint and mutual regard, persons are to be encouraged to exercise their own free and rational choices in deciding what best serves their interests, and how to best to secure these interests, while still being attentive to the welfare of others. Operating with a minimalist understanding of the state's role in this self-seeking process, Rawls maintains that allowing persons to select their own self-chosen ends is the best way to procure fair access to competing visions of the good for as many people as possible.[6]

Rawls's rational choice theory of social goods entails the corollary assumption that only the human person has the capacity to follow regulative principles of equal liberty and fair opportunity in its interactions with other members of the human community. According to Rawls, animals do not regulate their conduct by living in accordance with just laws and institutions. Therefore, since other living beings do not have the capacity for free, rational choice vis-à-vis common institutional structures, it follows that they are not to be accorded the same rights as those enjoyed by human beings. Rawls argues that reason is the basis of equality. Without reason, animals are not candidates for just and equal treatment within the social order. Rawls writes:

> I now turn to the basis of equality, the features of human beings in virtue of which they are to be treated in accordance with the principle of justice. Our conduct toward animals is not regulated by these principles, or so it is generally believed. On what grounds then do we distinguish between mankind and other living things and regard the constraints of justice as holding only in our relations to human per-

sons? . . . Here the meaning of equality is specified by the principles of justice which require that equal basic rights be assigned to all persons. Presumably this excludes animals; they have some protection certainly but their status is not that of human beings.[7]

For Rawls, the devaluation of plants' and animals' interests follows from the fact that these life-forms, in principle, cannot be members of a social order in which resources are equitably distributed through rational, moral procedures. As is the case with Kant, animals and other nonhuman beings, while possessing some degree of value in Rawls's thought, are finally excluded from the sphere of justice and equal rights because they are devoid of human reason.

The Problem of Universal Reason in Humanist Thought

Kant's position is the seedbed for Rawls's subordinationist treatment of animal rights. Both thinkers emphasize the capacity of human beings to make universal, rational choices as the grounds for elevating human value and depreciating the worth and dignity of beings that are not human. But Kant's (and by implication Rawls's) position is troubling on numerous grounds. Kant's theory rests on the twofold assumption that an action is moral when (a) the justification of a particular action can be applied universally and (b) the persons affected by this action are treated as ends and not as means. But at best this assumption can only guide decision making in circumstances in which a possible course of behavior is well suited to these two criteria. One can imagine particular courses of action that we would identify as moral but that do not fit either or both of these criteria. Unfortunately for Kant, therefore, in instances in which a course of moral action fails Kant's test, it may be that it is the test itself—not the action in question—that needs to be jettisoned.

Now, in some situations, to Kant's credit, it does make sense to consider whether the maxim of a particular course of action can be applied universally. It makes sense to ask myself the question, Am I acting in such a way that I would like the principle of my action to be the same principle that guides other people's activities as well? Using my powers of universally applicable rationality, Kant says that I should only act in such a way that the rationale for my action could be applied to all other persons' actions as well. In this manner, as Kant writes, the guidelines for my actions are "fit for universal legislation"[8]—that is, the reasons for my actions obligate everyone else, not just me, to perform the same action. The universal principle that I should always tell the truth, for example, means that no matter what the particular circumstances are at the time, I should never lie. I should not lie and no one else should lie as well, because truth telling is universally compulsive. I can justify the rightness of my action based on its binding force regarding all persons, not just me. Since no one should lie—lying everywhere and always is wrong whatever the circumstances, according to Kant—I should not lie as well.

Kant's universalism is a powerful impetus for good in some circumstances. But in other situations where I would like to do the right thing but cannot justify my choice based on its ubiquitous force, it is difficult to see the relevance of Kant's universal criterion for action. Let me offer two counterexamples to Kant's principle of universal reason regarding morality as cases in point.

First of all, let's take the question about whether it is right to save the earth no matter what the cost. Like telling the truth, should protecting earth community by all means necessary be a universal principle, what Kant calls a "maxim," that is compulsory on all persons to observe? Is radical ecodefense equally binding on all persons even when oneself (or other persons) might be harmed by such protective efforts? In the previous chapter we saw how passionate the commitments are of many pro-wilderness insurgents who commit to protecting the earth against development and degradation no matter the cost to themselves or others. But as we saw in the case of Craig "Critter" Marshall and Jeffrey "Free" Luers, the green militants who are serving long prison terms for their actions, the cost of this type of anticapitalist wilderness activism is sometimes very steep.

Indeed, some activists have sacrificed their own lives for the cause of ecodefense. On September 17, 1998, for example, David "Gypsy" Chain was killed by an errant tree felled by an angry logger while Gypsy was tree-sitting and tree-hopping to stop a timber operation in Humboldt County in Northern California. Gypsy and his fellow activists often played a "cat-and-mouse" game with loggers, jumping from tree to tree, sometimes on the ground and sometimes high in the overhead canopy, as giant redwoods and other trees were being cut and brought to the ground. Their immediate aim was to taunt and frustrate individual loggers to stop tree-cutting by putting themselves in harm's way. But their long-term plan was to find common moral ground with the loggers by appealing to the loggers' sense of common humanity: "You have no compunction about killing living trees, we see that, but you won't take the risk of killing us as well when you cut down the trees, will you?" Unfortunately for Gypsy, his gamble in this instance did not pay off, as he was mortally injured by a falling redwood during one of his many forest resistance efforts.[9]

Chain is a martyr to the cause of wilderness defense; he paid with his life to stop unsustainable logging practices. But should the rationale for his action—protect wild places at any price—be universally applied in every situation where forested areas are endangered by logging and development? I believe the decision to put oneself (or others) in harm's way in order to save wilderness areas should weigh a number of factors that should include (but not exclusively so) the universal applicability of the justification for this decision. In the case of wilderness defense efforts, such factors would include the following: How will this ultimate sacrifice preserve the welfare of a particular bioregion? What is the emotional cost to family and friends in the event a life is lost in the fight against exploitative forces? And what is the relevance of my or other persons' deeply held political, moral, and religious beliefs in making the decision about possibly forfeiting my life for a higher cause? Other factors need to be integrated into the decision-making process before one risks an ultimate sacrifice.

Thus, the criterion of universalizability alone is not enough to fill out and complete the complicated moral judgments required by this type of excruciatingly difficult decision-making process. In the situation of earth-centered self-sacrifice, while I myself might be convinced that I am always and everywhere obligated to defend the integrity of natural systems at all costs, it does not follow that my warrant for this obligation is equally binding on everyone else, nor need it be. Just because I am obligated to protest unnecessary damage to the earth, it does not follow that this impulse should be obligatory for others; by the same token, insofar as this impulse is universally binding, it does not follow that I should act on it irrespective of other important factors (practical utility and sensibilities of others) that must be accounted for before such a decision is made.

Kant's universal ethics requires that any particular action is morally valid only when such action can be grounded on a rationally justified foundation that is applicable to all persons. But, again, some decisions are morally praiseworthy that do not seem, in principle, universally compulsory, while other moral decisions, that do seem to be universally binding, still must factor in a range of issues important to a full-bodied appraisal of the merits of the decision in question. In my mind, therefore, Kant's

reach exceeds his grasp. A decision about a particular course of environmental action is morally praiseworthy if this decision is personally compelling and informed by the range of factors adumbrated above (welfare
of the planet, cost to family and friends, and relevance to deeply held
beliefs). It is not necessary that this decision be rooted in a universally
binding rationale for the action in question; on the contrary, what is necessary from an ethical point of view is that the decision-making process
weigh in the balance as many of the relevant factors as possible that have
some bearing on the decision in question. And yet it is precisely this perspectival and contextual character of moral judgment making that Kant's
universalist theory tries to avoid—and for which it cannot adequately
account.

One of the problems, then, of Kant's humanism is that it is too thin
and general an account of the difficulties inherent in complicated moral
judgments. Kant's theory is noble in its universal ideal of only-do-some-
thing-if-you-can-generalize-the-principle-of-your-action, but it is fundamentally ill-equipped to handle the complexities and contestations of
everyday life. As Alasdair MacIntyre puts it, Kant's "formulation clearly
does have a moral content, although one that is not very precise, if it is
not supplemented by a good deal of further elucidation."[10] Kant's theory,
in my mind, fails to provide a sufficiently broad-minded and flexible set
of guidelines for informing the varieties of moral conflicts and ethical
choices that persons regularly face in everyday situations.

The Problem of Species Chauvinism in Humanist Thought

The other problem with Kant's approach is his insistence that only human
persons are to be treated as ends and not as means. This is a problem in
Rawls's philosophy as well. This problem stems from a particular blind
spot in humanism—namely, its failure to come to terms with the ecosystemic responsibilities that have a hold on us apart from the loyalties
we owe to other persons as ends in themselves. Treating other people as
bearers of value and worth is important to maintaining healthy human
relationships, but there is a prior obligation to a larger order of being that
takes precedence over interhuman value responsibilities. Kant's and Rawls's inability to speak to this wider concern illuminates why Enlightenment moral theory cannot account for the fundamental moral obligation
that precedes and envelops one's obligation to other persons—namely,

the primary responsibility we human denizens of the biosphere have to other beings, human and nonhuman, by maintaining the integrity of the lifeweb.

My thesis is that the interdependence we share with all creation is the primary fact that should ground human moral choices. The humanist position that because humans are rational and free moral agents they are both superior to and responsible for the rest of the biotic order cannot account for the primordial reality of interspecies interdependence. As natural beings—albeit beings with the capacity for reason and moral choice—we are fundamentally implicated in a web of ecological relationships that claims our loyalties antecedent to the moral duties we owe other persons. Far from the self being primarily and singularly obligated to protect the rights and dignity of other humans—as important as this obligation is—the self is always already burdened with loyalties and responsibilities for the integrity of the natural order. The self is first bound to care for the created order that makes all life possible prior to any obligations the self has to other persons. We may think of ourselves as autonomous moral agents, blessed with godlike reason and having responsibilities limited to the welfare of our own kind. We are not independent subjects, however, but "thickly constituted, encumbered selves" with obligations to the whole ecosystem that precede our duties to other humans.[11] This holistic position, as ecophilosopher Laura Westra puts it, "recognizes intrinsic value in wholes which are life-supporting. It is also a position that proposes such value as the focus of moral considerability before all other individual considerations and before interpersonal morality."[12] Our kind survives based on its symbiotic relationship with otherkind. Our very existence depends upon the integrity of earth community. This primitive fact of total dependence upon the vitality of the lifeweb, however disruptive this fact may be to our antinature self-definitions, obliges us to nurture and protect wider earth community as the grounds for caring for our own kind.

Assigning moral priority to the welfare of ecosystemic wholes rather than individual human needs is a challenge to Western humanist thought. Green biocentrism reverses Kant's and Rawls's hierarchy of value: now not only is the nonhuman order invested with inherent worth but its valuation is given priority status as basic to the protection of the dignity of individual human beings. Without the maintenance of the health of the entire biotic order—without the defense of the earth's common life-support systems—it is not possible to preserve human well-being, much less the rational liberties of individual human moral agents, the highest ideals in Kant's and Rawls's thought. The whole humanist edifice of fair-minded and equal regard for other persons in a free and open society depends upon the preservation of natural systems as the basis for robust and egalitarian interhuman interactions. *Unless ecosystemic life is vigorously protected, the human person's rights to individual life and liberty cannot be secured.*

Kant and Rawls argue that our superior value to other life-forms inheres in our capacity for rational moral choice. Indeed, the rational ability to choose an infinite number of ends is a unique and valuable attribute of the human being. But (contrary to Kant and Rawls) why does it follow that because human beings are endowed with this particular capacity—and thereby different from other life-forms—humans are therefore superior to other beings in value and worth? Why should the power of human intelligence and not, say, the ability to thrive and subsist under adverse circumstance, be the primary yardstick for measuring basic value and worth? Many grasses and insects, for example, are more fit for species survival than humans.[13] But we do not invest disproportionate value in these biotic communities because of their tenacious resilience even in the face of sometimes chronic loss of habitat. The vision of green Christianity I have offered here has sought to demonstrate that the Spirit's indwelling and love of all things render impossible the assignation of superior worth to human beings. On the contrary, green spirituality affirms the intrinsic value, indeed, the coequality, of all members of the biotic world.

All life-forms depend upon healthy patterns of reciprocal interaction in order to sustain the integrity of earth community. It does not make sense to argue that the particular difference enjoyed by humans—namely, reason—substantially divides human needs from, and prioritizes them in relation to, the needs of nonhuman biota. On the contrary, ecosystemic integrity is the necessary condition for the maintenance of human reason and human worth. Unless we are able to preserve the integrity of the natural world around us, humanism's celebration of human freedom and value will lack the vital and necessary support system essential to the protection of human dignity as we know it. A crisis is brewing, a crisis brought about in large part by our humanist legacy, and we need a paradigm shift in our thinking. The rich teachings of a revitalized green Christian faith is a living fund of ecological images and ideas that has the potential to transform the contemporary debate about the human-nature relationship in our time.

Extending the Horizon of Morality to Include All Life-forms

In this chapter I have emphasized the need to widen the circle of moral concern to include the well-being of Mother Earth's entire family. But working to ensure the health of whole ecosystems may appear to devalue the worth and importance of individual life-forms. My argument has centered on the welfare of biotic communities to make the point that individuals, human or otherwise, depend upon a state of harmony among themselves and the plants and soils, the animals and watersources that make up the wider natural world. Ethically, what I have sought to do is to extend the boundaries of moral interest beyond the human order to include all of nature. But this extension of ethics to biotic wholes may appear to put too much emphasis on "the whole" and not enough on "the parts," that is, those particular life-forms that constitute the larger aggregate in question.

Aldo Leopold is the activist and thinker most notably associated with emphasizing the value of ecosystems rather than the rights of individual plants and animals to survive and flourish. Born in 1887 and active in the early wilderness conservation movement in the first half of the twentieth century, Leopold was a national forestry expert, cofounder of the Wilderness Society, and professor of game management, a profession he helped to found, at the University of Wisconsin.

Leopold was a gifted chronicler of the lifeways of original American landscapes. He is well known for articulating the moral rule that "A thing is right when it tends to preserve the integrity, stability, and beauty of the biotic community. It is wrong when it tends otherwise."[14] This deep ecology principle—what Leopold referred to as a "land ethic"—expresses his high regard for healthy land use as basic to moral life and thought. The stress here does fall on the whole and not the parts, but Leopold's love of the land includes his respect and admiration for the particular members of a landscape or watershed that constitute the larger biotic community. Leopold argues that a land ethic firmly grounds human beings within the wider natural order and that preserving the integrity of both the individual participants within the ecosystem *and* the ecosystem itself are the focal concerns of such an ethic. He writes, "In short, a land ethic changes the role of *Homo sapiens* from a conqueror of the land-community to plain member and citizen of it. It implies respect for his fellow-members, and also respect for the community as such."[15] In biocentric thought, it is a false choice to say one must choose either the biotic community or its constituents as the focus of moral concern. Rather, seeking to preserve the welfare of the whole enables local attention to particular life-forms and, in kind, caring for individual living things opens up to a wider concern for the preservation of the abiotic and biotic whole that supports its fellow members.

Personally speaking, my own environmental work has often traveled more in the direction of caring for ecosystems rather than particular plants and animals. But being a father of a girl who is passionate about the welfare of individual living beings—a baby robin whose damaged wing needs medical care, a groundhog who needs lots to eat, including her father's vegetable garden, a worker ant carrying bread crumbs across the doorstep—has taught me that a seamless ethic that moves beyond the boundaries of human goods to include the goods of all things, in their wholeness and in their particularity, is vitally necessary.

In recent years our home in Swarthmore, Pennsylvania, has been a safe and warm environment not only for me and my wife, Ellen, and our children, Christopher and Katy, but also for many families of field mice. Our neighbors have cats while we do not, so my hunch is that the mice have found our home to be a natural refuge for their growing families. During the day we see signs of the mice in our kitchen and elsewhere; at night we hear the mice in the walls of the house scurrying back and forth. I have experimented with a variety of humane traps for our expanding mouse population, and over time I have settled on a small boxlike trap with a lid that falls shut when the unsuspecting mouse ventures inside the trap to eat the bait I have placed there. Recently, however, while on vacation spent in a small cottage in Little Compton, Rhode Island, the seashore community where we look for Turk's-cap lilies in the summer, I discovered once again that our place of residence was a haven for mice. In the rural community where we were staying I could not find for purchase any humane traps. In an unreflective moment I resorted to purchasing and using a traditional spring-snap mousetrap.

The trap worked all too well. I had some scruples about using the trap, and I told eight-year-old Katy what I had done. She was hurt and offended. "How would you like it if someone killed you in a trap?" "What if the little mouse has a family?" "Who is going to take care of its babies?" "What gives you the right to kill an innocent creature that has never done anything to harm you?" "Why do you get to decide who lives and dies?" I held my daughter while she cried about the death of the mouse. Begrudgingly, she was marginally glad for the comfort, but it did not change her mind about what I had done. In light of my purported value system that all things have the right to live and flourish, my killing of the mouse in our beach cottage was a breach of this value system.

A gesture of equal regard toward other life-forms is the foundation for robust and egalitarian human community—both physically and emotionally. Not only do we humans need the lifeweb to be secure for our own physical survival, but the quality of our human-to-human relationships depends upon our compassionate interactions with other living things. Care for the ecological family is necessary for our biological and relational well-being. Summary disregard, then, for the well-being of plants and animals eventually corrodes our ability to care for one another as well. Ecologically as well as ethically, we depend on the web of more-than-human life that surrounds us as the life-giving wellspring of our daily face-to-face human interactions with one another. By recommitting myself not to kill the mice I find around me, in Swarthmore and Little Compton, I not only give these small rodents the opportunity again to play the important role they perform in the surrounding ecosystem, but also improve the quality of life I enjoy with my family, and especially my daughter.

Living with mice everywhere, then, leads me to three conclusions: all forms of life need one another; no life-form is better or worse than any other; and the foundation of morality is care and compassion for all of God's good creation—an orientation that grounds, but does not privilege in the manner of humanism, human social relationships.

At this writing it is fall and my family and I are back now from summertime Little Compton and enjoying our home in Swarthmore. Alas, our Swarthmore home is once again a perfect habitat for the local mouse population. And so now again as before—in fact as recently as last night—I occasionally hear the door click shut on the humane mousetraps around our house. When this happens, I get out of bed and wake up my daughter from a deep sleep. It is time for another adventure in suburban environmental maintenance. In our pajamas we creep out of the house for a midnight car ride to a large field near our home where we release the captured mouse into a grassy area that I hope will become its permanent home, rather than our kitchen or bedroom. In an oddly compelling way, I now look forward to these late-night meetings involving me, Katy, and the field mice in our home—they are reminders to me that the web of life, when it is nurtured and protected, has a strange and wondrous way of bringing everyone together, humankind and otherkind, to form lasting relationships.

Chapter Five

Green Spirituality and the Invitation of Postmodernism

The Challenge of Deconstructionism

IN THE PREVIOUS CHAPTER I sought to defend the primary value of healthy biological communities as the foundation for preserving basic human freedoms. Since human welfare is not possible without careful attention to the welfare of the surrounding natural world, humanism, as a free-standing value system, is untenable because it separates human well-being from the integrity of the larger order of things. Again, consider the Native American proverb that says that the frog does not drink up the pond in which it lives. In other words, the health and restoration of our common humanity rests on a healthy and restored earth community. Sadly, while the stated intent of humanist theory is not to despoil the natural world, the inevitable outcome of this theory is just such a scenario because it is predicated on the devaluation of the very lifeweb that makes every form of existence on the planet possible in the first place.

A human-centered system of value is *morally* problematic because it is tone deaf to the special role ecosystems perform in supporting life as such. But this value system is also a *theological* problem because it cannot account for the role of the Spirit to fill up and thereby bring together all the good things God has made. Christian deep ecology envisions all things as bearers of God's presence through the agency of the Spirit. This approach regards the modern humanist assignation of privilege to human welfare in the wider scheme of things to be an expression of human arrogance. Not only does such an assignment not make sense from the vantage point of ecosystemic integrity, but it is also opaque to the mystery of the biblical Earth God who infuses all things with her power and presence.

If nature, therefore, is the primary focus of an earthen theological perspective, what do we mean by the term "nature" when we valorize it in this way? Along with humanism, postmodern "deconstructionism" is another fundamental worldview in our time that challenges green spirituality to reexamine its basic suppositions. The postmodern project seeks to show how knowledge about the world is generated through language and culture. If the task of an earlier modernism was to uncover the nature of reality as stable and ordered, the task of postmodernism today is to destabilize or deconstruct our notions of reality by showing us that the ways we understand things are always a product of our interpretive activities.[1]

Postmodernism's challenge to religious ecology is to question whether green spirituality's "turn to nature" betrays a crude understanding of the natural world as a self-evident set of facts, when the meaning and significance of the so-called facts that make up reality are actually imposed upon the world based on our prized cultural assumptions. Postmodern critics contend there is no such thing as nature as such. In a manner of speaking, then, "nature" should be written in quotation marks to signal that our understanding of the term is always conditioned by the frameworks of meaning we bring to our experience of anything, including our experience of the natural world. Postmodernists maintain that nature is as much a product of our "in here" cultural presuppositions as it is an "out there" world that imposes itself on us apart from our interpretive frameworks. There is no empirically obvious "raw" nature that tells us what reality is really like. Rather, according to postmodernism, we import into the natural world our own socially mediated presumptions about our proper role in nature in relation to the wider world around us.[2]

This debate has important religious consequences. If appeals to nature among religious thinkers naively presuppose a self-revealing environmental order independent from human imagination, then such appeals appear to trade on an objectivist understanding of the natural world that does not recognize our dependence on language and culture for formulating understandings of the environment. But if the meaning of the external world relies upon our internal modes of understanding, then is green spirituality fated to forever chase its own tail, so to speak, so that it can never really know anything about reality as such but can only articulate its own cultural assumptions? Is green spirituality just talk? That is, is green spirituality just a form of solipsism—a self-referential exercise that can know nothing but its own opinions about things, including nature? Does deconstruction, then, fundamentally undermine a green Christian spirituality by revealing it to be nothing more than a self-contained rhetorical exercise with no stable referent—such as the natural world itself—to ground its discourse?

Human self-centeredness in moral decision making, as we saw in the last chapter, and the role of language and culture in formulating understandings of nature, as we will consider in this chapter, are potent challenges to the task of green Christianity responsive to the ecocrisis in our time. In this chapter I will take up the role of postmodern deconstructionism—or what I will also refer to as "constructivism" or "constructionism"—to emphasize the role of human imagination and social formation in building the conceptual schematas by which we discern the meaning of the natural world. I will critically correlate postmodernism in relation to a Spirit-centered vision of earth healing in a manner that both rejects and appropriates some of this perspective's basic insights.

Is Nature Real?

So what is nature, or, in religious terms, what is creation exactly? Is nature or creation an observable, empirical "fact"—the secure, external world about which we can say "nature reveals itself as such and such" or "creation teaches us this or that"? Or is nature a humanly constructed picture or narrative that only has meaning within the context of particular presuppositions? Even though it appears to us as "out there," is nature finally one more "in here" repository of our cultural assumptions and conceptual schemes? If, however, the natural world is not a hard-and-fast reality but a social construct resting on the shifting sands of language and culture, is it still possible to have reliable, even testable, knowledge about the external world?

Posed in this binary manner—Is nature a human construct or objectively real?—this question has generated considerable debate within contemporary environmental thought, religious and otherwise. On the one side are what we might call the objectivists, who contend that the natural world is more like an empirical datum waiting to be *discovered* rather than something constituted by the language schemes *invented* by social groups.

On the other side we have constructivists or constructionists, who focus on the role *culturally embedded representations of reality* play in the formation of what we take nature to be. Weighing in on the constructivist side of the discussion is William Cronon, a history professor at the University of Wisconsin, and a group of interdisciplinary scholars whose 1994 seminar with Cronon at the University of California at Irvine explored the theme "Reinventing Nature."[3] Cronon and his colleagues argue that nature is a term loaded with cultural baggage. Nature is not a fixed reality but a value-laden concept whose meanings undergo dramatic shifts over time. Ironically, there is little if anything that is natural about nature because both the term "nature" and the reality to which it corresponds have been ineluctably shaped by human desires and imaginings.

In this vein the Irvine scholars are somewhat at odds with deep ecologists and other direct-action environmentalists who assume (without argument) that nature is self-evidentially a center of ultimate value and should be correspondingly protected at all costs. Ironically, it is not that Cronon and his colleagues disagree with this deep ecology valuation of nature. In fact, interestingly enough, the Irvine scholars appear to be either outright environmentalists themselves or at least deeply sympathetic with the aims of the environmental movement. It is rather that the deep ecology valuation of nature as a supreme good is just that—an ethically motivated interpretation, by particular human beings, of the purported worth and importance of the natural world. One cannot "read off" of nature its inherent values and meanings; rather, the nonhuman world—while being fundamentally real—is nevertheless the catchall of human dreams and projections. Any hope of uncovering true nature through, for example, politically engaged wilderness recovery activities—even though such activities are laudable in themselves—is always an exercise in constructing the idea of nature in a manner that best fits the ideals of the activists in question.

Cronon's deconstruction of the concept of "nature" is a frontal challenge to left environmentalism. All knowledge about nature, he argues, is local and positioned. That is, when we ask the question about what nature truly is we must account for the situated ideologies and concerns of the person who puts forward this question in the first place. The query, "What is nature?" can only be addressed by first responding to the prior question, "Whose nature are we discussing here?" Though Cronon shares the core concerns of progressive green activists, he hopes to problematize and complicate the moral authority now invested in environmental movers and shakers whose raison d'être is the protection of wild habitats and species. Popular environmentalism, according to Cronon, successfully trades on a naive realist notion of a universal nature whose true essence is available to any honest inquiry. But this notion of nature as a stable, external reality scrubbed clean of its cultural contexts is a dangerous chimera because no reality—even nature—can be rightly understood if it is seen as divorced from its social formation. Cronon's hope is to interrogate critically the generally unexamined ideal of "nature-is-good" while at the same time acknowledging that it is this very ideal that is the animating force behind much of the good work within contemporary environmental activism. He writes:

> Popular concern about the environment often implicitly appeals to a kind of naive realism for its intellectual foundation, more or less assuming that we can pretty easily recognize nature when we see it and thereby make uncomplicated choices between natural things, which are good, and unnatural things, which are bad. Much of the moral authority that has made environmentalism so compelling as a popular movement flows from its appeal to nature as a stable external source of nonhuman values against which human actions can be judged without much ambiguity. If it now turns out that the nature to which we appeal as the source of our own values has in fact been contaminated or even invented by those values, this would seem to have serious implications for the moral and political authority people ascribe to their own environmental concerns.[4]

Cronon's point is that eco-activists' unexamined assumptions about the nature of nature—which they assume to be a self-revealing order of being imbued with inherent worth—mask the highly imaginative constructions of nature crafted by human cultures. This "essentializing" orientation toward nature is generally taken for granted. Of course, this orientation is pragmatically useful as it serves as the basis for the moral exhortations by environmentalists to take up the plight of nature and fight against the destruction of our planet home. Thus the understandable fear by some environmentalists is that by moving away from regarding nature as a self-evidential good to redefining nature as a cultural construction, the grounds for action in defense of the earth will be effectively undermined.

Not only do Cronon's critics regard his constructivism, therefore, as undercutting green activism, but they regard his position as a stalking horse for pro-development forces opposed to systemic environmental protection. By examining nature within the confines of cultural relativism and projectionism, Cronon provides intellectual backing for conservative policy makers and developers who maintain that nature is not an absolute good to be defended at all costs but, instead, a resource to be used to serve the ideal of human flourishing. "Nature" is morally ambiguous, since "nature" is not "naturally" good or bad. Cronon's critics argue that if you say nature is not an intrinsic, self-evident good that cries out for our protection, you are then giving tacit permission to antienvironmental forces to exploit the natural world in whatever way they deem necessary in order to serve their commercial interests.

The argument of Cronon's critics is that (a) once nature is deconstructed as a project of discourse with (b) no inherent capacity for providing criteria to adjudicate which projections are better than others, then it follows that (c) nature can be used and abused to serve selfish human ends since its true essence is always filtered through the lens of imaginal activity. If nature is not a fixed, objective fact that tells us what to do, then it becomes a candidate for exploitation and depredation. This is the main point environmentalists make in opposition to Cronon. In a trenchant criticism of Cronon and his ilk, deep ecologist George Sessions writes that "for most postmodernists, there is no standpoint beyond human cultures . . . there is no objective truth—all theories and statements (even by scientists) reflect only the interests of power elites; and that since Nature is a human construction, humans can 'reinvent Nature' . . . in any way that suits our immediate interests and desires."[5] Earth First! and Wilderness Society cofounder Dave Foreman writes similarly that "the irony of Cronon is that he is the kind of intellectual the anti-wilderness populists decry in their red-faced anti-intellectualism, yet he gives these people arguments to use against wilderness (and they *are* using Cronon's arguments)."[6]

Green activist Bill Willers avers that because Cronon writes about nature "purely in terms of social and cultural values," he has "dealt quite a blow to the environmental movement" that is "all the more pernicious in that it is being widely reproduced and excerpted."[7] And environmental academic Michael Soulé, who, along with his University of California at Santa Cruz colleague Gary Lease, has coedited a volume entitled *Reinventing Nature?*, a critical takeoff written against the reputed constructivist excesses of Cronon and the Irvine group, writes in the same vein that "the nihilism and relativism of radically constructionist critiques of science and the materiality of nature, while popular in some academic circles, is sophomoric. Further, it is harmful because . . . it undermines efforts to save wilderness and biodiversity."[8]

The criticism directed at Cronon and other environmental constructivists is understandable. The thesis that nature is a cultural invention seems to fall prey to the *idealist fallacy* that the external world has no existence apart from human perception.[9] As a species of idealism, or so it seems, constructivism serves to undercut efforts by green radicals to appeal to the reality of threatened ecosystems as the basis for activism. Why struggle hard to counteract environmental degradation if nature is nothing more than the product of human culture and discourse? Why work hard to save the biosphere if the material world is simply the imaginary repository of human hopes and dreams? To be sure, Cronon's thesis does spell difficulties for the founding rationales eco-activists assume as the basis for green philosophy and action. But is the anti-Cronon sentiment as wellfounded as it appears to be at first glance? I do not think so.

It is important to note Cronon's claim that his attention to the value-laden character of nature discourse is intended to strengthen, not undermine, environmental thinking and action. Cronon believes that the commitment to earth healing will become more honest and effective when environmentalists learn to become more nuanced and self-reflective in their use of the term "nature" in their moral language and ethical engagements. Though unadulterated nature is beyond our reach, Cronon's hope is that by examining the rhetorical constructions of nature within human cultures, environmentalists will become more sensitive to the various uses *and* abuses to which the idea of nature has been put. With this new sensitivity in place, the fight for nature can proceed with renewed vigor as it attends to the terminological and political shades of meaning employed on behalf of—and against—the integrity of the natural world.

In my mind, while Cronon and the Irvine group are at pains to argue that the concept of nature is a human idea, they are not thoroughgoing idealists. Their opposition to naive realism—the commonsense notion that the external world is fully knowable apart from cultural mediation—does not entail subscription to the extreme antirealist or idealist position that the material world either does not exist or is fundamentally unknowable. Cronon and his supporters do not argue that physical objects and places like rocks and trees and wetlands have no reality apart from our perception of these objects and places; rather, their point is that the meaning we attach to these things as cultural icons is largely a human affair and cannot be divorced from any supposed inherent qualities these objects and places have apart from our interpretation of them. In spite of the dismissals by his critics, Cronon for his part labors to make clear his desire to hold in tension the *constructivist* thesis that the concept of nature is a cultural invention with the *realist* notion that the actual material world exists independently of being perceived. In this sense, neither is Cronon, philosophically speaking, an extreme idealist nor, politically speaking, is he opposed to reclaiming the integrity of the natural world. He says:

> Asserting that "nature" is an idea is far from saying that it is only an idea, that there is no concrete referent out there in the world for the many human meanings we attach to the word "nature" . . . Yosemite is a real place in nature—but its venerated status as a sacred landscape and national symbol is very much a human invention. The objects one can buy in stores like The Nature Company certainly exist in nature—but that does not begin to explain how they came to inhabit some of the most upscale malls in modern America.[10]

Riding the Cusp

The status of the external world in the debates between realists and constructivists has a long history in Western thought. Realists claim that material things have a real, objective existence and exist independently of our sense experience. In the history of philosophy, otherwise disparate thinkers such as John Locke, G. E. Moore, and Hilary Putnam have agreed that there is a world of independently real objects that exists beyond our perceptions and about which we can have reliable knowledge. Constructivists respond that we can have no direct and immediate knowledge about the world beyond our perceptions. They reply that knowledge of physical things—mountains and trees and lakes and so forth—is dependent on sense impressions or mental images in the mind of the perceiver that rely on overarching conceptual frameworks for their meaning and understanding. Once it is recognized that what we perceive are not raw, material things *in themselves* but rather the *ideas* of such things—ideas that may or may not neatly correspond to the things that are actually out there—then the move is made to arguing that all such ideas can only be understood relative to a particular conceptual scheme.

Constructivists have sometimes been confused with idealists, but the two positions are not equivalent. Whereas classical idealists such as

George Berkeley reduce the material world to mental activity, constructivist thinkers such as Ludwig Wittgenstein, Thomas Kuhn, Richard Rorty, Jacques Derrida, and Sandra Harding argue that the material world, while certainly "out there," depends upon the perceiver's "in here" conceptual schematas for making sense of that world. As philosopher Richard Rorty puts it, "The world is out there, but descriptions of the world are not. . . . The world does not speak. Only we do. The world can, once we have programmed ourselves with a language, cause us to hold beliefs. But it cannot propose a language for us to speak. Only other human beings can do that."[11] The world does not communicate its essential nature unadulterated to the keen empirical observer. The world is not a mind-independent reality with a determinate essence yielding self-subsistent facts available to the neutral spectator. On the contrary, while constructivists do not deny the existence of the material world, they aver that what this world *is* and its *meaning* for human beings are dependent on the working deep vocabularies—or, in philosopher Jacques Derrida's parlance, the inherited "sign-systems"—that particular cultures rely on to organize the data of experience.

Twentieth-century Austrian philosopher Ludwig Wittgenstein uses his colleague G. E. Moore's famous "proof" of the external world as grounds for questioning commonsense realism. Moore is a straight-ahead realist. In philosophical circles, he is well remembered for holding up his hand in front of his face and declaring, "This is my hand," as proof of the independent existence of the external world.[12] What could be more obvious, says Moore, than that I know the character of reality as such based on looking at my outstretched hand and simply telling you what I see? One does not need a culturally nuanced, conceptual scheme of meaning to make sense of this fact. One just needs to observe one's own hand and explain in direct, straightforward language what one sees. Thus, reality or nature is not the object of any broad framework of meaning that I use to make sense of the world; rather, reality tells us what it is on its own terms. Telling you what I see when I look at my hand in front of my face is all the proof one needs to demonstrate that realism makes the most sense and that constructivism makes things unnecessarily complicated.

Wittgenstein does not question the inherent *plausibility* of Moore's claim that "This is my hand," but he does argue that establishing the *meaning* of any such claim relies on the inherited background beliefs that allow the claim to be made and rendered intelligible in the first place. Wittgenstein writes, "All testing, all confirmation and disconfirmation of a hypothesis takes place already within a system. . . The system is not so much the point of departure [for an argument], as the element in which arguments have their life."[13] The test of the truth of the declaration "This is my hand" is not based on the claim's capacity to somehow "correspond" to the object in question, the outstretched hand, independent from the speaker's belief system. Rather, the confirmation or disconfirmation of this claim relies on the speaker's ability to locate and make sense of this claim within the context of a body of beliefs that generate the meaning of the claim at the outset. "When we first begin to *believe* anything," Wittgenstein says, "what we believe is not a single proposition, it is a whole system of propositions. (Light gradually dawns over the whole.)"[14]

According to Wittgenstein, then, the truth of propositions about the external world can only be established by first accounting for the entire web of beliefs that support the propositions in question. In his later writings Wittgenstein coined the phrase "language games" to refer to the symbiotic process by which assertions (or "moves," to continue with the "playing a game" analogy) are rendered intelligible on the basis of their fidelity to a body of cultural assumptions (or "rules") about the world.[15] So, to make sense of reality, in Wittgenstein's world, our task is to "play" different "language games" according to the "rules" our cultural group lays down as basic to comprehending the way things are. At first glance this might seem like a strange approach for testing the truth of Moore's claim about his outstretched hand, because Moore's contention seems patently true in relation to any belief system and not in need of any type of broader framework analysis. But oddly enough, even Moore's truth-claim about his hand, the "move" Moore makes, only makes sense against the backdrop of his own cultural assumptions about reality—that is, it only makes sense against the background of the assumed "language game" Moore is committed to "playing." If one were to alter the inherited and generally unexamined network of beliefs that support Moore's claim, then the truth and meaning of the proposition itself would be radically altered.

For a hard-boiled empirical realist such as G. E. Moore, the observation "This is my hand" proves the self-subsistent existence of said hand and correspondingly offers direct proof for the external world as well. But we can imagine radically different understandings of the meaning of Moore's hand depending on differing cultural contexts for making sense of reality. Take, for example, the contrasting worldview of a devotee of Vedantic Indian philosophy, such as the celebrated philosopher Ramakrishna, who presumably might claim that Moore's hand should be regarded as an exercise in make-believe because the so-called external world is unreal in relation to the true reality of what Hindus refer to as *moksa*, or illusion. By the same token, a quantum physicist such as David Bohm might argue that the outstretched hand is not a solid independent thing but a composition of microparticular "processes" or "events" whose subsistence is dependent on every other process or event in the universe. Of course, these alternative explications of the outstretched hand are not incommensurable—that is, no one explanation rules out the plausibility of any of the other explanations of Moore's hand, including Moore's own explanation—but these alternatives do make clear that Moore's claim is not as obvious and straightforward as it might appear at first glance.

Thus, there is no God's-eye perspective, so to speak, by which to adjudicate once and for all the truth or falsity of these discrete interpretations of the raised hand divorced from the language games upon which they rely. Thus to say, as Moore does, that holding up my hand and observing it ineluctably proves the reality of external things is to say, indeed, that the claim is "proven"—but only insofar as this claim is dependent upon an empirical-physicalist set of assumptions for its meaning and coherence. (As Wittgenstein puts it, a proposition is true because it "follows the rules" of its own internal language game.)[16] To insist, however, as Moore in fact does, that this truth-claim is now incorrigibly certain irrespective of particular conceptual schemes is to slide into a philosophical hubris that Wittgenstein finds culturally and linguistically impossible to sustain. As he puts it, "To say of man, in Moore's sense, that he *knows* something; that what he says is therefore unconditionally the truth, seems wrong to me.—It is the truth only inasmuch as it is an unmoving foundation of his language-games."[17]

As we have seen, Wittgenstein argues that reality claims, by following the rules of a particular language game, are dependent upon a network of cultural assumptions for their meaningfulness. Akin to Cronon's thesis that the idea of nature is figurally produced, Wittgenstein's opposition to Moore's realism on this score would seem to land him in the constructivist camp. But Wittgenstein eschews any such labels for his work, and often stresses that his orientation is neither consistently realist nor idealist—or, in our terms, his position is neither consistently objectivist nor constructivist.[18] Wittgenstein's hope, rather, is to dissolve this binary distinction by maintaining that the so-called external world is *constituted* in the interface between what we consider to be the world and the background beliefs that we rely on for understanding. Reality, then, is composed and organized in our self-reflexive interactions with the physical environment from the vantage point of our own inherited languages and cultures. This dissolution of the realist-idealist distinction does not solve the disagreement between the exponents of the two positions. Instead, it recasts the discussion in favor of focusing on the vital, living dialectic—the dynamic interaction between self and other, or mind and world—operative in the subject's perspectival encounters with the data of everyday experience.

Focusing on this dialectical relationship between self and other, Wittgenstein aspires to undercut the pairing of the conventional oppositional terms—subject/object, inner/outer, perception/reality, scheme/content, language/world, and so forth—used to breathe life into the realist-idealist divide in Western theories of knowledge. Of course, Wittgenstein admits, our use of language and its predicative conventions betrays our habitual attachments to the very set of distinctions that we argue are so blinding to our understanding of the elusive and intricate interplays between self and other constitutive of our everyday life. But it is not possible to step outside language and articulate the complete overcoming of these familiar oppositions. Thus to use language against itself in striving to undercut the seeming obviousness of the realist-idealist polarity is the best strategy for realizing the subtle exchanges between self and world that make up daily experience.

Wittgenstein's obviation of the realist-idealist debate undergirds many contemporary thinkers' attempts to negotiate the objectivist-constructivist debate in contemporary environmental discussion. In particular, philosopher N. Katherine Hayles's proposal of a "constrained constructivist" model for breaking the impasse between the two groups has real promise. Hayles's proposal mediates the opposition between scientists and activists who appeal to dependable, testable knowledge about the world as the basis for study and action, on the one hand, and nature deconstructionists who maintain that the physical world can only be understood within the confines of particular belief systems, on the other. She proposes that we construe the external world as unmediated *flux*—that is, ever-changing flow patterns that do not "exist" in any cognizable fashion until they are first organized and processed by a perceiving subject. Hayles writes:

> Suppose that we think about what is "out there" as unmediated flux. The term emphasizes that the flux does not exist in any of the usual conceptual terms we might construct (reality, nature, the universe, the world) until it is processed by an observer. It interacts with and

comes into consciousness through self-organizing, transformative processes that include sensory, contextual, and cognitive components. The processes I call the cusp.[19]

Like Wittgenstein, Hayles is wary of trading on dyadic terminology to advance a dialectical understanding of mind and world, to use the conventional pairing. So, instead of erecting one more binary system, she employs two terms—"flux" and "consciousness"—in order to sublate them in favor of a third term—"cusp"—that stands for the all-encompassing reality that relativizes all other pairings. The "cusp," in her words, is constituted in the interface between the ebb and flow of natural processes and the positioned assumptions and contextual experiences of the observer.

The purpose of Hayles's work is to encourage scientists, activists, and critics alike to "ride the cusp," as she puts it, by accounting for *both* one's localized and embodied presumptions about the world *and* the reality-based limits imposed on the observer by the data of experiential, scientific evidence.[20] In the betwixt and between environment of the cusp, the struggle for environmental renewal is relativized by the recognition of one's positioned and partial interpretations of the world, and it is constrained by the availability of relatively adequate research concerning the organic flow patterns of the flux. Hayles writes that "constrained constructivism points to the interplay between representation and constraints. Neither cut free from reality nor existing independent of human perception, the world as constrained constructivism sees it is the result of complex and active engagements between the unmediated flux and human beings."[21] Thus Hayles's mediatory view challenges the realist assumption that nature-in-itself is directly and readily understandable to any neutral observer; as well, it challenges the sometimes overly zealous constructivist thesis that there are no external checks and balances that the subject must come to terms with in the interpretive process. In the model of constrained constructivism, the understanding of the world is neither "cut free from reality," in the manner of vulgar constructivism, nor "existing independent of human perception," in the style of naive realism.[22]

Indebted to theorists such as Wittgenstein and Hayles, the conceptual resources are now at hand for mediating the realist-constructivist debate. The world is formed on the basis of one's culturally positioned deep vocabularies about reality in dialogue with natural processes and the insights gleaned from other persons' belief systems—be those systems scientific, religious, philosophical, or what have you. In earth-centered terms, this constrained constructivist model, as Hayles calls her approach, construes nature or reality as constituted at the intersection of the observer's conceptual schematas and the ebb and flow of ecosystem dynamics. This model avoids, then, the one extreme of naive realism where the understanding of reality is divorced from one's conceptual schemes, and the other extreme of solipsism where reality is captive to one's assumptions and has no independent existence. Thus, while no *one* construal of nature is incorrigibly certain and unrevisable, it is also not the case that *all* construals are equally valid since competing language games do provide criteria by which to judge a construal's relative adequacy.

The constrained constructivist model preserves the environmental scientists' and activists' concern that empirical evidence about threatened ecosystems can be acquired and relied upon as the basis for action, and it preserves the constructivist position that value commitments and ingrained assumptions must always be critically taken into account whenever knowledge is gained and actions are taken on behalf of wildspaces or other threatened bioregions. Constructivism, therefore, seeks to incorporate scientific evidence about the natural world as well as stay attuned to the power of culture and language to shape the interpretation of this evidence—evidence that is critical for understanding responsible green thought and action.

Green Theology in a Postmodern, Constructionist Context

So far in this chapter I have sought to show that nature is real, indeed, but only insofar as it can be described within the belief systems of particular cultures. This recognition that nature is alternately external to and dependent upon the play of situated experiences within particular social groups spells significant consequences for the task of theology—the task of critical reflection upon the sources and nature of religious experience. In this final section I take up the question of theological method in an age of environmental passion—the question concerning how theology should be done in relation to deep ecology spirituality. The focus of this section—green theology—investigates the claims to meaning and truth within earth-centered religious experience. My basic point is that with the recognition that all critical thought is generated within particular languages and cultures—including thought about the natural world—it follows that theology, now understood as biophilic theology, should rely on the fertile resources of its own specific belief system to articulate its distinctive vision of the world. For green theology this worldview, rooted in the good creation God has made, takes flight within the strange and wonderful universe of the biblical literatures. From this perspective, John Calvin is right to say that the Bible provides the spectacles through which Christians view nature.[23] With a nod to Calvin, it follows that earth-loving theology operates within the gravitational space of two important sources for the practice of green spirituality: the socially mediated reality of the natural world and the fruitful language and figures of the biblical scriptures. Green theology is nourished and sustained by sinking its roots deep into the fertile soil of the fecund earth, on the one hand, and the rich imagery of the biblical texts, on the other.

Nevertheless, much of historical Western theology has sought to square its proposals not with earth wisdom or biblical teachings, but with various metaphysical or ontological systems of thought. By metaphysics or ontology I mean here grand, totalizing thought systems that try to demonstrate the nature of ultimate reality, sometimes referred to as God or Being, through abstract, philosophical reason and language. Green theology moves away from this enterprise by celebrating the wonder and magic of the natural world, now understood through the optics of the biblical witness, as its primary source for understanding reality. Green theology eschews dependence on any grandiose philosophical thought system in favor of discerning the lineaments of emancipatory, eco-friendly spirituality within the biblical texts. In this way, green theology steps away from dependence on metaphysics or ontology and relies instead on the biblical texts' ancient earth wisdom as its inspiration for construing healthy relations between humankind and otherkind.

Such a move outside metaphysics signals a sea change in contemporary theology. Historically speaking, much of Western thought about God and the world has been dominated by philosophical assumptions. Classical expressions of this tradition are arguments made by Aristotle and Thomas Aquinas that the human experience of contingent selfhood proves the existence of God as a necessary being, an unmoved mover, who is the necessary source and end of all particular beings. In Thomas's metaphysics, for example, God's being (*ens*) is God's existence (*esse*)—God's essence is "to be"—whereas other beings exist not in themselves but only by virtue of their participation in God.[24] The reality of contingent existence, therefore, leads one backward in a chain of iron logic to self-subsistent Being-itself as the noncontingent source of all dependent beings. Not only, then, is God shown to exist, but God's existence has the force of logical necessity: God *must* exist. This type of thinking is often referred to as "ontotheology", that is, the rational attempt to prove and define the reality of a higher power according to philosophical notions of Being. Such speculative reasoning grounds the long-held desire of historical philosophical theology to develop a metaphysically rooted system of beliefs with enough certitude to be considered a science. Unless and until theology becomes grounded in a universally compelling rational foundation, so the argument goes, it runs the risk of remaining mired in the parochial origins of the early faith communities that gave rise to primitive theological reflection in the first place.

As the natural sciences have been able to secure foundational knowledge about the order and predictability of physical objects, so philosophical theology, historically understood, seeks to specify the necessary conditions for the possibility of every form of being and existence, including the being and existence of God. The dream of philosophical theology, therefore, has always been the ideal of metaphysics, that is, "inquiry beyond or over beings which claims to recover them as such and as a whole for our grasp."[25] This metaphysical tradition continues into the present. For many contemporary Christian theologians and philosophers of religion, belief in God should have the same intellectual status as other incorrigible, self-evident truths. Many of the primary exponents of normative theology today maintain that the problem of theology is that it has not adequately patterned its efforts after the models of its counterparts in philosophy and science. They argue that the development of the right conceptual system for establishing the cognitive claims of Christianity has gone begging and that without an adequate intellectual undercarriage the authority of the scriptures, and the faith of believing communities, will retreat into the twilight world of private belief untouched by the light of reason and argument.

The called-for reliance of theology on metaphysical presuppositions raises a number of questions, however, for a theology that seeks primary fidelity to earth-centered biblical testimony. Should theology seek to ground its proposals on a metaphysical foundation, or should it abandon its quest for such foundations? Even if theology chooses the latter, can it do so? Can theology and metaphysics be disentangled so easily? As Martin Heidegger asks, can theology "overcome" or "step back" beyond "ontotheology"—as we have seen, the philosophical fusion of grand philosophy and biblical notions of God—by asserting its independence from any and all metaphysical influences?[26] Or, as Jacques Derrida insists, "if one does not have to philosophize, one still has to philosophize"—in other words, even when one seeks to think outside the question of being, must not all thought, nevertheless, still circulate within a metaphysical economy?[27] Even if theology could ensure its autonomy from the question of being, should it do so? Will theology not slide into tribalism and privatism unless it allows itself to be disciplined by ontotheology? Or does the practice of theology under the horizon of Being threaten to undermine the distinctive expressions of authentic religious life that should characterize all theology, including green theology?

In my mind, Heidegger is right that the question of Being in theology has saddled Christianity with a philosopher's God, the metaphysically certain God of supreme causality who mechanically functions as the philosophical ground and unity of all beings in the world. In this system metaphysics is the all-knowing monarch that tells theology what it can and cannot say. When God is relegated to the part of a placeholder in a chain of cosmic causality, theology becomes captive to "ontotheological" assumptions that limit God, in the language of all-supreme philosophy, to the role of "highest existent," "pure actuality," "being-itself," and "first cause"—a distant, frozen, and abstract deity who, as "the god of philosophy," again as Heidegger says, is such that one "can neither pray nor sacrifice to this god. Before the *causa sui* [supreme cause], man can neither fall to his knees in awe nor can he play music and dance before this god."[28] Using Heidegger's formulation, it is critical for theology that it engages, ironically, in what Heidegger calls "god-less thinking which must abandon the god of philosophy" in order to approach the God of biblical faith.[29] One must deny the God of Reason in order to embrace the Earth God of the biblical witness. In this model God is not the *Being* known within the horizon of metaphysics but the *occasion* for fostering new modes of ecologically and scripturally enriched existence that are no longer founded on the metaphysical securities of Western thought.

Green theology becomes a vital undertaking when it avoids the temptation to ground its enterprise on a philosophical foundation and returns instead to the living wellspring—the vitalities of nature and the founding images of biblical faith—from which a sustainable spirituality, based on a new partnership between humankind and otherkind, can be founded. Theology today is best served by returning to its roots in the creation-based biblical narratives and cutting its moorings to the ontotheological tradition of understanding God as supreme cause and ultimate Being. This metaphysical tradition is sterile and fruitless because it has imparted to modern religious life and thought a distant and unfeeling deity, an apathetic unmoved mover, who can be neither feared nor loved, pleaded with nor danced to, blasphemed nor glorified. Such a deity has no relationship to the earth-rooted God witnessed to in the biblical texts. This philosophical deity cannot be wrestled with and struggled against, as was the God of Jacob at the river Jabbok in Genesis; venerated in awe and wonder, as was the God of Moses in the burning bush in Exodus; railed against in anger and bitterness, as was the Creator of the Earth who overwhelmed Job in a violent whirlwind; nor petitioned in blood, as was the God of Jesus in Gethsemane in the Gospels.

While recognizing that the metaphysical tradition has no resonance with the rich and variegated portraits of Earth God within the biblical heritage, we may remain anxious that without the public security of an all-encompassing philosophical substructure, theology will lose its standing in the academy and the wider culture and sink back into the netherworlds of privatism and tribalism. But this worry about the universal versus private status of theology presupposes a sterile binary distinction that obscures a hidden middle path beyond the impasse generated by this false opposition. As an alternative to understanding theology in either universal, philosophical terms or private, sectarian terms, my proposal is for a green theology with an emancipatory intent that uses a variety of tools borrowed from contemporary critical theories for recovering from the biblical sources models for sustainable living in a broken world.

Seeking a third way beyond universalism and tribalism, green theology emphasizes both general intellectual rigor and creative fidelity to the particularities of the texts that ground historical Christian faith.

On the one hand, green theology abides by communal norms of argument and rationality in order to articulate a body of beliefs that are credible within the contemporary intellectual milieu. In so doing, however, it refuses to be held hostage to any philosophical assumptions (metaphysical or otherwise) that will blunt its move toward understanding the complexity of its rich subject matter, God in nature. On the other, green theology seeks rhetorical resonance with its scriptural sources in order to construct a full-bodied vision of the divine life that can engender earth-friendly vitality and well-being. At the same time, a biblically sonorous theology is vigilant in resisting the sectarian temptation to limit theology to the role of defending biblical or church orthodoxy. Eschewing both artificial philosophical limits and deadening ecclesial conformity, green theology seeks creative and at times subversive fidelity to the biblical and historical traditions that can fund visions of liberation and change for a world in crisis.

In the previous section I argued that the constrained constructivist schemes of Wittgenstein and Hayles help us to understand the nature of reality as the result of daily mediations between the flux of natural processes and our ingrained value commitments and worldviews. Constructivism maintains there is no one universal and objective model of the natural world but a series of perspectival understandings of reality specific to the language and culture of particular groups. In turn, this perspective opens up a new vision of theology as an exercise in imagining God in green terms through the optics of the biblical texts rather than as an operation in universal metaphysics.

In this way green theology is akin to other similar movements in contemporary thought. On one level it bears affinities with postmodern architecture, which eclectically uses historical quotation in order to bring together materials, motifs, and styles from the past into a new urban aesthetic.[30] Like postmodern architecture, green theology is an imaginative fusion of different sources and ideas into a new composition that seeks to be both highly original and historically vibrant. It is a self-consciously *constructive* enterprise that selects from previous works thought-forms and vocabulary that can be usefully recombined and refashioned in an idiom expressive of the hopes and desires of our age.[31] On another level, however, green theology goes beyond innovative thinking and biblical-historical quotation with its explicit commitment to enabling transformative, sustainable practice. Green theology utilizes a wide variety of historical styles and motifs in order to craft a new spiritual practice that can unleash productive engagements with the critical environmental challenges of our time.

Kenneth Gergen's Social Constructionism

To further refine this model of theology, I propose the "social constructionist" project of psychologist Kenneth Gergen, a colleague of mine at Swarthmore College, as a valuable resource for filling out the type of emancipatory green spirituality envisioned in this book. As a social scientist, Gergen's "constructionist" thought, as he calls it, additionally develops the constructivist projects of the philosophers of science we have just considered. Like Wittgenstein and Hayles, Gergen's central insight is that truth and rationality are constructed within social groups. Our assumptions about "'the nature of things" or "what the world is really like" are not a result of individual minds having reliable sense impressions of hard facts, but a product of shared experiences and tacit assumptions generated over time by particular communities. Wittgenstein and Hayles would be sympathetic to Gergen's point that

> knowledge is derived from value-interested conceptual standpoints rather than accurate mappings of the facts of nature. . . . In contrast to the empiricist position . . . the locus of knowledge [is] not in the minds of single individuals, but in the collectivity. It is not the internal processes of the individual that generate what is taken for knowledge, but a social process of communication. It is within the process of social interchange that rationality is generated. . . . *Interpersonal* colloquy is necessary to determine "the nature of things."[32]

As was previously argued, the world does not communicate its essential nature unadulterated to the keen empirical observer. The world is not a mind-independent reality yielding self-subsistent facts available to the neutral spectator. On the contrary, while not denying the reality of the world "out there," constructionists such as Gergen contend that the world only has meaning and value based on the culturally embedded "in here" conceptual schematas particular social groups rely on to organize the data of experience.

The recognition that all forms of inquiry are relative to intercommunal assumptions frees contemporary theology to reimagine God, self, and nature through a very particular retrieval of the transforming, earthen imagery within the biblical texts that gave rise to Christian traditions in the first place. Theology can avoid, therefore, the hoary task of trying to ground its enterprise on the security of a metaphysical foundation in the hopes that such a foundation can provide a universally secure perspective on the whole of human experience. With the realization, as Gergen writes, that "nothing exists for us—as an intelligible world of objects and persons—until there are relationships"[33] and that with attention to new patterns of relationship, "constructionism offers a bold invitation to transform social life, to build new futures,"[34] green theology is freed to pay renewed attention to those potentially revolutionary patterns of relationship narrated within the biblical witness as models for sustainable living. In a constructionist framework, appeals to timeless ontotheological notions such as "God as Being," "eternal truth," or "the human being as such" are supplanted by close biblical readings of how the Spirit of God transformatively interacts with earth community to realize truth and goodness within specific, historical social settings.

In the constructionist framework green theology, as a situated discourse rather than a philosophical system, is liberated to enter with confidence the public square of competing ideologies and thereby offer its scripturally rich visions of reality without relying on the pseudo-protection of metaphysics to trump the competitor thought systems that surround it. Theology, then, becomes essentially an activity in rhetoric and persuasion, a richly imaginative and poetic exercise in the art of conversation with people and communities from all walks of life. It is no longer an in-house discipline only for the benefit of true believers. Here theology is reenvisioned as a form of dialogical engagement with the wider culture that offers the biblical ideal of earth friendship as a paradigm for speaking to the hearts and imaginations of persons committed to faith-based social change. As a type of communicative practice, the potentially revolutionary intent of green theology becomes a player to be reckoned with in the marketplace of competing mores and worldviews.

Of course, without the bulwark of ontotheology, it may appear that green theology is just one more minority voice in the cacophony of viewpoints that vie for the loyalty of contemporary persons. This is a serious concern for many traditional theologians. Many religious thinkers suffer from legitimation anxiety that unless theology grounds itself on a universal, metaphysical vocabulary, it will continue to lose ground to other perspectives and further find that its once vaunted status as queen of the sciences is in terminal jeopardy. Some religious leaders are intimidated by diversity and continue to rely on universal appeals to truth and dogma in order to protect the threatened role of church teaching in the wider society.

Nevertheless, a vibrant and robust biblical faith need not feel threatened by ideological differences and social change but instead can learn to embrace diversity and change as opportunities for new growth. Still, the nagging question remains—namely, are assertions about meaning and truth still possible in the current reality of our radically pluralistic environment? Gergen maintains that social constructionism does not disallow claims about the real and the good, but he emphasizes that such claims always emerge within a contingent and historically located tradition that must appeal to its own intercommunal norms and warrants for the plausibility of the claims it advances. As Gergen says, "The generation of good reasons, good evidence and good values is always *from within a tradition*; already accepted are certain constructions of the real and the good, and implicit rejections of alternatives."[35] Constructionism enables us to be self-reflexive about competing constructions of value; it encourages a multi-positioned, cross-cultural, and polyvocal awareness of the wide web of working assumptions that support the fragile relations within the global village that is our common postmodern reality. Gergen puts it this way:

> For constructionists such considerations lead to a celebration of *reflexivity*, that is, the attempt to place one's premises into question, to suspend the "obvious," to listen to alternative framings of reality, and to grapple with the comparative outcomes of multiple standpoints. . . . This kind of critical reflection is not necessarily a prelude to rejecting our major traditions. It is simply to recognize them as traditions—historically and culturally situated.[36]

A wide number of contemporary thinkers—including, as we have seen, Wittgenstein and Hayles, to name two—agree with Gergen's constructionist thesis that all modes of understanding the world are products of intersubjective agreements about what does and does not count as reality. We saw that Wittgenstein is the progenitor of the constructivist position that inherited frames of reference constitute what a culturally situated subject understands to be the nature of things. Rationality is always generated and sustained within the "worldviews," "language games," or "forms of life" shared by persons in particular social relationships. Gaining knowledge about the world (what philosophers call "epistemology") is, in short, a relational rather than an individual task, according to Wittgenstein. Whether in psychology, science, literary criticism, or theology, claims about meaning and truth only make sense against the background of the received beliefs that allow such claims to be made and rendered intelligible in the first place.

Constructionism, then, is not a beachhead for pernicious relativism, but rather a recognition of the interdependence of language and culture in judgments about the nature of reality. In theology this orientation permits serious, reflective dialogue with time-honored traditions, including the biblical traditions, that have engaged many persons' hearts and minds for centuries. It encourages critics and practitioners alike to be honest and self-critical about the healing power as well as the destructive underside of these ancient revealed texts and beliefs. Green theology and social construction share, therefore, a deep affinity. Both modes of inquiry are committed to preserving the health and vitality of living traditions without insulating these traditions from serious scrutiny, vigorous criticism, and, at times, wholesale reconstruction. From this angle, the constructionist project is not a threat to the integrity of religious faith and tradition—though metaphysical and fundamentalist religious thinkers might think so—but an exercise in intellectual hygiene that helps theology purge itself of its desire for ahistorical or philosophical security in a pluralistic, postmodern world.

In the last two chapters we have seen that green spirituality is confronted by rival worldviews, humanism and deconstruction, that question its fundamental assumptions. In the first case, is not the great legacy of the human species our capacity for rational judgment? Is not the free exercise of this capacity the guarantor of essential human freedoms? And does not the valorization of this special capacity both signal our superior difference from other life-forms and ensure our care of their basic needs? On the contrary, I have argued, presupposing that humans are bearers of more value than other life-forms, far from being an obvious fact in nature, generally leads to nonsustainable patterns of thinking and behavior that blunt our ability to understand the essential importance of biotic interdependence as the key to protecting the interests of all natural kinds, human and nonhuman. If our genuine concern is to ensure fair treatment for all members of the human community—and, by extension, equitable treatment for other abiotic and biotic communities as well—then developing habits of heart and mind that better comprehend the mutual dependence of all beings on healthy ecosystems is the real demand of the moment. Again, the frog does not drink up the pond in which it lives. From my perspective, therefore, the verdict against humanism is clear. By self-servingly protecting the interests of *one* particular species at the expense of others, anthropocentrism is an outmoded and dangerous worldview that undermines the very support system necessary for maintaining the quality of life for *all* natural species. Ironically, humanism's purported aim, to secure human well-being, is foiled by its own skewed worldview.

In the second case, as we have seen in this chapter, what happens to green theology in its encounter with deconstruction? Deconstruction attempts to pull back the veil of our most prized notions—notions such as "nature" or "the world"—and show us that such notions betray our attachments to hidden assumptions about what makes up our picture of reality. Whenever theorists (including religious theorists) claim to delineate "how things really are," they are, in fact, representing their own presuppositions and convictions as much as they are describing the so-called real world. There is nothing wrong with this sort of value-laden mode of analysis as long as scientists, theologians, activists, and others recognize how their own personal worldviews and beliefs are implicated in the accounts they give of the realities they describe. In this vein, nature is not natural: nature is not raw and ready to be *discovered* by the individual observer because nature is always being *constructed* according to the socially mediated partisan convictions of the observer in question.

Green theology finds this constructionist model of knowing to be a healthy tonic in its attempt to articulate an earth-friendly religious vision. Constructionism helps to keep theology honest in its reminder that all claims to reality are partial and reformable. Now fully aware that the meaning of the natural world is partially based on cultural assumptions, green theology enters the public fray clearheaded about its own founding assumptions and clear-sighted in its distinctive vision of an interdependent world charged with the healing power of the Spirit in all things. Green theology, as an antidote to ecocidal thinking and lifestyles, calls for the conversion of each of us to sustainable living. This call for conversion does not need the pseudo-security of a philosophical foundation to be heard; instead, it utilizes the always original and richly fecund earth language of the Bible for its hortative power.

As green theology enters the public square and seeks to make its case to religious and nonreligious persons alike, it meets face-to-face with competing worldviews that have the potential to challenge, sharpen, and at times deepen the message of God's earthen love for all members of the biosphere. In these meetings the vision of a renewed earth where all of God's creatures live in harmony with their surroundings can be put forward with clarity and compassion.

Chapter Six

Earth God as the Wounded Spirit

In the Vatican Museums

SOME YEARS AGO, my wife, Ellen, and I lived in Europe during the spring while we were on sabbatical from Swarthmore College. We stayed in a stone cottage in an olive grove just outside a medieval hill town in central Italy. During the day we traveled to different historical and cultural sites to expand our understanding of historical Christianity and Italian culture. Our children were young then and Ellen and I would bundle them into strollers and infant backpacks in order to move about from site to site. On one such trip we visited the Vatican Museums. As our children needed our regular attention on this trip—diaper changes, bottle feedings, rest stops—I recall moving with some dispatch through room after room of stunning art treasures. As we walked briskly along the well-worn route many art pilgrims like ourselves had traveled for generations, we came upon the Vatican's Gallery of Modern Art. Moving quickly through this gallery with our children and equipment in tow, I was arrested by a painting unlike anything I had ever seen before.

The painting is entitled *The Baptism of Christ* and was finished in 1961 by French artist Bernard Buffet (see plates 6–9). It is part of a series of large paintings depicting the life of Christ that Buffet completed in the early 1960s intended to decorate the Chapelle de Château l'Arc in southern France. In 1971, at the request of the secretary to Pope Paul VI, the paintings were moved to the Vatican Museums, where they remain on permanent display. *The Baptism of Christ* portrays the baptism of Jesus by John the Baptist surrounded by robed supplicant women, a ministering angel, and the Holy Spirit in flight just over the head of Jesus. What arrested my attention in this painting, however, was Buffet's depiction of the Spirit as a wounded dove hovering over the newly baptized Savior (see plate 6). Buffet imagines the Spirit as thoroughly Christlike. The Spirit's wings are in full extension, stretched out to their limits, looking almost as if they have been pinned (or nailed) to their gold background. Intersecting the horizontal line of the Spirit's elongated wing pattern is an equally strong vertical line. Along this vertical line the Spirit, with bowed head and beak pointing down, is shown with its legs, like its wings, again fully extended and seemingly pinned (or nailed) to its lower abdomen and undertail, and pointing straight down like its beak. This crosswise depiction of the Spirit is repeated in the manner Buffet paints the Spirit's name in Latin, *Spiritus Sanctus*, by using sharp, angular, crisscrossing lines that look like a series of crosses perched high over the outstretched wings of the sacred bird.

But what I found most astonishing about Buffet's Spirit art is the depiction of the dark red wound in the Spirit's breast. Running with blood, the Spirit is pierced in its right side. I have never seen a similar crucifixion-styled, or "cruciform" figuration, of the Spirit in Western art. Whatever Buffet's intent in imagining the Spirit in this fashion, to me the message in this work is strikingly clear: the Spirit, like Jesus, is a victim who experiences the same suffering as does Jesus on the cross. This connection between the Spirit and Jesus is made clearer in the companion painting to the Spirit painting, in which Buffet shows John the Baptist bearing a cross as he comes to baptize Jesus (see plate 7). This scene falls directly underneath Buffet's image of the bleeding aviary Spirit. With the wounded Spirit above his head and the cross-bearing John the Baptist at his side, Jesus inaugurates his public ministry through his baptism by John and, at the same time, is preparing himself for his death on the cross. Jesus' baptism is a baptism into both his life and his death.

Buffet's crucifixion imagery in these paintings is further strengthened by a corollary set of two other paintings that he placed opposite the baptismal scene under study here. Paralleling the baptismal panel is a second panel entitled *The Crucifixion of Jesus*, which shows the lamb of God (*Agnus Dei*) in repose and positioned above the head of Jesus (see plate 8), who suffers in agony his death on the cross (see plate 9). In the book of Isaiah and the Gospel of John the lamb of God is the sacrificial victim who suffers in order to secure salvation for all creation. Indeed, it is John the Baptist in

John 1:29 who sees Jesus at his baptism and proclaims, "Behold, the lamb of God, who takes away the sin of the world!" Viewing the two panels side by side in the Vatican Museums in their original X-like, chiasmatic arrangement, I saw that Buffet's depiction of Jesus' baptism intersects with the lamb of God symbolism even as the wounded Spirit painting intersects with the crucifixion symbolism. Aesthetically and theologically, the juxtapositions between the two sets of images are telling: the cross that John the Baptist carries in the lower-left panel is pitched at the same right angle as the shepherd's hook carried by the lamb of God in the upper-right panel; in the same manner, the outstretched wings of the pierced Spirit in the upper-left panel are paralleled by the outstretched arms of the dying Jesus in the lower-right panel. Crucifixion imagery is the red thread that ties together the complementary thematic elements in this related set of four paintings by Bernard Buffet.

Buffet's portrayal of the crucified Spirit is an oddity in Christian art and theology. Based on the Gospel texts, the Spirit is often viewed as alighting upon Jesus at his baptism; however, I know of no visual or textual sources that depict the Spirit as crucified like Jesus. But however strange or unorthodox Buffet's religious art might seem at first glance, I believe his image of the bleeding Spirit conveys a profound religious truth—indeed, a profoundly earth-centered religious truth—that calls out for further reflection. Can the Spirit be imagined as wounded like Jesus? And if so, how does this novel depiction illuminate the task of green spirituality for our time? In response to these questions, I will consider further in this chapter the relationship between the Spirit and the earth as an entry point into the important theme of the wounded Spirit as figured in Buffet's art.

The Cruciform Spirit

Buffet's unusual painting of the Spirit cut and bleeding raises an interesting theological problem. If it is Jesus on the cross that is traditionally portrayed as pierced and crucified, then how can the Spirit be pictured by Buffet in this Christlike fashion? If the Gospels singularly describe Jesus, not the Spirit, as the victim of crucifixion, then what is the theological justification for Buffet's depiction of the Spirit in like manner?

My instincts tell me that the legitimating source for explaining Buffet's original illustration of the cruciform Spirit is the doctrine of the Trinity. In the Trinity the three members of the Godhead are neither divided from one another nor confused with one another. Coeternal and coequal, Father, Son, and Spirit share mutual joys and common sorrows in an intimate society of love and affection. From a trinitarian perspective, the depiction of the cruciform Spirit makes sense as one member of the Godhead, namely, the Spirit, expresses in her wounded body solidarity and shared feelings with another member of the Godhead, namely, the suffering Christ. Looking, therefore, at the four paintings in a crisscross pattern, I believe Buffet's juxtaposition of bleeding Spirit and crucified Christ, on the one hand, and lamb of God and baptized Christ, on the other, is intended, among other things, to signal the coparticipation of the Spirit in the crucifixion event that grounds and centers each of the four images in the two panels in question—bleeding Spirit, baptized Christ, lamb of God, and crucified Christ. In the Trinity of God's inner family life, Holy Spirit and Son of God suffer together the world's sin and degradation in a mutual experience of loss and victimization.

But there is another sense—a green spirituality sense—in which the Spirit can be understood as suffering in Christlike fashion that I think is pointed to by Buffet's paintings (even if Buffet himself did not paint these images with this interpretation in mind). From the vantage point of green spirituality, the Spirit, like Jesus, also suffers loss and deprivation because the Spirit, as God's abiding and sustaining presence within nature, experiences in the depths of her person the corrosive impact of environmental depredation in our time. *Jesus suffers on the cross the sins of the world; the Spirit in the earth suffers the despoilment of the world.* Jesus suffers because he bears the sins of the world in his human flesh. The Spirit, as coeternal and coparticipatory with Jesus in the eternal Godhead, also experiences this suffering (even as does God the Father, for that matter). But the Spirit also suffers in a way distinctive of her role in creation because she feels the pain of a degraded earth in her more-than-human body. The Spirit is the bird God. The Spirit is the earthen God who indwells all things. The Spirit is the God enfleshed within all the life-forms that swim and fly and crawl and run upon the earth. Whenever, then, these life-forms suffer loss and pain, the Spirit suffers loss and pain. Whenever these life-forms are threatened and destroyed, the Spirit feels threatened and experiences death and trauma in herself. Whenever earth community is laid waste, the Spirit deeply mourns this loss and fragmentation.

In this book I have emphasized that to say that the Spirit is the bird God, in the manner of the scriptures, is not an empty metaphor. Christians do not think identifying Christ with the man Jesus is simply a figure of speech, but rather a vital description of God actually becoming human in the person of one solitary individual two thousand years ago. Likewise, the biblical descriptions of the Spirit as earthen being (bird) or natural element (wind or fire) are not an ornamental trope, but rather a living description of the manner in which God becomes real and enfleshed in our time and place today. In Jesus, according to the Gospels, God became flesh and dwelled among us; in the Spirit, we can now say, God continually becomes flesh and dwells among us again.

The reason, therefore, that the Spirit suffers like Jesus on the cross—the reason Buffet's painting sets forth such a profound theological truth—stems not only from the fact that the Spirit and Jesus are one in the life of God, as crucially important as that fact is. Building on Buffet's painting, we can also say that the origin of the Spirit's suffering is also in the fact that *the Spirit and the earth are one*, in a certain manner of speaking. In this book, I have put forward a model of the Spirit as the enfleshment of God's sustaining power in the biosphere in order to emphasize the mutual interdependence of the Spirit and the natural world. Whether manifesting herself as a living, breathing organism, like a dove, or an inanimate life force, such as wind or fire, the Spirit indwells nature as its interanimating power in order to bring all of creation into a harmonious relationship with itself. The Spirit is the vital *rûach*—God's breath—that gives life to all beings. All things—rocks, trees, plants, rivers, animals, and humans—are made of Spirit and are part of the continuous biological flow patterns that constitute life on our planet. The Spirit *ensouls* the earth as its life-giving breath, and the earth *embodies* the Spirit's mysterious interanimation of the whole creation.

Spirit and Earth, Union of Heart

This dialectical model of the Spirit's real and ongoing union with the earth is borrowed from the fifth-century vocabulary used in Christianity's early doctrine of Jesus Christ's "two natures." After generations of struggle over how exactly to formulate the ancient conviction that Jesus was both fully human and fully divine, in the year 451 a group of theologians convened an ecumenical synod in Chalcedon (in what is today eastern Turkey) in order to work out the proper understanding of the relationship between Jesus' two natures. In essence, the theologians of Chalcedon put forward a tension-ridden, interactional framework for understanding Jesus' two natures. As thoroughly divine and thoroughly human, Jesus' person is made up of two natures; each nature, divine and human, subsists in a deep and abiding interconnection with the other, while at the same time the distinctiveness and integrity of each nature is preserved as well. Jesus is an integrated, complete, and whole person, fully divine and fully human, and his two natures are understood as being neither confused with nor collapsed into one another.

I think of this Chalcedonian formula as an instance of a "productive contradiction." A productive contradiction imaginatively juxtaposes two apparently opposing ideas—in this case, the ideas of divinity and humanity in one person—in order to articulate a new vision of reality—in this case, the idea that this one person, Jesus, is a divine human being. Another way to refer to this type of tensive thinking is to speak of a "coincidence of opposites," an instance of "semantic impertinence," or a "non-oppositional dualism."[1] When dialectical thought is stretched to its limits, there is the possibility of discovering, ironically, a previously undisclosed unity, a blinding flash of new insight, that was not possible prior to an inventory of the oppositions in question. When apparent polar contradictions are pulled to their breaking points it becomes possible, paradoxically, to preserve the integrity of each of the opposing viewpoints and at the same time uncover a deeply rooted harmony between the two polar contradictions that had previously been hidden.

Borrowing from the ancient christological wisdom of the fifth century and applying it to the task of green spirituality today, we can see how important it is to hold together two seemingly opposing viewpoints in a tension-ridden unity that nevertheless preserves the independence of each individual viewpoint. Employing, then, the dialectical logic of Chalcedon, we can say that the Spirit indwells the earth and the earth enfleshes the Spirit. This formulation of the relationship between Spirit and earth signals an inseparable unity between the two realities without a consequent absorption of the one into the other. Another way to put this is to say that the Spirit and the earth are one and that the Spirit and the earth are not one. To be sure, Spirit and earth enjoy a permanent and living unity, one with the other: each reality internally conditions and permeates the other in a cosmic festival of love and harmony. Erotically charged, Spirit and earth dwell in oneness and fellowship with one another. But both modes of being live through and with one another without collapsing into confusion with, or separation from, one another. The reciprocal indwelling of Spirit and earth is neither an absorption of the one into the other nor an admixture of the two. By the same token, the mutual indwelling of Spirit and earth does not signify merely an outward and transitory connection between the two realities.

The point, rather, is that Spirit and earth enjoy an internal and abiding union in their common life together. Insofar as the Spirit abides in and with all living things, Spirit and earth are unified together, while, at the same time, each reality also possesses its own distinctive identity. Spirit and earth are internally inseparable because both modes of being are living realities with the same common goal of sustaining other life-forms. But Spirit and earth are also distinguishable insofar as the Spirit is the hidden source of life for all things, while the earth is the visible nesting ground, so to speak, where all things live and move and have their being.

The Spirit is the "soul" of the earth—the wild, life-giving breath of creation—empowering all life-forms to enter into a dynamic relationship with the greater whole. In turn, the earth is the "flesh" of the Spirit—the living landscapes of divine presence—making God palpable and viscous in nature's ever-widening circles of seasonal changes. To experience the full range of nature's birthing cycles, periods of growth, and seasons of death and decay—to know the joy and sadness of living in harmony with nature's cyclical processes and flow patterns—is to be empowered by the Spirit and nurtured by nature's bounty. The Spirit is the hidden, inner life of the world, and the earth is the outward manifestation of the Spirit's sustaining energies.

The Chalcedonian understanding of the interrelationship between Spirit and earth challenges the classical, philosophical model of God in Christian thought we discussed earlier. In the metaphysical model God is an immovable heavenly being insulated from this-worldly concerns. God is divorced from the passions and vagaries of transient existence. In the classical paradigm, God is unfeeling, self-subsistent, and independent from the ebb and flow of life and death that makes up our earthly habitations. Metaphysical doctrines about "divine apathy" and "divine impassibility"—the standard, philosophically influenced belief that God is a stolid, dispassionate being not susceptible to the whims and fancies of human emotions—achieved the status of obvious truth in early Christian thought as a reaction to the fire and fury characteristic of the gods and goddesses of pre-Christian Pagan mythology.[2] Here again, as we saw earlier, Christianity and Paganism, in their own respective historical development, go their separate ways. In the face of the malevolent and capricious actions of Pagan divinities, Christians envisioned their God as pure goodness and impassive to change and circumstance. Beyond life and death, the supreme God of Christianity is quintessentially self-possessed and far removed from the tumult and impermanence of mortal existence. All flesh is mortal, all flesh is grass, says the Bible. But God, according to classical Christianity, is not mortal; God is not fleshly being. God is the All-Powerful who is uniquely immortal, invisible, and unchangeable. God, in a word, is Being itself—eternal and immovable.

The Chalcedonian logic of the Spirit—that Spirit and earth, interactively conceived, are one—opposes this metaphysical idea of God as unchangeable and apathetic in the face of the suffering and turmoil within the creation that God has spun into existence. Earth God is not a distant abstraction but a living being who subsists in and through the natural world. Because God as Earth Spirit lives in the ground and circulates in water and wind, God suffers deeply the loss and abuse of our biological heritage through our continued assaults on our planet home. God as Spirit is pained by ongoing eco-squalor; God as Spirit undergoes deprivation and trauma through the stripping away of earth's bounty. As the earth heats up and melting polar ice fields flood shore communities and indigenous habitats, God suffers; as global economic imbalance imperils family stability and intensifies the quest for arable land in native forests, God suffers; as coral reefs bleach into decay and whole ecosystems of fish and marine life die off, God suffers; and as our planet endures what appears to be the era of the Sixth Great Extinction, like the great extinctions of the ice age and other mass death events, God suffers. When we plunder and lay waste to the earth, God suffers.

Because God and earth mutually indwell one another, God is vulnerable to the same loss and degradation the earth undergoes at the greedy hands of its human caretakers. This means that God as Spirit, Earth God, lives on "this side of eternity," as it were. Earth God lives on "this side" of the ecological squalor our global greed has spawned. God is not an inert, metaphysical concept but a living, suffering coparticipant in the pain of the world. God has cast her lot with a depredated planet and has entered into the fullness of the tragic history of humankind's abuse of our planet home. God has become, then, a tragic figure in our time. God is a tragic figure not in the sense that God, pitifully, arouses our sympathy because God is weak and ineffectual in the face of environmental terror—that God is somehow fated for destruction along with the destruction of the earth. No, rather, God is a tragic figure in our time in the sense that the tragedy of human rapaciousness is now God's own environmental tragedy as well. Who can say what profound torment is felt in the depths of the divine life itself when God surveys the devastation human avarice and stupidity have wrought? The sorry spectacle of an earth under siege and God's longing for a renewed biosphere are one. In union of heart, in agony of spirit, God and the earth are one.

In Jesus God enfleshed Godself at one time in one human being; in the Spirit God enfleshes Godself continually in the earth. In both instances, God decides in freedom and love for all beings, and not by any internal necessity, to enter into the fullness of human tragedy. In making this decision regarding our sad eco-drama, the Spirit puts herself in harm's way by becoming fully a part of a planet ravaged by human arrogance. *God is at risk in the world today.* It is not an extreme statement to say, then, that the threat of ecocide brings in its wake the specter of deicide: to wreak environmental havoc in the biosphere is to run the risk that we will inflict lasting injury on the source and ground of our common life together, Earth God. Spirit and earth are one. Spirit and earth are one in suffering. Spirit and earth are one in the tragedy of ecocide. Spirit and earth's common unity and life-centered identity raise the frightening possibility that despoiling our planet and chronically unsustainable living may result in permanent trauma to the divine life itself.

The Wounded God

In 1972 German theologian Jürgen Moltmann published a revolutionary new vision of Christian belief entitled *The Crucified God.* Moltmann had been conscripted into the German army at age seventeen and witnessed many of the horrors of the Second World War, including the Jewish Holocaust. Writing in the wake of the Shoah, Moltmann questioned whether the classical understanding of God as an independent, self-subsisting being divorced from earthly concerns was adequate in the light of the massive suffering spawned by the Nazi death camps. Where is God in the concentration camps? Moltmann asked. If God, as an active, agential being, decided not to intervene on behalf of God's people to stop the slaughter, then is God a distant, unfeeling deity unmoved by human misery? Or, in a manner that remains ultimately inscrutable and unfathomable, was God somehow present to and deeply affected by the suffering of millions even though God did not actively change the course of history in favor of the victims? But if God were somehow actively attending to the sufferers, if God is not a stranger to death and misery, in what manner did God perform this identity with the victims of the death camps? If God did not visibly enter into the tragedy and alter such a horrific course of events, but was somehow fundamentally affected by what happened, in what fashion did this occur?

Moltmann's answer to these questions is that the biblical God of love and compassion suffers the pain and loss of the victims insofar as God is really (but mysteriously) present in the lives of the many persons who died in the Shoah. God is not God unless God experiences the unspeakable torment and dashed hopes of the sufferers. Writing about the Spanish philosopher Miguel de Unamuno's theology of the sorrowful God, Moltmann says, "A God who cannot suffer cannot love either. A God who cannot love is a dead God. . . . The living God is the loving God. The loving God shows that he is a loving God through his suffering."[3]

Since the biblical God, in compassion and like-minded empathy, is alive through suffering, it remains unanswerable as to why God did not break the evil chain of historical causality that led to the mass suffering of millions of persons. This inactivity of God at that time remains inscrutable. Be that as it may, however, the question remains, If God is alive in the suffering of the victims, in what manner is God present to the victims? The answer to this profoundly disturbing question is grounded in the crucifixion of the Son of God at the hands of his human tormentors. In the cross of Jesus, Moltmann answers, God experiences sorrow and abandonment, and in that experience, an experience that continues well into the present, God is actively present in the lives of fellow and sister sufferers. Moltmann maintains that the long-ago crucifixion of Jesus introduces God to the history of human suffering that persists today, manifesting its ugly face in the Nazi death camps and continuing into the present. As God in Jesus suffers the godforsaken death of the cross, God continues to suffer grief and injury through God's sympathy and identification with the persons and communities brutalized by the National Socialists.

If Jesus died on the cross, and if Jesus is the incarnation of God in the world, does it follow that God died as well? Moltmann says not. The cross does not signify the "death *of* God," as if God somehow perished at Calvary, but the death of Jesus does inaugurate "death *in* God" as a terrifying event of suffering and destitution within the inner life of Godself. The cross is not an instance of God dying, but a death event in Godself where the divine life takes into itself the demise of the godless son of God crucified for the sins of the world. In the cross God now becomes radically discontinuous with Godself by taking up the broken, murdered body of the crucified one. Moltmann writes:

What happened on the cross was an event between God and God. It was a deep division in God himself, insofar as God abandoned God and contradicted himself, and at the same time a unity in God, insofar as God was at one with God and corresponded to himself. In that case one would have to put the formula in a paradoxical way: God died the death of the godless on the cross and yet did not die. God is dead and yet is not dead.[4]

In the cross, God splits Godself by incorporating the godless death of Jesus into the inner life of the Godhead. In this rift caused by Jesus' death, God now undergoes a permanent and fundamental change by becoming a willing victim of death itself. In the cross God is not a far-removed, self-contained, unchangeable heavenly being. Rather, God now enters into the fullness of human history, the vagaries of earthly existence, with all its ambiguities, uncertainties, and messy and senseless suffering. In Jesus and continuing into our troubled present, God now becomes one of us.

In becoming one of us God takes the death camps—the loneliness, the betrayal, the abandonment, the deprivation—into Godself. The dying Son of God is part of the inner life and history of Godself. God knows, therefore, what it is like to experience death and despair. It is for this reason that it is now possible for the helplessness and anguish of those preyed upon by their tormentors to enter into the eternal grief of God. The failed hopes of God's covenant people are now God's failed hope as well. In Moltmann's barbed language, God and Auschwitz become one:

> It is necessary to remember the martyrs . . . that God himself hung on the gallows, as Elie Wiesel was able to say. If that is taken seriously, it must be said that, like the cross of Christ, even Auschwitz is in God himself. Even Auschwitz is taken up into the grief of the Father, the surrender of the Son and the power of the Spirit. That never means that Auschwitz and other grisly places can be justified, for it is the cross that is the beginning of the trinitarian history of God. . . . God in Auschwitz and Auschwitz in the crucified God—that is the basis for a real hope which both embraces and overcomes the world, and the ground for a love which is stronger than death and can sustain death.[5]

For Moltmann, the death cry of the crucified Jesus becomes the cry of all humanity. When Jesus wails on the cross, "My God! My God, why have you forsaken me?" he is calling out on behalf of everyone who suffers and is unjustly punished. The seeming "apathy" and "impassibility" of God in classical Christian theology is now subverted by a this-worldly theology of a suffering God who offers hope to an abandoned humanity. God is not up in heaven dispassionate in the face of human suffering and indifferent to the corrosion of body and soul in the horrors of the Shoah and other events of mass destruction. Rather, because God and the world are one, the world's agony and loss are now God's torment as well. It is this *identity* of God with the poor and destitute—the primal fact of "God in Auschwitz and Auschwitz in the crucified God," as Moltmann disturbingly puts it—that is the basis for hope in a fragmented world. Hope—however tenuous and fragile it appears—is religiously possible because God and our broken humanity are one. God is one of us: herein lies the basis of hope for our time.

Moltmann's affirmation of divine suffering opens new vistas into a deeper understanding of the Spirit's anguish over an endangered earth. Analogous to God in Jesus' undergoing agony and loss because human-kind suffers is the suffering God as Spirit experiences because the whole world is under siege. My point in this chapter is this: as Jesus' death on the cross brought death and loss into Godself, so the Spirit's suffering from persistent environmental trauma engenders chronic agony in the God-head. From the perspective of earthen spirituality, therefore, Moltmann's "crucified God" now has a double valence: death enters into the inner life of God through the cross of Jesus even as the prospect of mass ecological death enters into the life of God through the Spirit's communion with a despoiled planet. We see, then, as we saw in Buffet's crucifixion art, that the Spirit is truly Christlike or cruciform because she suffers the same violent fate as did Jesus—but now a suffering not confined to the onetime event of the cross, but a continuous suffering that the Spirit experiences daily based on the degradation of the earth and its inhabitants.

Because ecological trauma deeply grieves the Spirit, we can imagine that the Spirit today is pleading with the human community to nurture and protect the fragile bioregions we all share. When we drive high-emis-sion, gas-guzzling automobiles, refuse to recycle our waste, or eat fac-tory-farmed food that causes needless pain to the animals around us, do we not feel the Spirit in our hearts tugging at our conscience and urging us to cause less harm and suffering toward earth community? In a highly insightful discussion of the Spirit's relationship to nature, the apostle Paul writes that human arrogance has caused the whole creation to groan in agony as it awaits final deliverance. Nature is in bondage, Paul writes, as a result of human pride. Nature is troubled and groans for release from its captivity to humanly generated squalor. To update Paul's insights and correlate them with the contemporary ecocrisis, Paul's writings about the

Spirit appear uncannily prescient: our hostile treatment of the earth has now plunged all of creation into deep suffering and travail. Paul writes:

> The creation waits with eager longing for the revealing of the sons of God; for the creation was subjected to futility, not of its own will but by the will of him who subjected it in hope; because the creation itself will be set free from its bondage to decay and obtain the glorious liberty of the children of God. We know that the whole creation has been groaning in travail together until now; and not only the creation, but we ourselves, who have the first fruits of the Spirit, groan inwardly as we wait for adoption as sons, the redemption of our bodies. . . . Likewise the Spirit helps us in our weakness; for we do not know how to pray as we ought, but the Spirit himself intercedes for us with sighs too deep for words. (Romans 8: 19-23, 26)

Paul writes that as the creation sighs in pain, the Spirit likewise groans within us in sounds too deep for words. The Spirit intercedes on our behalf and teaches us to pray that God's love for all creation will be consummated. In the midst of the current crisis, all of creation groans under the weight of humankind's habitual ecoviolence. We feel the weight of this crisis, and we sense the Spirit alive within each of us, moaning out of pain and yearning for the renewal of a green, healthy, vibrant planet. In visceral sighs too deep for words, as Paul writes, Earth God inwardly calls on us to care for our planetary heritage. God as Spirit agonizes over the squalor we have caused, and through her abiding earthly presence implores us to stop the violence before it is too late.

Today, God as Spirit lives among us in great sorrow and deep anguish. From the viewpoint of green spirituality, as the God who knows death through the cross of Jesus is the crucified God, so also is the Spirit who enfleshes divine presence in nature the wounded Spirit. In antiquity, God's human body endured the cut marks of whips and nails; today and every day, the Spirit's earth body is injured by the deep trauma we ceaselessly inflict on the planet. In Jesus, God at one time suffered the wounds of human sin and error; in the earth body of the Spirit, God is continually lacerated by chronic and thoughtless assaults upon our planet home. Herein lie the sad parallels between the crucified Jesus and the cruciform Spirit: the lash marks of human sin cut into the body of the crucified God are now even more graphically displayed across the expanse of the whole planet as the earth body of the wounded Spirit bears the incisions of further abuse. Because God as Spirit is enfleshed within creation, God experiences within the core of her deepest self the agony and suffering of an earth under siege. *The Spirit, then, as the green body of God in the world, has also become in our time the wounded God.* Earth Spirit is the wounded God who daily suffers the environmental violence wrought by humankind's unremitting ecocidal attitudes and habits. The Spirit is the wounded God even as Christ is the crucified God. As God once suffered on a tree by taking into Godself humankind's sin, so God now continually suffers another sort of agony and loss by daily bringing into Godself the environmental squalor that humankind has wrought.

Eating the Body and Drinking the Blood of God

I have suggested that we refer to the Spirit in our time as the "wounded Spirit" or "cruciform Spirit" who, like Christ, takes into herself the burden of human sin and the deep ecological damage this sin has wrought in the biosphere. In this way I am reminded of the Christian practice of the Lord's Supper when I contemplate the analogy of suffering between the crucified Jesus and the cruciform Spirit. In corporate worship Christians regularly reactualize the power of Jesus' death by eating bread and drinking wine together in the ritual of the Eucharist, symbolically reenacting Jesus' own last meal, when he prophesied his coming arrest, trial, and execution. "Whenever you eat this bread and drink from this cup," says Jesus in the Gospels, "you remember my death until I come again." The message of Christianity is that this group meal in churches today, the practice of the Lord's Supper, brings into the living present the meaning and power of Jesus' life-giving sacrifice from long ago.

I want to make the following comparison between Christ and Spirit based on this eucharistic ritual. As Christ's wounds become the eucharistic blood that nourishes and inspires hope in the life of the believer—drawing the analogy here between Jesus' suffering and the Spirit's suffering—so also does the Spirit's agony over damage to the earth become a source of promise and new beginnings for communities facing seemingly hopeless environmental destitution. Bernard Buffet's avian God sacrifices herself for the welfare of others. Like Jesus' blood, the blood of the pierced Spirit Bird in Buffet's revolutionary art signals God's radical identity with the animal world and, by extension, God's desire for a green planet in balance with itself.

The message of the cross is that senseless death is not foreign to God because it is through the cross that God lives in solidarity with all who suffer. The promise of new life that flows from the suffering God hanging from a tree is now recapitulated in the ministry of the wounded Spirit, whose solidarity with a broken world is a token of divine forbearance and love. Hope, then, for a restored earth in our time is theologically rooted in the belief in the Spirit's benevolent cohabitation with all of the damaged and forgotten members of the biosphere—human and nonhuman alike. The Spirit's abiding presence in a world wracked by human greed is a constant reminder that God desires the welfare of all members of the lifeweb—indeed, that no population of life-forms is beyond the ken of divine love, no matter how serious, even permanent, the ecological damage is to these biotic communities.

One of the many ironies of Christian faith is the belief that out of death comes life; from loss and suffering comes the possibility of hope and renewal. This irony is symbolized in the Creator's emptying of herself in creation so that all beings may enjoy fullness of life; in Jesus' crucifixion, where the spilling of his lifeblood becomes the opportunity for all persons to experience the fullness of new life in him; and in the Spirit's desire for earth renewal and concomitant willingness to endure our ecological violence, so that we can be offered again and again the chance to change our habits and reenter the sorority of the earth and her Creator. The Spirit in and through the body of the earth groans in travail over our addictions to ecoviolence. Tragically, our rapacious habits daily wound afresh the Earth Spirit who breathes life into all things. And daily the Earth Spirit intercedes for us and groans in sounds too deep for words—imploring us to love our planet home.

But in the Spirit's wounds we have life because it is in the wounded Earth Spirit that we see God's love overabundant and outpouring on our behalf. In her wounds we see God's refusal to remain aloof from creation—apathetic, unmoved, uncaring—just insofar as God decided to enflesh Godself in all of the earth systems and life-forms that constitute life as we know it. We continue unabated in our ravaging of the earth body of the one who has given herself for us so that we might live. But to this point the cruciform Spirit has not withdrawn her sustaining presence from the planet—a reminder to us that God is a lover of all things bodily and earthly—and a call to a renewed passion on our part for nurturing and protecting the biosphere that is our common inheritance and common home.

We need today a conversion of the heart to a vision of a green earth, where all persons live in harmony with their natural environments. It is too wonderful to imagine, and our hearts overflow with joy and gratitude, but we continue to enjoy the Spirit's daily protection of our kind and otherkind by allowing all of us to remain richly alive in spite of our ecocidal behavior to the contrary. May the Holy Spirit, as divine force for sustenance and renewal in all things, come into our hearts and minds and persuade us to work toward a seamless social-environmental ethic of justice and love toward all of God's creatures.

Chapter Seven

The World Is Alive with Spirit

A Council of All Beings Ritual

I WONDERED WHETHER CLASSES should be canceled at Swarthmore College the day after the attacks on the New York World Trade Center on September 11, 2001. The emotional aftershock of that terrible event was still being felt on the Swarthmore campus the next day. The day after what we now call "9/11" I was scheduled to teach the second session of my class "Religion, the Environment, and Contemplative Practices." I had planned that afternoon for the three-hour class meeting to take place in the Crum Woods, a beautiful forest preserve adjacent to the Swarthmore campus. In addition to discussing the assigned readings, I had hoped that the students could begin a series of group meditation and ritual practices I had envisioned for this class throughout the semester. Under any circumstances, asking students to take the chance of practicing various meditation disciplines in an open classroom environment in full view of their peers is a risky proposition. But to take this risk immediately following such a traumatic event as 9/11 I now felt to be especially ill-timed. So I e-mailed the class before our meeting to see what they wanted to do, assuming they would prefer to cancel class for that day and make it up at a later date. To my surprise the students wanted to go ahead with the class as planned.

We first met in our regular classroom, and then, without speaking, we proceeded into the Crum Woods as a group, practicing a kind of silent walking meditation. Along the way I asked members of the group to experience being "summoned" by a particular life-form in the Crum Woods—red fox, clod of dirt, water strider, flatworm, gray squirrel, red oak, skunk-cabbage—and then to reimagine themselves as becoming that life-form. After the walk through the woods we gathered in a circle, thirty or so students and myself, in a grove of sycamore trees in an open meadow next to the Crum Creek.

At this juncture I asked the students to speak in the first person and give a message to our group from the perspective of the individual life-form they had become. (I explained that this was a voluntary exercise and that no one should feel compelled to speak if he or she did not want to.) If you could imagine yourself, for example, as a brook trout or mourning dove or dragonfly living in and around the Crum Creek, and the creek is threatened by suburban storm water runoff and other problems, what would you like to say to this group of us human beings in this circle? This group activity is a variation on a deep ecology, Neopagan ritual called a Council of All Beings, in which participants enact a mystical oneness with the flora and fauna in a particular area by speaking out in the first person on behalf of the being or place they have chosen to identify with. A Council of All Beings ritual enables members of the group to speak "as" and "for" other natural beings and to feel imaginatively what it might be like to be bacterium, bottle-nosed dolphin, alligator, old-growth forest, or gray wolf. Participants become this or that animal or plant or natural place and then share a message with the other human persons in the circle. The purpose of a Council is to foster compassion for all life-forms and heal the ugly splits that separate human beings from the natural world.

In principle, this sort of group activity seemed like a good idea for inaugurating a new class format that included academic religious studies along with earthen meditation practices such as a Council of All Beings ritual. But as we moved into the silent period of sitting in a circle waiting for someone in our group to speak "as" his or her adopted life-form, it became awkwardly clear to me that no one was ready to speak right away. How could I expect my students, shocked and traumatized by the day's previous events in New York, to openly perform this sort of strange ritual, especially since it appeared that some of my students, understandably, were uncomfortable "becoming" other life-forms in a public setting? It seemed to me that some of the students were shy, while others did not want to do or say anything that might embarrass themselves in a group setting. As the minutes drifted by, I feared that I had been asking too much of the class. After a half hour no one had spoken, and I could feel the perspiration running down the inside of my shirt. I had been preparing this class for months, but now I felt I should have proposed a more conventional alternative to a Council of All Beings ritual in light of the sad events at the World Trade Center the day before.

Then something magical happened.

"I am blue heron," said one member of the class. "I glide quietly though the creek in the early morning looking for something to eat. I break the calm of the late afternoon with my great wings as I take flight over the water and travel to new destinations. Humans, keep this watershed clean so that I can grace this place for years to come."

Soon other life-forms began to speak as well.

"I am red-backed salamander. I live under rocks and deep down in the moist, fertile ground. I need the protection of this forest to dig for food and raise my young. I am worried that contaminants in the soil I live in will make me sick to the point of death. Please care for the earth so that I can live."

"I am monarch butterfly. I migrate through the open meadows in your forest looking for the milkweed plant on which I lay my eggs and my caterpillars feed. I brighten your day with my beautiful orange and black wings; I help other plants grow and pollinate by nectaring here and there. Please don't pave over the meadows and cut down the milkweed that I need for my survival."

"I am black walnut tree. I add to the protective canopy of this forest. My heartwood is favored by you for your furniture making. The large nuts I drop to the ground are food for squirrels and mice and other forest critters. I purify the air and absorb the carbon dioxide you produce so that everyone can breathe. Protect this forest and all its inhabitants."

And the litany of voices continued: "I am lichen. . . ." "I am holly bush. . . ." "I am crayfish. . . ." "I am forest wildflower. . . ." "I am worm. . . ." "I am mourning dove. . . ." "I am furry caterpillar. . . ." "I am tulip tree. . . ." and so forth.

After the long period of silence members of the class shared their eco-stories in a polyphony of proclamatory speech, soft-spoken entreaties, tears, and laughter. I feared the initial silence had signaled class members' unease with group ritual. But what I now realized was that the time of silence at the beginning of class allowed participants to gather their thoughts and discern what they should say as they took on the identity of the particular life-form who had originally summoned them during our forest walk.

As I followed the pattern of the puzzlelike pieces of bark flaking off the trunk of the sycamore tree next to me, I became encircled by a medley of voices reminding me and other class members of our obligations to care for the forest. Sitting cross-legged in the open meadow, I saw yellow jackets buzzing low to the ground foraging for food; my skin felt warmed by the mid-afternoon sunlight; the low gurgle of the creek nearby provided background music to our gathering. Soon class would end, and we would be back on campus and away from the forest. But here for a moment we enacted our identities as fellow and sister members of this forest preserve in communion with all the other life-forms therein. We felt ourselves embedded in a sacred hoop greater than ourselves. As human citizens of this wider biotic community, we found ourselves surrounded by a cloud of witnesses calling us to our responsibilities for preserving the Crum Woods.[1]

Sojourning in the Crum Woods

The Crum Creek watershed is a thirty-eight-square-mile area of land that sits on the western edge of suburban Philadelphia. It is a network of streams, wetlands, and aquifers that supplies two hundred thousand households and businesses with drinking water as well as being a discharge area for wastewater effluent and a natural floodway for storm water events. The watershed is a scenic retreat for persons in the Philadelphia area who need a place of refuge from the strains and stresses of urban life. And it is an important habitat for many native plants and animals.

A variety of species of wildlife relies on the Crum Creek watershed for food and raising their young. Scarlet tanagers migrate from Colombia and Bolivia to lay their eggs in the old-growth forests surrounding the creek area. Spotted and red-backed salamanders are two of the twelve or so species of amphibians that live within and along the banks of the creek and its tributaries. Monarch butterflies migrate from Mexico to the open meadows of the watershed area, where they roost to feed on milkweed plants and lay their eggs. Ancient southern red oaks survive in a section of the Crum Woods near the Swarthmore College campus in an aboriginal forest relatively undisturbed by white settlement. American eels migrate downstream through the creek every fall to lay their eggs in the Sargasso Sea near Bermuda; in turn, their offspring then swim upstream to mature in the same creek area where their parents began their own journeys out to sea. And showy, large-flowered trillium wildflowers fade from white to pink each year in the deep, rich woods of the watershed.[2]

The Crum Woods near the Swarthmore campus is my favorite site for passive recreation and easy walking meditation. Living in a world awash in parking lots and strip malls, I find it healing and restorative to be able to take refuge in the dark quiet of the woods. Henry David Thoreau writes about the art of getting lost, the vertiginous pleasure of abandoning oneself to a natural place without the artificial supports of urban maps and street signs. Today many of us have cell phones and handheld global positioning devices so that no one need go missing and become confused about where they are. But in taming wild places and making them the quantifiable objects of our measurement and control, we have done harm to our basic humanity, our basic animal nature. We are animal beings at our core. Our need for sleep, hunger for food, drive for companionship, and desire for sex are telling signs of our carnal natures. To be sure, we are animals that are self-aware and self-conscious, animals whose conscience can burn with shame and guilt, animals who create art, engage in science, and produce grand mythologies that map the cosmos and set forth the roles each of us should play. But we are animals all the same.

To be divorced from our fleshly, bodily natures—not to see and hear the mad rush of a swollen river in the early spring or the smell of moist leaf litter in the autumn in the woods around us—is to be cut off from the vital tapsprings that make us who we are. We live and work in fixed-glass, temperature-controlled buildings sealed off from the natural world; we transport ourselves in fossil-fuel machines that require ever-widening incursions into undisturbed habitats; we eat processed food that has been genetically manipulated, irradiated, and then sealed in airtight packaging in order to preserve its interminable shelf life. We have replaced lives lived in sustainable harmony with the rhythms and vitalities of the natural order with soul-deadening, consumption-intensive lifestyles that leave us emotionally depleted and spiritually empty. We need untamed places to return us to our animal identities, and I am deeply grateful for the role the Crum Woods plays in my own return to the wildness within me.

The Crum Woods is a celebration of the natural amity that characterizes the human and the more-than-human spheres of existence. It is a place of scenic beauty, sensual delight, and spiritual sustenance. Like the ancient groundwater aquifers in the woods that are recharged by winter snows and spring rains, the depths of my own inner life are recharged by regular sojourns along the forested banks of the streams and tributaries that make up the watershed.

In addition to being a healing refuge for visitors to the woods such as myself, the Crum Woods also functions as an extraordinary outdoor classroom and laboratory for Swarthmore College faculty and students. I noted above in the Council of All Beings ritual the importance of the Crum watershed as an inspirational setting for my religious studies classes at Swarthmore. But other members of the college community rely on the woods as an irreplaceable teaching and research site as well. In particular, for faculty and students whose academic work is field-based, the Crum Woods is an unparalleled resource. A dozen or so Swarthmore faculty and hundreds of students each year journey into the Crum Creek area to perform hands-on field research in native ecosystems and animal behavior, temporarily gather animal and plant specimens for laboratory observations and experiments, collect stream water and soil samples for water quality and habitat analysis, and engage in drawing exercises and creative writing by using the woods as the subject matter for landscape painting, poetry, and other forms of art. At Swarthmore College, faculty and students get their hands dirty studying the actual living environments of trees, shrubs, insects, amphibians, reptiles, birds, and mammals. In recent years, biological and scientific inquiry has increasingly devoted itself to digital simulation of the natural world as a replacement for on-the-ground field research due to the increasing scarcity of functioning habitats and native ecosystems. The Crum Woods is a priceless treasure that enhances field-based education at Swarthmore by giving faculty and students access to an immeasurably rich, real-world learning environment.

The Crum Woods under Siege

There are few activities more exhilarating than swimming in a stream or lake in a mountainous or forested area. This past summer my children were tired of swimming in the sanitized confines of our town's municipal pool and wanted instead to take a dip in the Crum Creek. I knew the fish in the creek were not safe for eating, and I had also heard rumors that the water was not safe for swimming. But it was a warm, humid day, and the cool water of the creek seemed especially inviting. Christopher and Katy picked a soft bend in the river downstream from a small waterfall for their trip into the creek. They jumped into the water with the abandon of childhood, howling and screaming with delight as the cold dark water electrified their senses. Fearing the rumors I had heard about the creek's unsafe swimming conditions, I asked the kids not to put their faces into the water and to get out after a few minutes. Reluctantly, they did so, and we headed home from the creek area, renewed and refreshed.

I wanted to take the kids for another plunge into the river, but is the Crum Creek a safe swimming area? I wondered. Katy and Christopher were thrilled with their brief splash in the water, but I needed to find out more about the stream's water quality. It was hard to imagine that such an apparently healthy living environment could be polluted but I had my doubts and questions. To answer this question I contacted Swarthmore College's Environmental Laboratory and requested that the area where we had gone swimming be tested for pollution levels. Swarthmore College is a member of the Crum Creek Watershed Partnership, which is committed to protecting and improving the health of the Crum Woods ecosystem. The college and watershed partnership together monitor the well-being of this natural resource, and they graciously agreed to test our swimming area. To my sadness and disappointment, the results of the water quality testing were not good: the Crum Creek, at least in the area where Christopher and Katy entered the water, is a badly degraded stream with high levels of E. coli and other bacteria that make it an unsafe environment for fish consumption or drinking water. Indeed, according to the test results, it is also not a safe place for swimming.

Since this time I have become a volunteer water monitor with the Chester-Ridley-Crum Watersheds Association, another conservation agency determined to safeguard the health of the Crum ecosystem, and I have learned that not all of the Crum Creek watershed is a badly degraded area. For example, the upper portion of the creek at its headwaters is a high-quality, almost pristine waterway with low levels of pollution and diverse aquatic fish life and varied plant and animal life along its stream banks. Nevertheless, the lower watershed of the Crum Creek where I live and teach at Swarthmore College has been badly degraded by generations of residential and commercial development, threatening the ability of the lower watershed to support a healthy ecosystem of diverse plants and animals. A by-product of this degradation is poor water quality, rendering already my recollection of my children's splashing and frolicking in the Crum Creek a distant memory of a wonderful summer interlude now tainted by my current realization that the lower Crum Creek, as beautiful as it is, carries trace elements of dangerous toxins harmful to the health of all of us.

The many threats to the Crum Woods seem almost too numerous to mention.

Overall development pressures pose the largest perils to the integrity of the watershed. In the upper portion of the creek area, housing construction, shopping centers, office parks, and parking lots have fragmented natural habitats and increased the amount of paved areas, leading to storm water runoff problems. In the lower portion of the creek near Swarthmore College, continued institutional development by the college along the edges of the watershed has created the same sorts of problems. Ironically, while Swarthmore College has been a relatively benign caretaker of the woods near its campus for many generations, in recent years the college's growth pattern has made it a threat to the preservation of species and habitat in the lower Crum Creek. This troubling growth pattern entails cutting down edges of the forest preserve to open up space for college facilities. Since the 1960s new townhouses for faculty, expanded student dormitories, additions to existing academic buildings, new access roads, and construction of surface parking lots have shrunk the perimeter of the forest. A new proposal now under study by Swarthmore College focuses on the construction of a series of athletic fields, along with a span bridge for foot and light vehicular traffic, to be built across the breadth of the creek and surrounding forest.

These past and future uses of forest near the college campus raise troubling questions about the long-term health of the Crum Creek watershed. Within Delaware County, the suburban area that includes Swarthmore College just west of Philadelphia, the Crum Woods includes the last remaining old-growth forest in the county, with remaining strands of native trees and deep-woods habitat for threatened and endangered species of plants and animals. This wealth of wildlife habitat—including a southern red oak forest, spotted salamander breeding ponds, scarlet tanager nesting grounds, and migrating American eel populations, among others—relies on the protected forest interior to survive. Historically a good neighbor of the forest, Swarthmore College's institutional growth trajectory will further shrink the rich heartland of the forest that supports these and other plant and animal populations. By cutting into the woods, the college makes more compact the woodland core and thereby diminishes its strength and vitality. The shrinking of this deep-woods core makes forest-interior plant and animal life more vulnerable to temperature and weather changes and the invasion of exotic species.

Along with the construction of new facilities comes the inevitable growth of paved areas and rooftops that sends storm water streaming off of developed sites and into the Crum Creek watershed. Unfiltered storm water carries pollution that runs off oil-slicked roads and parking lots and pesticide-treated lawns on the Swarthmore College campus. While older sections of the college campus have not been retrofitted to treat storm water runoff at the site, new building construction at the college is now required by the local municipality to mitigate the impact of such runoff on-site. Along with treated effluent from wastewater plants and failed septic system discharges, untreated storm water runoff reduces the amount of clean water, which is needed to recharge underground aquifers, and it further degrades stream quality and wildlife habitats by sending toxins into the watershed.

The wooded open space managed by Swarthmore College in the lower watershed of the Crum Creek is a unique island of old-growth forest and protected habitat in an ocean of suburban sprawl and commercial development. Traditionally, the college has been a good steward of its portion of the watershed. But without an extensive plan for protecting the forest perimeter, and a comprehensive storm water management program, continued institutional growth on campus is at odds with the college's wildlife-friendly relationship to the lower Crum Creek. The Crum Woods is a premier research, teaching, and recreational site. It needs to be protected from further institutional encroachments and restored as a living and diverse ecosystem for the sake of the plants and animals that live there and for the education and enjoyment of future generations of Pennsylvania residents.

The Crum Woods as the Wounded Sacred

Degraded but still glorious, wounded but still alive—the Crum Creek watershed is an impaired wildlife area that continues to supply water, food, and other basic elements to the many communities, human and nonhuman, that flourish alongside and within its banks and streams. The Crum Creek suffers regular abuse from suburban storm water runoff, sewage discharges, dams and other stream impediments that create low flow conditions, and the cutting down of perimeter forest that supports interior habitat networks for threatened plants and animals. But to me the Crum Woods is a sacred place, a place where I am nourished and affirmed in my religious quest, a place where I find God.

Does it make sense to say that the Crum Woods is a sacred place?

Today our common discourse has expanded to make almost anything we do and believe in sacred. Special periods spent with our families are sacred time. The important responsibilities we assign to law enforcement officers or child care workers is a sacred trust. And almost anyplace we might venture—from a graveyard to a churchyard, from a memorable site in our childhood to a battlefield or even a football stadium—can be a candidate for a sacred place. But if anything or any place can be sacred, then what is not sacred? If the term is so elastic as to include virtually any activity or place we might imagine, then does the term any longer carry any meaningful significance?

I grant that to honor the Crum watershed as a sacred place appears, at first glance, to continue to expand the use of this term to include locales that might not obviously appear to be sacred sites. The Crum Creek is not a built religious structure like a church or a temple. It is not a time-honored legacy site such as a war memorial or historic battleground. It is not even a widely recognized natural place of extraordinary beauty and grandeur, such as the Grand Canyon or Yellowstone National Park. Nevertheless, the Crum watershed is a living system that supports an astonishing wealth of native wildlife, and insofar as it continues to function as a vital habitat for a variety of species and their young, it is a sacred place. Health and vitality are the highest ideals that make life on Mother Earth possible and worth living. Plant and animal well-being in harmony with natural systems is the supreme value that supports human and nonhuman flourishing on our fragile planet. A place where God especially dwells, a place that is sacred, is a place where nature subsists in harmony with diverse ecosystems. God as Spirit inhabits the biotic support systems on which all life depends, invigorating these systems with divine energy and compassion. The Crum Creek is not a pristine watershed; it will not win any virgin forest or clean water awards. But it is a site for the landed sacred, a place that God inhabits, because it is a small, and increasingly rare, patch of earth and river in harmony with itself that supports the well-being of its living inhabitants.

Wherever there are places left on earth where natural ecosystems are in balance with their surroundings, there is God's presence. God is the giver of life, the sustainer of all that is good, the benevolent power in the universe who ensures the health and vitality of all living things. The Crum Creek watershed—battered and degraded though it may be—continues to function as a balanced and self-sustaining network of life-giving habitat for plant, animal, and human well-being. The life-giving role the Crum Creek performs is divine in the truest sense of the word because it describes precisely the role God performs in and through the earth:

to give life, to make all beings come into fruition, to sustain the zest and vigor of creation. In this sense, the Crum Creek and God are one because they both are sources of life and health for earthen beings. To say, then, that the Crum watershed is a sacred place does not debase the meaning of the word "sacred" by designating just any such place as sacred or religious based on personal whim or fancy. On the contrary, to celebrate the Crum Woods as a sacred place is to drop to one's knees on the ground, and extends one's arms to the sky, in order to honor this place of God's indwelling as one of the remaining life-giving habitats on our planet that make our existence, indeed the existence of all of us, possible at all.

The Crum Woods is sacred, indeed, but the Crum Woods survives today as the *wounded sacred*.

In the previous chapter I discussed Bernard Buffet's painting *The Baptism of Christ* as an artistic portrayal of the wounded sacred. This painting depicts the Holy Spirit as a crucified bird stretched out in a cross-like manner with a bleeding gash mark in its upper breast. Like Jesus on the cross, the Spirit in Buffet's painting also endures agony and dies on behalf of a suffering world. I said that this portrayal has deep ecological implications: as Jesus suffered one time two thousand years ago on behalf of the whole human community in need of a savior, so also does the Spirit continually suffer today as God's presence on a planet that is enduring degradation of natural resources and rapid species extinction. The Spirit is the injured sacred, the enfleshed reality of the divine life who grieves over what may become a lost planet, at least for human habitation. As the Spirit is the bleeding, suffering God, so also is the body, so to speak, of the Spirit's worldly presence, the earth itself, the wounded sacred. Together in a common passion and common destiny, the Spirit of God and an earth scarred by human greed body forth the wounded sacred in our time.

From the perspective of green Christianity, the Crum Woods, a small fragment of aboriginal forest still functioning as a relatively hearty ecosystem on the edge of urban Philadelphia, is one of many surviving networks of life-giving habitat that show forth God's bounty and compassion in the earth. But the Crum Woods also displays God's suffering in our present time as well. As toxins from ruptured sewer lines and storm water leech into the creek, as the edges of the forest are cut down to make way for more suburban sprawl and commercial and institutional growth, God as Spirit experiences the loss and depredation of this delicate watershed in the depths of Godself. God is harmed by what we do. God is injured by the ways in which we despoil the natural systems that have supported life in many bioregions, including the Crum Woods, for tens of thousands of years. Spirit in love with the land—God in friendship with this small strip of Pennsylvania greenway—are codetermined, fellow sufferers in a unified effort to bring sustainable well-being to earth community. The Crum Woods is a small but important member of the Spirit's earthen body; as is all of creation, this forest fragment is part of the body of God's material presence. When the Crum Woods suffer, God suffers as well, reminding all of us to travel lightly on the earth as we participate in the evolution of particular ecosystems, including the evolution of this particular watershed.

Is the Crum Woods an Idol?

In traditional Christian thought only God is sacred. God alone is supremely absolute and sovereign over the whole created order. All other beings, while valuable as products of God's creative love and bearers of God's image, only have value and worth relative to God. God alone possesses absolute value as the ultimate source of life in the cosmos. The author and arbiter of life and death itself, God is the principal power in the universe who rules with authority, judgment, and compassion over all of the human and nonhuman subjects in God's care and domain. In this classically feudal picture of God's relationship to his creaturely vassals, sacredness belongs to God and God alone.

This feudal model of the God-world relationship has undergone serious modification in contemporary Christian thought. Nevertheless, it remains the regnant model in theology today. The dominance of this model is entirely understandable given the important theological images in the Bible and Christian liturgy that focus on God as Lord, King, Sovereign, Ruler, Monarch, and Judge. In Exodus Moses praises God for his greatness and majesty in destroying Israel's Egyptian enemies. In Joshua the Almighty is the God of Battles who prosecutes a holy war against the armies who occupy the promised land. In Kings and Chronicles God is the ruler who establishes and sustains theocratic monarchies and then destroys earthly kingdoms when their human rulers become unfaithful and corrupt. In the Gospels God is the Most High who punishes the wicked and rewards the righteous with eternal life in heavenly bliss. And in Revelation God is the Sovereign Lord, holy and true, who sits on a royal throne and avenges the blood of the martyrs in a paroxysm of religious violence. It should not come as a surprise that the feudal depiction of God as King has deep and lasting resonance in the Christian imagination today. This kingly depiction of the divine life speaks volumes about what properly can and cannot be said of God and what can and cannot be said of the earthly domain under God's charge. From a monarchical vantage point the biblical message is clear: God is sovereign, just, and good, and all of God's creaturely subjects—plants and trees, human beings and other beings, ocean, land, and sky—have value and goodness only derivatively in relation to the supreme life source of God in Godself.

A nuanced articulation of a modified feudal view of God and the world is put forth by John B. Cobb Jr. In many respects, Cobb, along with Joseph A. Sittler, is the father of Christian environmental theology. His 1972 book *Is it Too Late? A Theology of Ecology*, written in the wake of first-wave environmental awareness during the social justice movements of the 1960s, is a searching indictment of Christianity's complicity with ecological destruction and a visionary proposal for an earth-friendly theological agenda.[3] This pathbreaking book was followed by *For the Common Good: Redirecting the Economy toward Community, the Environment, and a Sustainable Future*, coauthored with Herman E. Daly, which further refines Cobb's ecological vision in dialogue with process philosophy, natural science, and holistic economics.[4] Cobb laments Christianity's myopic focus on the salvation of human beings to the exclusion of concern for the well-being of nonhuman plant and animal communities. This anthropocentric bias has blinded Christianity to the degradation of the biosphere and the cry of animal suffering that defines human history. A new vision of Christianity in harmony with nature is the demand of our time.

Cobb's move to a thoroughgoing green Christianity in harmony with a deep ecology sensibility would seem to be the natural trajectory of his thought. And in many important respects, Cobb does share certain fundamental assumptions with deep ecology. Like deep ecologists, Cobb argues for a basic revaluation of nature as a bearer of intrinsic and not simply instrumental value: nature is worthwhile in and for itself and is not merely an extension of human need and utility. Likewise, all beings, including and especially human beings, are radically and mutually interdependent on natural systems: to wantonly destroy plant and animal life is to threaten and diminish the life quality and well-being of all of us, human and nonhuman alike.

But in spite of these basic areas of agreement, Cobb also carefully distinguishes his project from that of deep ecology. In particular, Cobb, while investing nature with spiritual power and sacramental meaning, disagrees with the tendency in religious deep ecology to honor nature as sacred in itself. While God is in the world and benevolent toward creation, God alone is sacred. It is a dangerous misnomer, even blasphemous, to confuse the Creator and the creation and to venerate the earth as sacred along with God. In a word, God alone is holy. Cobb writes:

> Nevertheless, [the sacredness of all creatures] language is, from a historic Protestant perspective, dangerously misleading. Speaking rigorously, the line between the sacred and the profane is better drawn between God and creatures. To place any creatures on the sacred side of the line is to be in danger of idolatry. For many Protestants . . . the right way to speak is incarnational, immanental, or sacramental. God is present in the world—in every creature. But no creature is divine. Every creature has intrinsic value, but to call it sacred is in danger of attributing to it absolute value. That is wrong.[5]

Cobb's case against religious deep ecology is twofold. First, Cobb's objection is theological: deep ecology blurs the line of distinction needed to separate beings of relative value from the divine being itself, the bearer of absolute value. Unless theology polices the borderland that divides creation and Creator, there is the danger that religious faith will slip into the worship of a false divinity, an idol. Idolatry for Cobb is the confusion of realms of reality that need to be kept apart. Cobb's theology operates within a binary, either-or logical field: one worships either God or nature but not both. One should worship God alone as sacred. While nature is charged with God's presence, nature itself is not a divine reality alongside or internal to God that is the right object of our devotion and worship. To call the created order sacred is dangerous and idolatrous: it is to deify and revere the earth as equal in worth and value to God. To do this is to displace God's unique role as humankind's proper object of worship.

Second, Cobb's objection to Christian deep ecology is practical: unless one can refer to a being of absolute, transcendent value, judgments of relative value are impossible to make. If all beings—everything from megafauna such as human beings and blue whales to microflora such as mold spores and green algae—are sacred, if everything is equal in value and worth, then on what basis can decisions be made about what should be saved and protected and what can be used and destroyed? Without some hierarchical system that grades the relative value of different life-forms, there is no coherent foundation on which to base preservation of species, resource allocations, food production, biomedical research, and so forth. Cobb writes that one "cannot give up the affirmation of gradations of value. All creatures have intrinsic value, but some have greater intrinsic value than others. That is to say, the inner life of some creatures is more complex, deeper, and richer than that of others."[6] For Cobb, God alone is sacred and the highest expression of absolute value; after God, human beings follow God in this ordering hierarchy as centers of complex rationality and rich experience; after humans, other communities of animals and plants are graded according to the depths of their cognitive functions and range of feelings and abilities. Without this sort of pecking order, moral decision making is impossible. For Cobb, extreme green spirituality is well-meaning but wrongheaded. By affirming the sacredness of all creation, religious deep ecology plunges us into a night in which all things are black and there is no way to distinguish between which use patterns are healthy and sustainable and which are not.[7]

What Cobb neglects in his critique of religious deep ecology is sustained attention to the privileged role of the predator-prey relationship in deep ecological understandings of the life cycle. In this model, value is inherent in the vitality of the food web, the natural life process of biocommunal eating and being eaten; it is not a characteristic of this or that life-form over and against other life-forms. The task of Christian earth healing would be to ensure, therefore, the health and dynamism of the life cycle rather than protect the interests of added-value beings (such as human beings) whose inner life is more complex than other beings. Thus green spirituality is able to make highly nuanced and sophisticated *practical* judgments about use and value, but it does so in biocentric rather than anthropocentric terms. Such judgments are made not in relation to the putative supreme value of human beings but on the basis of maintaining healthy predator-prey relationships within the food web. All energy in the natural world is obtained and transmitted through a series of predatory and mutualistic relationships among different and interconnected living things. Aldo Leopold, the Wisconsin conservationist whose thought we briefly looked at in chapter 4, alternately refers to this flow of energy according to highly organized systems of biotic relationships as the food chain, the energy cycle, or the land pyramid:

Plants absorb energy from the sun. This energy flows through a circuit called the biota, which may be represented by a pyramid consisting of layers. The bottom layer is the soil. A plant layer rests on the soil, an insect layer on the plants, a bird and rodent layer on the insects, and so on up through various animal groups to the apex layer, which consists of the larger carnivores.

The lines of dependency for food and other services are called food chains. Thus soil-oak-deer-Indian is a chain that has now been largely converted to soil-corn-cow-farmer. Each species, including ourselves, is a link in many chains. The deer eats a hundred plants other than oak, and the cow a hundred plants other than corn. Both, then, are links in a hundred chains. The pyramid is a tangle of chains so complex as to seem disorderly, yet the stability of the system proves it to be a highly organized structure. Its functioning depends on the co-operation and competition of its diverse parts.[8]

The basic idea is that the sun provides food or energy for microorganisms in soil and water, which correspondingly provide energy for insects and smaller plants and animals; in turn, these life-forms feed the family of larger animals, of which human beings are one among many members, until death and decay again return unexpended energy to soil and water. This energy circuit is a continuous flow pattern that makes life possible. In the one case the sun furnishes energy for pond algae to grow, which then feed minnows which then become food for trout which bears then eat for their sustenance. In another case energy from the sun is absorbed by the soil and the grains that depend on it, which in turn feed cattle, which then become food for human beings.

Green spirituality can learn a lot from conservation biology about the food web. Scientifically speaking, in the natural order, everyone is food for everyone else. Human beings, for example, both eat and then are eaten by fungi, bacteria, and often insects and other anthropods as well. Everyone is predator and prey in relation to other living things. All of us, from the smallest bug to the largest carnivore, rely on this complicated flow mechanism for our daily bread. Moreover, all beings play an equal and vital role in maintaining the integrity of the energy cycle; no one member of this integrated plant and animal community is any more important in sustaining the cycle than any other member. Theologically speaking, then, judgments about value should be based on keeping open the living channels of energy that make life possible. This is the point Leopold makes in his general maxim for a land ethic: "A thing is right when it tends to preserve the integrity, stability, and beauty of the biotic community. It is wrong when it tends otherwise."[9] Value accrues to the health and vitality of the food web; it is not a property of particular organisms—more complex creatures do not get more intrinsic value than less complex creatures.

Contrary to Cobb's emphasis on subjective experience as the criterion for making comparative judgments about value, the food-web model makes clear that value inheres in the integrity and well-being of the web itself. Correspondingly, practical decisions about resource allocations and the like should focus on ensuring the dynamism and vitality of the energy cycle, not on the particular needs of individual participants within the cycle, including the needs of individual human participants. As humans, we should see ourselves as equal citizens of the biotic order, rather than as overlords of creation who possess more value than other beings. Some critics regard this subordination of human concerns to the welfare of the whole as a type of misanthropic thinking, even a kind of ecofascism in which human interests are now located in (or subordinated to) the wider orbit of ecosystemic interests. But, as we saw earlier in the discussion of Enlightenment humanism, the point is not that human happiness is unimportant in green systems thinking but rather that, without the well-being of the whole as the paramount concern, attention to human needs and interests is not possible. To put the point bluntly, if the worldwide system of energy flow patterns collapses due to ecocatastrophe of our own making, then our discussions about whether human beings have more value than other beings will seem academic at best and, at worst, contributory to the very mind-set that gave rise to the collapse in the first place.

In green spirituality, the warp and woof of everyday natural life is sacred. All life is sacred because the earth is a natural system, alive with God's presence, that supports the well-being of all created things. God's gift to all beings is this highly complex, biologically diverse earth where life itself is celebrated in all its fecundity and passion. Sacredness inheres in the God-given capacity of native plants and animals to stock and replenish the food web on which we all depend. Value inheres in the dynamism and elasticity of the energy cycle that makes our human lives and the lives of other created beings endlessly rich and potent with new possibilities. God as Spirit is the green force in the earth who animates the living food chains that make possible the flow of energy for all of us.

It is not blasphemous, therefore, to say that nature is sacred. It is not wrong to find God's presence in all things. It is not idolatry to enjoy the Crum Creek, degraded though it may be, as a sacred place that plays a crucial role in maintaining the health and well-being of humankind and otherkind in eastern Pennsylvania. God as Spirit is the gift of life to all creation, and where life is birthed and cared for, there God is present, and there God is to be celebrated. God is holy, and by extension all that God has made participates in that holiness. Thus, when we labor to protect and nurture the good creation God has made, we invest all things with inherent, supreme value as a loving extension of God's bounty and compassion.

My Return to the River

As I close this book I am fresh from a six-month sabbatical spent with my family in a mountain village in rural Costa Rica called Monteverde ("green mountain"). Monteverde was founded by a group of North American Quakers who left the United States in 1949–50 because they opposed the military mind-set and consumer values that were becoming increasingly prevalent in American culture. Some of the young men in this community had been arrested and sentenced to yearlong prison terms for refusing out of conscience to register for the draft to supply troops for the Korean War. After serving their prison time these men and their families emigrated to Costa Rica to start a new life. Costa Rica had just abolished its military at the time of this immigration and it provided a hospitable home environment for the Quaker settlers. The Quakers that Ellen, Katy, Christopher, and I lived with this past year have dedicated themselves to living in peace with their Costa Rican neighbors and to living sustainably in the midst of the spectacular cathedral rain forest that surrounds their mountain home.

I have many enduring memories of my time in the tropics, but my favorite is a hike my family and I took one morning to a breathtaking waterfall in the Monteverde Cloud Forest. Hidden away in the remote highlands of Costa Rica, I felt I was reentering the Garden of Eden. Butterflies were everywhere. Full-hand-sized brilliant morpho butterflies flashed iridescent blue along our path; see-through glasswing butterflies that transparently refract the light of the sun flitted by along our way. We stopped at the river en route to the waterfall and took a long draft of mountain refreshment. We picked and ate wild oranges; their tart flavor had a zesty kick we were not used to in the States. We found large woody vines hanging from a giant strangler fig tree and we swung on the vines through the forest Tarzan-like. As we climbed the path to the cascade, black vultures and swallow-tailed kites swooped down overhead, seeming to announce our arrival into the forest. Suddenly, a small band of white-faced monkeys bounded into view, almost flying, it seemed, from treetop to treetop, using their prehensile tails to grab tree limbs, chatting loudly with other members of their group, reaching into this or that branch for something good to eat. The white-faced monkeys are called "Capuchins" because they look like little versions of the medieval monks who wore black robes with white cowls. The monkeys' human-like pink-fleshed faces, intense with an amazing range of expressions and emotions, are framed by white fur around their faces and shoulders and then topped off by black skullcaps: primates with yarmulkes.

When we reached the Monteverde waterfall we stood in amazement at the sight. We howled at the spectacular display: a torrent of water cascading down through an earthen vault climbing hundreds of feet into the air. At the mouth of the vault above, brightly colored birds, clouds, and mist swirled, obscuring the view of the waters' initial descent; but down below where we stood, the warm sun fully illuminated the clear water in the pool at the base of the cascade, inviting us in for a swim. The cold mountain water felt good against our hot skin. Ellen and I played games of hide-and-seek with Katy and Christopher amid the large rocks nestled in the river; we ate avocado sandwiches and drank deeply from the river water at our feet. Wanting to be alone, I swam downriver by myself. A spiny lizard, its pebbly skin mottled in green and brown, was basking on a rock in the midday sun. I was startled by the bubbling song of a mountain wren, singing loudly as she defended what I then discovered to be her territory—she had built a small nest in the nook of a low cliff face along the water's edge. Singing loudly and flying rapidly back and forth from the nest area, I watched her frantic movements for a few moments and then slid back into the water, happy that I did not have to disrupt further this bird's normal caregiving routine with her young.

It is difficult for me to describe the spiritual emotions and sensual delights I felt entering this sacred place high in the cloud forests of Costa Rica. Spirit and earth, God and nature felt one to me in the bracing spray of the waterfall overhead and the river all around me. I felt the erotic passion of the Spirit's love for this place and all other places she has made and sustained; I felt God's greening, earthen presence pulsing through the glassy water, dense foliage, and sheltering animal life that surrounded me. Once more, I was reminded of my childhood swims in the Singing River. In the Singing River I heard God's moral voice in the music of the river calling me to live a life in peace and benevolence toward others. In this different—but also the same—river experience in Costa Rica, I encountered again the green face of God. In the tropical high country the Spirit was summoning me to recover the lost innocence I felt as a child toward the river God who moved through the watershed that sustained the Pascagoula and Biloxi for generations. Down in the river in Monteverde I felt I was recovering a religious naïveté toward nature, a childlike innocence toward the world—not the same naïveté I felt in the Singing River years ago, but a second naïveté, an adult innocence, won in my middle years through a faith tempered by grown-up experience but still rooted in my hope to live in the fullness of primal childhood openness.

Something else happened in the Monteverde forest as well.

I not only sensed I was back again in the Singing River, but I also experienced swimming in the river as a renewal of my baptism as an infant. Like a baby in the baptismal font, but now under the roar of this awesome waterfall, I felt I was being bathed again in the ocean of God's benevolence and love. As is the case in Christian faith, water symbolism is crucial in the experience of the world's varied religious traditions. Native Americans pour water over fire-heated rocks to release sacred powers in traditional earthen sweat lodges. Muslims perform *tahara* by washing their heads, hands, and feet before entering a mosque. Jewish women, and sometimes men, ritually immerse themselves in a ritual bath or mikvah for purification purposes. In Buddhist funerals water is poured out of a bowl symbolizing the return of the soul to its original source. And the Ganges River, Mother Ganges, is a sacred river that purifies all followers of God, and makes possible the attainment of enlightenment, in the practice of Hinduism. As with Christian faith, water plays a central role in world religious expression as the primal element that washes away any signs of impurity or defilement and offers life-giving energy for persons and communities seeking a closer relationship with the sacred.

Christian baptism stands in this long lineage of water-based practices that cleanse and restore a person in order to prepare her to enjoy the presence of God. In most churches today baptism is a sacrament—a means of grace by which God's love is made real within the community of believers. It signifies the forgiveness of sins and full membership in the family of God. It is a sacrament of memory by which the healing power of Jesus' original baptism is reactualized in a contemporary setting. It is a ritual of remembrance by which the renewing energy experienced by Jesus in his own baptism two millennia ago is felt again by the believer who goes into the water and then resurfaces again in newness of life. Most important, baptism is a regenerating practice that promises a new life—a fresh and clean, spanking-new mode of existence—for the initiate who is bathed in the healing energies of this sacrament.

I experienced swimming in this Edenic garden as a type of sacramental reawakening, a sort of little baptism that allowed me to experience again the grace and forgiveness I enjoyed at the Presbyterian church in Southern California where I was first baptized as an infant. But for any sacrament to be effective—including water baptism—there must be a special union between God's word and natural elements. In the case of the Eucharist, those elements are wine and bread; in the case of baptism, the element is water. Without water there can be no baptism—there can be no special means by which children and adults experience the cleansing, renewing power of God's grace. My wading and swimming in the Monteverde waterfall deeply enriched my original experience of baptism. I was grateful for this experience, but I was also reminded of how fragile and ephemeral sacred places such as this river have become in an increasingly tenuous and often degraded biosphere. Like so many other riverine habitats, if the area around this Costa Rican waterfall had been developed for industrial or commercial purposes, or the waters upriver of the cascade had been dammed, would I have been able to enjoy this baptismal renewal? More than fifty years ago a small group of expatriated North American Quakers and local Monteverde townspeople got together to preserve this waterfall and its surrounding environs. My little baptism was made possible by the farsighted vision of people who recognized this ancient river and its supporting headwaters to be a vital ecological resource worthy of preservation for future generations. By doing the right thing, by keeping this river wild and free as a common good, these early river keepers indirectly gave me an extraordinary gift: a powerfully sensual and deeply restorative experience that reactualized the grace and love promised to me in my baptism as an infant.

Now I am back in eastern Pennsylvania and I think to myself, I am happy to be alive in this place where God is also present. Sacred is the ground I stand on; holy is the earth where I am planted. The world is the abode of God, the dwelling place of life-giving Spirit. God is not a dispassionate and distant potentate who exercises dominion over the universe from some far-removed place. Rather, in and through this planet that is our common home, God is earnestly working with us to heal the earth, but God also suffers deeply from the agony of this unlifted burden. The earthen Spirit who infuses all things with her benevolent presence is also the wounded Spirit who implores us, in groans too deep for words, to practice heartfelt sustainable living in harmony with the natural world around us. We can do this and I hope that it is not too late for us to do so. In the warmth of the sun, the shelter of the encircling sky, the strength of the great oceans, and the fecundity of the good land, we have everything we need to recover our kinship with Spirit and earth here and now.

Notes

Introduction

1. The story is told in music composed by Josie Gautier, *The Singing River: The Mysterious Music of the Pascagoula* (Gautier, MS: Singing River Originals, 1952).

2. On one level the story of the Pascagoula's mass death is an ugly story. Unless put into context, it seems to counsel group suicide as an answer to intractable social problems. While sensitive to its disturbing implications, I understood the story then, and again now, as an irreducible tragedy—as a survival tale, oddly enough, about how one group of people, in order to prevent certain disaster for themselves and another group, were forced into a course of action that was strangely moral and immoral as well. Like Simone Weil, the French mystic who likely starved herself during World War II as an expression of solidarity with deprived Allied troops on the front lines of the war, or like the Buddhist monks in the 1960s who publicly immolated themselves in protest of the American war in Vietnam, this Gulf Coast native community sought to break the cycle of violence that surrounded them by putting themselves in harm's way. Be this as it may, this story is fundamentally irredeemable in certain respects. Daniel T. Spencer, partly relying on religious ecofeminists' criticism of self-sacrifice as a warped male ideal used to justify the need for self-denial among women and minority persons, writes that it is deeply troubling to emphasize "self-sacrificial love as imaging the divine in the incarnation with no reference to the social consequences of this teaching for historically marginalized groups, particularly women and people of color" (*Gay and Gaia: Ethics, Ecology, and the Erotic* [Cleveland: Pilgrim Press, 1996], 154). I have always been troubled by what is said to have happened on the banks of the Singing River. While I agree with Spencer and others that sacrifice is not the royal road to authentic religion because it is a dangerous and unhealthy model for persons who have been told to value others more than themselves, I do think such extreme action is understandable, if not justifiable, on rare occasions and under certain severe social conditions when exceptional human communities are stretched to their breaking points and possess no other options.

3. See the expressions of Christian spirituality based in nature in Sallie McFague, *Super, Natural Christians: How We Should Love Nature* (Minneapolis: Fortress Press, 1997); James Nash, *Loving Nature: Ecological Integrity and Christian Responsibility* (Nashville: Abingdon, 1991); and Rosemary Radford Ruether, *Gaia and God: An Ecofeminist Theology of Earth Healing* (San Francisco: HarperSanFrancisco, 1992).

4. See Niles Eldredge, *Life in the Balance: Humanity and the Biodiversity Crisis* (Princeton, NJ: Princeton University Press, 1998). For an overview of the environmental crisis see Leslie Roberts et al., *World Resources 1998–99: A Guide to the Global Environment* (New York: Oxford University Press, 1998), and Jeremy Rifkin, *Biosphere Politics: A Cultural Odyssey from the Middle Ages to the New Age* (San Francisco: HarperSanFrancisco, 1991). See Lynn White Jr., "The Historic Roots of Our Ecological Crisis," *Science* 155 (1967): 1203–07, for a seminal discussion of Christianity's complicity with modern environmental degradation.

5. See Dieter T. Hessel and Rosemary Radford Ruether, *Christianity and Ecology: Seeking the Well-Being of Earth and Humans* (Cambridge: Harvard University Press, 2000). This lavish collection of articles with extensive bibliography is the best compendium of contemporary green spirituality currently available.

6. On the history of the tension in Christianity between Earth-God and Sky-God religion, see Steven Bouma-Prediger, *For the Beauty of the Earth: A Christian Vision for Creation Care* (Grand Rapids, MI: Baker Academic, 2001); H. Paul Santmire, *The Travail of Nature: The Ambiguous Ecological Promise of Christian Theology*, Theology and the Sciences (Philadelphia: Fortress Press, 1985); and Max Oelschlaeger, *Caring for Creation: An Ecumenical Approach to the Environmental Crisis* (New Haven: Yale University Press, 1994).

7. A lack of experience in and understanding of the Spirit in our time may be changing, however, in light of the numerous works on the Spirit in recent years from a variety of disciplinary perspectives. Many of these works have been essential to my own thinking about the Spirit in nature in writing this book. In theology, see José Comblin, *The Holy Spirit and Liberation*, trans. Paul Burns (Maryknoll, NY: Orbis Books, 1989); Peter C. Hodgson, *Winds of the Spirit: A Constructive Christian Theology* (Louisville: Westminster John Knox, 1994); Adolf Holl, *The Left Hand of God: A Biography of the Holy Spirit*, trans. John Cullen (New York: Doubleday, 1998); Chung Hyun-Kyung, "Welcome the Spirit; Hear Her Cries: The Holy Spirit, Creation, and the Culture of Life," *Christianity and Crisis* 51 (July 15, 1991): 220–23; Elizabeth A. Johnson, *She Who Is: The Mystery of God in Feminist Theological Discourse* (New York: Crossroad, 1992); idem, *Friends of God and Prophets: A Feminist Theological Reading of the Communion of Saints* (New York: Continuum, 1998); Catherine Keller, *Apocalypse Now and Then: A Feminist Guide to the End of the World* (Boston: Beacon Press, 1996); idem, *Face of the Deep: A Theology of Becoming* (London: Routledge, 2003); Veli-Matti Kärkkäinen, *Pneumatology: The Holy Spirit in Ecumenical, International, and Contextual Perspective* (Grand Rapids, MI: Baker Academic, 2002); Jürgen Moltmann, *God in Creation: A New Theology of Creation and the Spirit of God*, trans. Margaret Kohl (Minneapolis: Fortress Press, 1993); idem, *The Spirit of Life: A Universal Affirmation*, trans. Margaret Kohl (Minneapolis: Fortress Press, 1992); idem, *The Source of Life: The Holy Spirit and the Theology of Life*, trans. Margaret Kohl (Minneapolis: Fortress Press, 1997); Geiko Müller-Fahrenholz, *God's Spirit: Transforming a World in Crisis*, trans. John Cumming (New York: Continuum, 1995); Nancy Victorin-

Vangerud, *The Raging Hearth: Spirit in the Household of God* (St. Louis: Chalice Press, 2000); Mark I. Wallace, *Fragments of the Spirit: Nature,Violence, and the Renewal of Creation* (Harrisburg, PA: Trinity Press International, 2002); and Michael Welker, *God the Spirit*, trans. John F. Hoffmeyer (Minneapolis: Fortress Press, 1994). In philosophy, see Jacques Derrida, *Of Spirit: Heidegger and the Question*, trans. Geoffrey Bennington and Rachel Bowlby (Chicago: University of Chicago Press, 1989); idem, *Specters of Marx: The State of the Debt, the Work of Mourning, and the New International*, trans. Peggy Kampf (New York: Routledge, 1994); and Steven G. Smith, *The Concept of the Spiritual: An Essay in First Philosophy* (Philadelphia: Temple University Press, 1988). In cultural studies, see Joel Kovel, *History and Spirit: An Inquiry into the Philosophy of Liberation* (Boston: Beacon Press, 1991).

8. The literature on the question of the value hierarchy concerning spirit and matter is extensive. See, for example, Caroline Walker Bynum, *Fragmentation and Redemption: Essays on Gender and the Human Body in Medieval Religion* (New York: Zone, 1991); Susan Griffin, *Woman and Nature: The Roaring inside Her* (New York: Harper & Row, 1978); Mark Johnson, *The Body in the Mind: The Bodily Basis of Meaning, Imagination, and Reason* (Chicago: University of Chicago Press, 1987); and William R. LaFleur, "Body," in *Critical Terms for Religious Studies*, ed. Mark C. Taylor (Chicago: University of Chicago Press, 1998), 36–54.

9. The hope for a recovery of Christian love and passion for flesh and the body is to go back to the future, to retrieve the Bible's fecund earth symbols for God as the beginning of a new ecological Christianity. Deep strains within Christian spirituality are marked by indifference (or even hostility) to "this world" in favor of "the world to come." But not all Christian thinkers have suffered from this debilitating dualism. In the thirteenth century CE, St. Francis of Assisi celebrated the four cardinal elements, along with human beings and animal beings, as members of the same cosmic family parented by a caring creator God. St. Francis's poetry is suffused with biophilic earth imagery. "Be praised my lord for Brother Wind and for the air and cloudy days/ Be praised my lord for Sister Water because she shows great use and humbleness in herself and preciousness and depth/ Be praised my lord for Brother Fire through whom you light all nights upon the earth/ Be praised my lord because our sister Mother Earth sustains and rules us and raises food to feed us" (St. Francis of Assisi, "Be Praised My Lord with All Your Creatures," in *Earth Prayers: From Around the World*, ed. Elizabeth Roberts and Elias Amidon [San Francisco: HarperSanFrancisco, 1991], 226–27).

10. See this discussion in Comblin, *The Holy Spirit and Liberation*, 39, and Kärkkäinen, *Pneumatology*, 164–70.

11. On the history of Syriac feminine language and imagery for the Spirit, see Susan Ashbrook Harvey, "Feminine Imagery for the Divine: The Holy Spirit, the Odes of Solomon, and Early Syriac Tradition," *Saint Vladimir's Theological Quarterly* 37 (1993): 111–40.

12. For studies of reader response theory, the notion that literary meaning occurs in the space between reader and text, see, in comparative literature studies, Hans-Georg Gadamer, *Truth and Method*, trans. Garret Barden and John Cumming (New York: Continuum, 1975), and Hans-Robert Jauss, *Toward an Aesthetic of Reception*, trans. Timothy Bahti (Minneapolis: University of Minnesota Press, 1982); in biblical studies, see Mark I. Wallace, *The Second Naiveté: Barth, Ricoeur, and the New Yale Theology* (Macon, GA: Mercer University Press, 1990).

13. For recent works that interpret the Bible from a green perspective, see Ian Bradley, *God Is Green: Ecology for Christians* (New York: Doubleday, Image Books, 1990), Norman C. Habel, ed., *Readings from the Perspective of Earth*, The Earth Bible, vol. 1 (Cleveland: Pilgrim, 2001), and Matthew Scully, *Dominion: The Power of Man, the Suffering of Animals, and the Call to Mercy* (New York: St. Martin's, 2002).

14. See Margot Adler, *Drawing Down the Moon: Witches, Druids, Goddess-Worshippers, and Other Pagans in America Today*, rev. ed. (Boston: Beacon Press, 1997); Helen A. Berger, *A Community of Witches: Contemporary Neo-Paganism and Witchcraft in the United States* (Columbia: University of South Carolina Press, 1999); Graham Harvey, *Contemporary Paganism: Listening People, Speaking Earth* (New York: New York University Press, 1997); and Starhawk, *The Spiral Dance* (New York: Harper & Row, 1979).

15. Carl E. Braaten, "The Gospel for a Neopagan Culture," in *Either/Or: The Gospel or Neopaganism*, ed. Carl E. Braaten and Robert W. Jenson (Grand Rapids, MI: Eerdmans, 1995), 7.

16. Loretta Orion, *Never Again the Burning Times: Paganism Revived* (Prospect Heights, IL: Waveland, 1995), 226.

17. See David Abram, *The Spell of the Sensuous: Perception and Language in a More-Than-Human World* (New York: Pantheon, 1996); Bill Devall and George Sessions, eds., *Deep Ecology: Living as if Nature Mattered* (Salt Lake City: Peregrine Smith, 1985); and Roger S. Gottlieb and David Landis Barnhill, eds., *Deep Ecology and World Religions: New Essays on Sacred Ground* (Albany: State University of New York Press, 2001).

18. It is not an understatement to say that many Christian thinkers, including Christian environmental thinkers, are not happy with deep ecology's understanding of this radically intimate God-nature-human relationship because, among other reasons, it undermines the special (putatively biblical) stewardship role human beings are to perform in relation to the natural world. One commentator writes that well-known theologian "Loren Wilkinson argues that any proper understanding of Christian stewardship necessarily implies that humans are different from the rest of creation. While they may be the source of our ecological problem, they are also special creations of God and have distinct stewardship responsibilities. By no means should we think they may be conflated with the rest of nature" (Robert Booth Fowler, *The Greening of Protestant Thought* [Chapel Hill: University of North Carolina Press, 1995], 78). While generally cautious about the notion of stewardship, Peter Scott

labels deep ecology authoritarian because it posits a strict identity between God, nature, and humankind that effaces their important differences (see *A Political Theology of Nature* [Cambridge: Cambridge University Press, 2003], 63–88). On the history of Christian exceptionalist (stewardship) thinking regarding nature and the historic theological importance of policing the boundaries between humankind and otherkind, see Paul Waldau, *The Specter of Speciesism: Buddhist and Christian Views of Animals* (Oxford: Oxford University Press, 2002), 157–218.

Chapter One: God Is Green

1. See "Pascagoula River Basin: Paradise in Peril," *Sun Herald*, November 16, 2003.

2. Larry L. Rasmussen, *Earth Community, Earth Ethics* (Maryknoll, NY: Orbis Books, 1996), 5–14.

3. Sallie McFague, *Models of God: Theology for an Ecological, Nuclear Age* (Philadelphia: Fortress Press, 1987), 59–87.

4. Lynn White Jr., "The Historic Roots of Our Ecological Crisis," *Science* 155 (1967): 1203–7.

5. Ibid., 1205.

6. On Jung's position concerning the spiritual origins of alcoholism, see Ernest Kurtz, "Twelve Step Programs," in *Spirituality and the Secular Quest*, ed. Peter H. Van Ness (New York: Crossroad, 1996), 277–302.

7. The classical articulations of the "bondage of the will" are Augustine, "The Spirit and the Letter," in *Augustine: Later Works*, trans. and ed. John Burnaby, Library of Christian Classics (Philadelphia: Westminster Press, 1955), and Martin Luther, *The Bondage of the Will*, trans. Henry Cole (Grand Rapids, MI: Baker, 1976).

8. In this regard, the role of market-driven media in shaping public perceptions of nature is critical. A quick perusal of most magazines at any local supermarket will reveal a rash of clever advertisements by major industrial firms touting their environmental credentials. Is it really credible, as one global oil company contends in its advertisements, that offshore drilling platforms are environmentally benign habitat enclosures for a variety of sea creatures? On the use and abuse of nature in global media, see Susan G. Davis, "Touch the Magic," in *Uncommon Ground: Rethinking the Human Place in Nature*, ed. William Cronon (New York: Norton, 1995), 204–17; Judith Williams, *Decoding Advertisements: Ideology and Meaning in Advertising* (New York: Marion Byars, 1984); and Raymond Williams, "Ideas of Nature," in *Problems in Materialism and Culture* (London: Verso, 1980).

9. In this vein let me make a stylistic comment about writing the Spirit. Throughout this book I will capitalize "Spirit" in order to distinguish the divine personality (Holy Spirit or Spirit of the Lord) from other similar spirit-term significations (spirit of the times, public spirit, and so forth). Nevertheless, I suggest that the realities of Spirit and spirit should often be viewed

as active on the same continuum, as when, for example, the *Spirit of God* empowers the embattled *spirit* of an urban community to resist the forces of ecocidal oppression (as I will suggest in a later chapter in my discussion of Chester, Pennsylvania).

10. This definition is from the entry "spiritus" by Richard A. Muller, *Dictionary of Latin and Greek Theological Terms* (Grand Rapids, MI: Baker, 1985), 286.

11. The literature on this question is extensive. See, for example, Caroline Walker Bynum, *Fragmentation and Redemption: Essays on Gender and the Human Body in Medieval Religion* (New York: Zone, 1991); Susan Griffin, *Woman and Nature:The Roaring inside Her* (New York: Harper & Row, 1978); Mark Johnson, *The Body in the Mind:The Bodily Basis of Meaning, Imagination, and Reason* (Chicago: University of Chicago Press, 1987); and William R. LaFleur, "Body," in *Critical Terms for Religious Studies*, ed. Mark C. Taylor (Chicago: University of Chicago Press, 1998), 36–54.

12. Plato, *Timaeus* 42–49, 89–92.

13. Peter Brown, *The Body and Society: Men,Women, and Sexual Renunciation in Early Christianity* (New York: Columbia University Press, 1988), 160–89.

14. Augustine, *The Confessions* 7–8. Also see Peter Brown, *Augustine of Hippo* (Berkeley: University of California Press, 1969), 158–81, 340–97, and Elaine Pagels, *Adam, Eve, and the Serpent* (New York: Random House, 1988), 98–154.

15. On Paul's anthropology, see J. Christiaan Beker, *Paul the Apostle:The Triumph of God in Life and Thought* (Philadelphia: Fortress Press, 1980), 213–302.

Chapter Two: The Mother Bird God

1. Basil of Caesarea, *De Spiritu Sancto* bk. 16.

2. Augustine, *De Trinitate* bk. 15.

3. Ibid., bk. 15, 37 (xix).

4. For reproductions and commentary, see Jeffrey F. Hamburger, *The Rothschild Canticles:Art and Mysticism in Flanders and the Rhineland circa 1300* (New Haven:Yale University Press, 1990), 118–42. I am grateful to Ellen Ross for directing my attention to this volume.

5. *Perichoresis* is the doctrine that teaches the coinherence of each member of the Trinity in the other. For a fuller discussion of this term and its relevance to contemporary theology, see Catherine Mowry LaCugna, *God for Us:The Trinity and Christian Life* (San Francisco: HarperSanFrancisco, 1991), 270–78. See the contemporary articulation of the relational interdependence of the trinitarian members from an earth-centered perspective in Jay B. McDaniel, *Earth, Sky, Gods and Mortals:A Theology of Ecology for the 21st Century* (Mystic, CT:Twenty-Third Publications, 1990), 149–51.

6. For reproductions of and commentary on Father Giuliani's nativist trinitarian art, contact Bridge Building Images, Inc., P.O. Box 1048, Burlington,VT 05402: telephone 800-325-6263: Web site www.bridgebuilding.com.

7. Luce Irigaray, "Divine Women," in *Sexes and Genealogies*, trans. Gillian C. Gill (New York: Columbia University Press, 1993), 57.

8. Frederick Charles Copleston, *Greece and Rome*, vol. 1 of *A History of Philosophy* (Garden City, NY: Image, 1962), 29–97.

9. Irigaray, "Divine Women," 63–64.

10. Ibid., 67.

11. Ibid.

12. Ibid., 61–63.

13. On the history of Syriac feminine language and imagery for the Spirit, see Susan Ashbrook Harvey, "Feminine Imagery for the Divine: The Holy Spirit, the Odes of Solomon, and Early Syriac Tradition," *Saint Vladimir's Theological Quarterly* 37 (1993): 111–40; quote here is from pp. 115–16. Also regarding feminine language for the Spirit, see Gary Steven Kinkel, *Our Dear Mother the Spirit: An Investigation of Count Zinzendorf's Theology and Praxis* (Lanham, MD: University Press of America, 1990), and Elizabeth A. Johnson, *She Who Is: The Mystery of God in Feminist Theological Discourse* (New York: Crossroad, 1992), 128–31.

14. Harvey, "Feminine Imagery for the Divine," 123.

15. Catherine Keller, *Face of the Deep: A Theology of Becoming* (London: Routledge, 2003), 233.

Chapter Three: Green Spirituality, Brownfields, and Wilderness Recovery

1. Bob Edwards, "With Liberty and Environmental Justice for All: The Emergence and Challenge of Grassroots Environmentalism in the United States," in *Ecological Resistance Movements: The Global Emergence of Radical and Popular Environmentalism*, ed. Bron Raymond Taylor (Albany: State University of New York Press, 1995), 37.

2. "The Wildlands Project Mission Statement," *Wild Earth* 5 (winter 1995/96): inside front cover, n.a.

3. See this discussion in Charlene Spretnak, *The Spiritual Dimensions of Green Politics* (Santa Fe, NM: Bear, 1986), 25–53; cf. Catherine L. Albanese, *Nature Religion in America: From the Algonkian Indians to the New Age* (Chicago: University of Chicago Press, 1990), 171–78.

4. I have used Christian resources to put forward sustainable, green spirituality in this book. Nevertheless, many other historical religious traditions have articulated this vision in their own idiom, underscoring that such a vision is not the province of any one tradition. Green spirituality is a generic sensibility available to any person—Christian or not, religious or not—interested in crafting a holistic vision of life on the planet. Its roots are deep in the soil of various earth-friendly spiritualities, and it generates crucial motivation for and insight into the process of earth healing. For a wide introduction to green spirituality and global religions, see Richard Foltz, *Worldviews, Religion, and the Environment: A Global Anthology* (Belmont, CA: Wadsworth, 2002).

5. Edwards, "With Liberty and Environmental Justice for All," 37.

6. See Robert Gottlieb, *Forcing the Spring: The Transformation of the American Environmental Movement* (Washington, DC: Island, 1993), 184–91.

7. See Carolyn Merchant, *Radical Ecology: The Search for a Livable World* (New York: Routledge, 1992), 162–67.

8. "US High Court Takes Waste Case from Chester," *Philadelphia Inquirer*, June 9, 1998.

9. I have drawn this information from "Chester Decides It's Tired of Being a Wasteland," *Philadelphia Inquirer*, July 26, 1994; and Chester Residents Concerned for Quality Living, "Environmental Justice Fact Sheet" and "Pollution and Industry in Chester's 'West End,'" pamphlets, n.d. I am grateful to former Swarthmore College students Laird Hedlund and Ryan Peterson for making available to me their expertise and research concerning the Chester waste facilities.

10. "Plant Asks to Burn Waste Tires for Fuel," *Philadelphia Inquirer,* September 11, 2001, and "Chester Residents Angry about Plant's Quiet Move," *Philadelphia Inquirer,* September 28, 2003.

11. Maryanne Voller, "Everyone Has Got to Breathe," *Audubon*, March–April 1995.

12. Editorial, "Chester a Proving Ground," *Delaware County Daily Times*, December 8, 1994, and "EPA Cites Lead in City Kids, Bad Fish," *Delaware County Daily Times*, December 2, 1994.

13. Voller, "Everyone Has Got to Breathe," and Chester Residents Concerned for Quality Living, "Environmental Justice Fact Sheet."

14. "Problems in Chester," *Delaware County Daily Times*, August 1, 1995.

15. Howard Goodman, "Politically Incorrect," *Philadelphia Inquirer Magazine*, February 11, 1996.

16. The term "sacrific zone" belongs to Carolyn Merchant, who uses it in her *Radical Ecology*, 163.

17. Chester Residents Concerned for Quality Living, "Pollution and Industry in Chester's 'West End.'"

18. Barbara Bohannan-Sheppard, "Remarks" (Department of Environmental Resources Public Hearing, February 17, 1994, transcript).

19. Bill Clinton, Executive Order Number 12898, February 1995; cf. Gretchen Leslie and Colleen Casper, "Environmental Equity: An Issue for the 90s?" *Environmental Insight*, 1995.

20. The First National People of Color Environmental Leadership Summit, "Principles of Environmental Justice," in *This Sacred Earth: Religion, Nature, Environment*, ed. Roger S. Gottlieb (New York: Routledge, 1996), 634.

21. See, for example, Arthur Green, "God, World, Person: A Jewish Theology of Creation, Part I," *Melton Journal* 24 (spring 1991): 4–7.

22. See Tu Wei-ming, "The Continuity of Being: Chinese Visions of Nature," in *Nature in Asian Traditions of Thought: Essays in Environmental Philosophy*, ed. Roger T. Ames and J. Baird Callicott (Albany: State University of New York Press, 1989), 67–78.

23. On Native American traditions, see John A. Grim, "Native North American Worldviews and Ecology," in *Worldviews and Ecology*, ed. Mary Evelyn Tucker and John A. Grim (Lewisburg, PA: Bucknell University Press, 1990), 41–54.
24. For a collection of source material and analysis on green religion, see Gottlieb, *This Sacred Earth*; for general analysis, see David Kinsley, *Ecology and Religion: Ecological Spirituality in Cross-Cultural Perspective* (Englewood Cliffs, NJ: Prentice-Hall, 1995), and Tucker and Grim, *Worldviews and Ecology*.
25. On Edwards's spirituality, see Jonathan Edwards, *The Nature of True Virtue* (Ann Arbor: University of Michigan Press, 1960), 1–26; cf. William A. Clebsch, *American Religious Thought: A History* (Chicago: University of Chicago Press, 1973), 11–56.
26. See Arne Naess, "The Shallow and the Deep, Long-Range Ecology Movement," *Inquiry* 16 (1973): 95–100.
27. Thich Nhat Hanh, "The Last Tree," in *Dharma Gaia: A Harvest of Essays in Buddhism and Ecology*, ed. Allan Hunt Badiner (Berkeley, CA: Parallax Press, 1990), 218.
28. John Seed, "Anthropocentrism," Appendix E in *Deep Ecology: Living as if Nature Mattered,* ed. Bill Devall and George Sessions (Salt Lake City: Peregrine Smith, 1985), 243.
29. The articulation of this rule is quoted from Paul W. Taylor, *Respect for Nature: A Theory of Environmental Ethics* (Princeton, NJ: Princeton University Press, 1986), 174; Devall and Sessions, *Deep Ecology* 68; and Tom Regan, "The Nature and Possibility of an Environmental Ethic," *Environmental Ethics* 3 (1981): 31–32. In the vein of the noninterference maxim, Taylor provides a helpful list of five principles—self-defense, proportionality, minimum wrong, distributive justice, and restitutive justice—for resolving conflicting "claims" between human and nonhuman populations. He also provides a number of case studies illustrating the relevance of these principles to different hypothetical conflict scenarios. See Taylor, *Respect for Nature*, 256–313.
30. On the history of Earth First! see Dave Foreman, *Confessions of an Eco-Warrior* (New York: Harmony, 1990); Christopher Manes, *Green Rage: Radical Environmentalism and the Unmaking of Civilization* (Boston: Little, Brown, 1990); and Bron Raymond Taylor, "Earth First! and Global Narratives of Popular Ecological Resistance," in *Ecological Resistance Movements: The Global Emergence of Radical and Popular Environmentalism,* ed. Bron Raymond Taylor (Albany: State University of New York Press, 1995), 11–34.
31. Edward Abbey, *The Monkey Wrench Gang* (New York: Avon, 1975), 100–101.
32. A moving example of an Earth First!–inspired tree-sit is Julia Butterfly Hill, *The Legacy of Luna: The Story of a Tree, a Woman, and the Struggle to Save the Redwoods* (San Francisco: HarperSanFrancisco, 2000). In the late 1990s in the Northern California Humboldt County Headwaters region, Hill lived for two years on a platform perched precariously within a giant redwood tree forest activists named "Luna." Initially facilitated by Earth First! Hill's goal was to preserve this tree and the larger habitat of old-growth forest in its immediate environment. She was partly successful in her efforts through

brokering with PacificLumber/Maxxam, owner of that portion of the forest, a preservation agreement for Luna and a small buffer zone in the immediate area of the Luna site. While her tree-sit was technically illegal, her story of courage and endurance is a public morality tale intended to inspire other persons' creative commitments to protecting the planet. In contrast to Hill's open crusade against nonsustainable forestry practices, see Bruce Barcott, "From Tree-Hugger to Terrorist," *New York Times Magazine,* April 7, 2002, which examines the secretive world of radical green ecotage intent less on nonviolent efforts to preserve wildlands and more on employing shocking acts of destruction against potent symbols of the world economic order that advance environmental degradation.

33. The journal *Earth First!* regularly publishes accounts of ecotage undertaken by members of ELF and other radical groups, such as the Animal Liberation Front (ALF), which employ similarly aggressive tactics in order to set free and disrupt biogenetic engineering and animal testing facilities, among other things. See *Earth First! Journal* (Eostar/March–April 2001) and (Mabon/September–October 2001), for example.

34. Barcott, "From Tree-Hugger to Terrorist," 59. For a less strident reading of radical ecotage groups that defends such groups against the charge of terrorism by examining their militant rhetoric but, until now, consistent refusal to inflict bodily harm on other persons, see Bron Taylor, "Religion, Violence and Radical Environmentalism: From Earth First! to the Unabomber to the Earth Liberation Front," *Terrorism and Political Violence* 10 (winter 1998): 1–42.

35. Barcott, "From Tree-Hugger to Terrorist," 59.

36. Jeffrey "Free" Luers, Letter to the Editor, *Earth First! Journal* (Eostar/March–April 2003): 3. After writing these comments, Free attaches an addendum: "Disclaimer: I would never encourage or advocate criminal activity, even if it is the most effective means. This is simply my opinion. Make up your own minds." Other ELF activists have also sought to clarify their position on ecotage, making a distinction between destroying physical property and violence against other persons. Recent firebombings of SUV dealerships in Southern California generated this comment by one anonymous spokesperson for the movement: "We support destruction of property as a means of bringing attention to important issues. . . . The ELF is opposed to harming any form of life, much less human life" ("Environmental Activist Claims Role in Firebombings at Car Dealership," *Los Angeles Times,* October 2, 2003).

37. "The Wildlands Project Mission Statement."

38. On this point see Bron Taylor, "The Religion and Politics of Earth First!" *Ecologist* 21 (November/December 1991): 258–66.

39. Gottlieb, *Forcing the Spring*, 318.

40. Ibid., 197.

41. Roger S. Gottlieb, "Spiritual Deep Ecology and the Left: An Attempt at Reconciliation," in Gottlieb, *This Sacred Earth*, 529; cf. a similar attempt to resolve the conflicts between deep ecology–inspired wilderness advocates and

environmental justice proponents in Michael E. Zimmerman, "Ecofascism: A Threat to American Environmentalism?" in *The Ecological Community: Environmental Challenges for Philosophy, Politics, and Morality*, ed. Roger S. Gottlieb (New York: Routledge, 1997), 229–54.

42. The quotation is from Murray Bookchin, "What Is Social Ecology?" in *Environmental Philosophy: From Animal Rights to Radical Ecology*, ed. Michael E. Zimmerman (Englewood Cliffs, NJ: Prentice-Hall, 1993), 368. Much of my thinking about the relationship between environmental degradation and market liberalism has been inspired by the writings of social ecologists Bookchin, Janet Biehl, and John Clark. For a thoughtful counterpoint to this approach, see the argument for a modified "social liberalism" in Avner de-Shalit, "Is Liberalism Environment-Friendly?" in Gottlieb, *The Ecological Community*, 82–103.

Chapter Four: Green Spirituality and the Problem of Humanism

1. See David Ehrenfeld, *The Arrogance of Humanism* (Oxford: Oxford University Press, 1981).

2. Ibid., 5–6.

3. On the Enlightenment's privileged valuation of human well-being, see Peter Gay, *The Enlightenment: An Interpretation*, 2 vols. (New York: Knopf, 1967); Charles Taylor, *Sources of the Self: The Making of the Modern Identity* (Cambridge, MA: Harvard University Press, 1989); and Mark I. Wallace, "The European Enlightenment," in *Spirituality and the Secular Quest*, ed. Peter H. Van Ness (New York: Crossroad, 1996), 75–101.

4. The most extreme version of the early modernist attitude toward nature can be found in the writings of Francis Bacon (d. 1626). For Bacon, only insofar as the world of otherkind can enable the support and maintenance of humankind does it become a reference for moral concern. As an adjunct to human formation, nature has value because it serves the purpose of being the raw material, so to speak, for the development of human growth. On its own and apart from serving its role as a medium for human development, nature is devoid of moral interest. But as a vehicle for human growth—in the same manner that we consider today how the market economy or modern medicine or the textile industry might serve this mediatory role—the world of plants and animals is charged with moral value. Even for Bacon, however, to say that nature's value is derived from or parasitic upon human needs is not to say that nature has *no* value, or even that it is devoid of *intrinsic* value, but only that its value is less than the premier value we assign to human beings. On Bacon, see Carolyn Merchant, *Radical Ecology: The Search for a Livable World* (New York: Routledge, 1992), 45–55.

5. Immanuel Kant, *Groundwork of the Metaphysic of Morals*, trans. H. J. Paton (New York: Harper & Row, 1964), 105–6.

6. John Rawls, *A Theory of Justice* (Cambridge, MA: Harvard University Press, 1971), 11–192, 504–81.

7. Ibid., 504–505.

8. Kant, *Groundwork of the Metaphysic of Morals*, 105.

9. Strong Wood, "No Charges in Gypsy's Death," *Earth First! Journal* (Brigid/February–March 1999): 11, and Garlic, "Remembering Gypsy in the Redwoods," *Earth First! Journal* (Samhain/November–December 1999): 1, 32.

10. Alasdair MacIntyre, *After Virtue: A Study in Moral Theory* (Notre Dame, IN: University of Notre Dame Press, 1981), 44.

11. The phrase belongs to Michael J. Sandel, *Democracy's Discontent: America in Search of a Public Philosophy* (Cambridge, MA: Belknap, 1996), 15. Sandel does not take up the problem of the environment explicitly in his analysis of American political life, but his criticism of the liberal tradition as espousing the ideal of the free, ahistorical subject unburdened by its culturally embedded loyalties to particular human communities echoes my interest in relocating the self in the wider web of its basic loyalties to the *nonhuman* communities to which it always belongs.

12. Laura Westra, *An Environmental Proposal for Ethics: The Principle of Integrity*, Studies in Social and Political Philosophy (Lanham, MD: Rowman & Littlefield, 1994), 124.

13. On this question, see Mary Midgley, *Beast and Man: The Roots of Human Nature* (Ithaca, NY: Cornell University Press, 1978).

14. Aldo Leopold, *A Sand County Almanac* (New York: Ballantine Books, 1970), 262.

15. Ibid., 240.

Chapter Five: Green Spirituality and the Invitation of Postmodernism

1. See John D. Caputo and Michael J. Scanlon, eds., *God, the Gift, and Postmodernism* (Bloomington: Indiana University Press, 1999); Steven Connor, *Postmodernist Culture: An Introduction to Theories of the Contemporary* (Cambridge: Blackwell, 1989); David Harvey, *The Condition of Postmodernity: An Inquiry into the Origins of Cultural Change* (Cambridge: Blackwell, 1990); Allan Megill, *Prophets of Extremity: Nietzsche, Heidegger, Foucault, Derrida* (Berkeley: University of California Press, 1985); and Merold Westphal, "Blind Spots: Christianity and Postmodern Philosophy," *Christian Century* (June 14, 2003): 32–35.

2. On the question of religion, postmodernism, and the environment, see Max Oelschlaeger, ed., *Postmodern Environmental Ethics* (Albany: State University of New York Press, 1995); David Ray Griffin, *God and Religion in the Postmodern World: Essays in Postmodern Theology* (Albany: State University of New York Press, 1989); and Michael E. Zimmerman, *Contesting Earth's Future: Radical Ecology and Postmodernity* (Berkeley: University of California Press, 1994).

3. See the proceedings of this seminar in *Uncommon Ground: Rethinking the Human Place in Nature*, ed. William Cronon (New York: Norton, 1996).

4. William Cronon, "Introduction: In Search of Nature," in *Uncommon Ground*, 25–26.

5. George Sessions, "Reinventing Nature? The End of Wilderness? A Response to William Cronon's *Uncommon Ground*," *Wild Earth* 6 (winter 1996/97): 46. See the collection of articles in this number of *Wild Earth* for a biocentric reply to Cronon and other postmodern environmental writers.

6. Dave Foreman, "Around the Campfire," *Wild Earth* 6 (winter 1996/97): 4.

7. Bill Willers, "The Trouble with Cronon," *Wild Earth* 6 (winter 1996/97): 59. The reference here to the wide reporting of Cronon's views is to the piece "The Trouble with Wilderness," which is the lead essay in his *Uncommon Ground* collection and which was reprinted, in different forms, in the *New York Times* and the *Utne Reader*.

8. Michael E. Soulé, "The Social Siege of Nature," in *Reinventing Nature: Responses to Postmodern Deconstruction*, ed. Michael E. Soulé and Gary Lease (Washington, DC: Island, 1995), 154. The papers in this volume had their origin at a conference at the University of California at Santa Cruz that received major funding from the Reinventing Nature project, the same project that undergirded the efforts of Cronon and his seminar colleagues at Irvine. In reaction to the Irvine scholars' notion of nature as manipulable construct, Soulé and Lease provide a sustained critique of "certain kinds of 'postmodern deconstructionism' that question the concepts of nature and wilderness, sometimes in order to justify further exploitive tinkering with what little remains of wildness" (Soulé and Lease, "Preface," in *Reinventing Nature*, xv).

9. The so-called idealist fallacy is often associated with the eighteenth-century British philosopher George Berkeley. Berkeley is labeled an idealist because everything that is said to be is an idea; nothing exists unless it is humanly perceived. Nothing in the world can exist independently from its being observed by a rational knower. To say that something exists is to say that it appears to my rational faculties as an "idea" or an "object" that I can apprehend. Nothing, then, exists apart from my knowing activity. On Berkeley, see Frederick Copleston, *A History of Philosophy*, vol. 5: *Modern Philosophy: The British Philosophers*, Part 2: *Berkeley to Hume* (Garden City, NY: Image, 1964), 9–62.

10. Cronon, "Foreword to the Paperback Edition," in *Uncommon Ground*, 21.

11. Richard Rorty, *Contingency, Irony, and Solidarity* (Cambridge: Cambridge University Press, 1989), 5–6.

12. See G. E. Moore, *Philosophical Papers* (London: Allen and Unwin, 1959).

13. Ludwig Wittgenstein, *On Certainty*, ed. G. E. M. Anscombe and G. H. von Wright, trans. Denis Paul and G. E. M. Anscombe (New York: Harper & Row, 1969), 16e.

14. Ibid., 21e.

15. See Ludwig Wittgenstein, *Philosophical Investigations*, trans. G. E. M. Anscombe, 3d ed. (New York: Macmillan, 1953), 2–51, 112–44; cf. idem, *On Certainty*, 50–77.

16. Wittgenstein, *Philosophical Investigations*, 36–59.

17. Wittgenstein, *On Certainty*, 52e.

18. Ibid., 7e. Even for philosophers who do prefer the conventional epistemological labels, Wittgenstein's attempt to dissolve the debate casts a long shadow. Hilary Putnam identifies his project as "internal realism," by which he means "at bottom, just the insistence that realism is *not* incompatible with conceptual relativity. One can be *both* a realist *and* a conceptual relativist" (*The Many Faces of Realism* [LaSalle, IL: Open Court, 1987], 17); see also idem, *Meaning and the Moral Sciences* [London: Routledge & Kegan Paul, 1978], 123–38). Like Wittgenstein, Putnam seeks to understand the relationship between the world of commonsensical objects and the partisan vocabularies we use to understand these objects. But Putnam strikes me as more wedded to the naive realist model that there are external things independent of our descriptions of them than is Wittgenstein. Nevertheless, his thesis that things only have meaning relative to a conceptual scheme parallels Wittgenstein's point that all understanding is ineluctably formed or played within a language game.

19. N. Katherine Hayles, "Searching for Common Ground," in Soulé and Lease, *Reinventing Nature*, 49.

20. Ibid., 49–55.

21. Ibid., 53.

22. Ibid.

23. John Calvin, *Institutes of the Christian Religion* I:6.

24. Thomas Aquinas, *Summa Theologica* (New York: Benziger, 1916–37), 1.Q.3.art.4.

25. Martin Heidegger, "What Is Metaphysics?" in *Basic Writings*, trans. David Ferrell Krell (New York: Harper & Row, 1977), 109.

26. Martin Heidegger, "The Onto-theo-logical Constitution of Metaphysics," in *Identity and Difference*, trans. Joan Stamburgh (New York: Harper & Row, 1969), 42–76.

27. Jacques Derrida, "Violence and Metaphysics," in *Writing and Difference*, trans. Allan Bass (Chicago: University of Chicago Press, 1978), 152.

28. Heidegger, "The Onto-theo-logical Constitution of Metaphysics," 72.

29. Ibid.

30. Cf. David Harvey, *The Condition of Postmodernity* (Cambridge, MA: Blackwell, 1990), 66–98.

31. As a constructive discipline, postmodern green theology is methodologically parallel to Jeffrey Stout's notion of *bricolage* in contemporary moral philosophy. Quoting Claude Lévi-Strauss, Stout writes that *bricolage* is the process whereby a *bricoleur* constructs original artifacts (be they physical or conceptual constructs) based on the contingent resources and arbitrary materials at hand. The *bricoleur* takes the assorted odds and ends at her disposal and fash-

ions them into a useful product; the random tools and elements at hand are the raw materials for the construction of the new project envisioned by the *bricoleur*. Postmodern green theology is a *bricolage* activity wherein the theorist cobbles together a framework for conversation between ancient source materials and contemporary realities and problems. See Jeffrey Stout, *Ethics after Babel: The Languages of Morals and Their Discontents* (Boston: Beacon Press, 1988), 71–81.

32. Kenneth J. Gergen, *Toward a Transformation in Social Knowledge* (New York: Springer-Verlag, 1982), 207.

33. Kenneth J. Gergen, *An Invitation to Social Construction* (London: Sage, 1999), 48.

34. Ibid., 49.

35. Ibid., 50.

36. Ibid.

Chapter Six: Earth God as the Wounded Spirit

1. These phrases, which speak to the reconciliation of apparently opposing positions to form a burst of new insight into reality, are used, respectively, by Karl Barth, *The Epistle to the Romans*, trans. Edwyn C. Hoskins from the 6th German ed. (Oxford: Oxford University Press, 1933); Paul Ricoeur, *The Rule of Metaphor: Multidisciplinary Studies of the Creation of Meaning in Language,* trans. Robert Czerny with Kathleen McLaughlin and John Costello, SJ (Toronto: University of Toronto Press, 1977); and Walter Lowe, *Theology and Difference: The Wound of Reason* (Bloomington: Indiana University Press, 1993).

2. See Jaroslav Pelikan, *The Christian Tradition: A History of the Development of Doctrine*, vol. 1: *The Emergence of the Catholic Tradition (100–600)* (Chicago: University of Chicago Press, 1971), 172–277.

3. Jürgen Moltmann, *The Trinity and the Kingdom*, trans. Margaret Kohl (Minneapolis: Fortress Press, 1993 [1981]), 38.

4. Jürgen Moltmann, *The Crucified God: The Cross of Christ as the Foundation and Criticism of Christian Theology*, trans. R. A. Wilson and John Bowden (Minneapolis: Fortress Press [1974]), 244. On the topic of divine suffering, see also, for example, Edward Farley, *Divine Empathy: A Theology of God* (Minneapolis: Fortress Press, 1996); Joseph Halloran, *The Descent of God: Divine Suffering in History and Theology* (Minneapolis: Fortress Press, 1992); and Grace Jantzen, *God's World and God's Body* (Philadelphia: Westminster, 1984).

5. Moltmann, *The Crucified God*, 278.

Chapter Seven: The World Is Alive with Spirit

1. On the history and practice of the Council of All Beings ritual, see Joanna Macy, "The Council of All Beings ritual" in *The Encyclopedia of Religion and Nature*, Bron Taylor, editor-in-chief (New York: Continuum International), forthcoming.

2. I have drawn my knowledge about the Crum Creek watershed from Roger Latham, "The Crum Woods in Peril: Toward Reversing the Decline of an Irreplaceable Resource for Learning, Research, Recreation and Reflection," http://www.swarthmore.edu/NatSci/Biology/bio_professors/latham/crumwoods.html; "Crum Creek Watershed: A Protection Guide," Chester-Ridley-Crum Watersheds Association pamphlet; and "Crum Creek 1995," report by the Advanced Research Biology Students of Conestoga High School, Pennsylvania, under the direction of Norman E. Marriner.

3. John B. Cobb Jr., *Is It Too Late? A Theology of Ecology* (Berkeley: Bruce, 1972).

4. John B. Cobb Jr. and Herman E. Daly, *For the Common Good: Redirecting the Economy toward Community, the Environment, and a Sustainable Future* (Boston: Beacon Press, 1989).

5. John B. Cobb Jr., "Protestant Theology and Deep Ecology," in *Deep Ecology and World Religions: New Essays on Sacred Ground*, ed. David Landhis Barnhill and Roger S. Gottlieb (Albany: State University of New York Press, 2001), 223. Other environmental theologians make a similar point. James A. Nash says that while "only the Creator is worthy of worship, all God's creatures are worthy of moral consideration" (*Loving Nature: Ecological Integrity and Christian Responsibility* [Nashville: Abingdon, 1991], 96).

6. Cobb, "Protestant Theology and Deep Ecology," 224.

7. Most Christian environmentalists I read agree with Cobb that spiritual deep ecology goes too far in erasing the line of distinction they aver separates humankind from otherkind. For such thinkers it is inconceivable, in terms of both value and ethics, to imagine a world in which human beings are not both fundamentally different from and in some basic sense superior to other life-forms. In an otherwise insightful plea for Christian ecotheology, Steven Bouma-Prediger argues that "insofar as [deep ecology] proponents claim that all organisms have equal value and worth, it is unclear how to adjudicate competing interests or goods. . . . How can one consistently put into practice such a position? . . . [In] acting we presuppose a [human-centered] scale or hierarchy of values. Better to be honest about what that axiological scale is than to pretend that all organisms are of equal value" (*For the Beauty of the Earth: A Christian Vision for Creation Care* [Grand Rapids, MI: Baker Academic, 2001], 132). My suggestion is otherwise: that we act honestly, indeed, and that we wean ourselves away from this traditional humanist value scale. We are all equal—all living beings and other entities in the biosphere—and we all depend upon one another for meeting our vital needs in the food web. Decisions about resource allocations should focus on how best to preserve the integrity of this web through sustainable predation patterns without appealing to a value hierarchy with human needs at the top of the hierarchy. Our needs do not trump the needs of other communities of beings. Or, to put it another way, all of our needs come first because we all depend upon each other for our daily survival. When we put our desires first, what we forget is that what we truly need is the preservation of a series of interdependent, healthy green belts across the planet for our, and our biological

neighbors', present and future sustenance. Environmental ethical decisions should not be made with primary reference to human needs, but in consideration of the health of entire ecosystems and their residential populations of plants and animals. Biocentric rather than anthropocentric criteria, ironically and wonderfully, ensure the good life for all of us. A robust and healthy food web is the primary value that should guide resource allocation decisions; this value, not Cobb's and Bouma-Prediger's benign humanism, is the core value upon which human health, and the health of all other beings, is best secured.

8. Aldo Leopold, *A Sand County Almanac* (New York: Ballantine, 1970), 252–53.
9. Ibid., 262.

Index